▼▼▼▼▼▼▼▼▼▼▼▼

Managing Professionals in Research and Development

A Guide for Improving Productivity and Organizational Effectiveness

▼▼▼▼▼▼▼▼▼▼▼▼

Donald Britton Miller

▼▼▼▼▼▼▼▼▼▼▼▼

Managing Professionals in Research and Development

Jossey-Bass Publishers

San Francisco • London • 1986

MANAGING PROFESSIONALS IN RESEARCH AND DEVELOPMENT
A Guide for Improving Productivity and Organizational Effectiveness
by Donald Britton Miller

Copyright © 1986 by: Jossey-Bass Inc., Publishers
433 California Street
San Francisco, California 94104
&
Jossey-Bass Limited
28 Banner Street
London EC1Y 8QE

Library of Congress Cataloging-in-Publication Data

Miller, Donald Britton.
  Managing professionals in research and development.

  (The Jossey-Bass management series)
  Bibliography: p. 387
  Includes index.
  1. Research, Industrial—Management. I. Title.
II. Series.
T175.5.M55   1986   658.5′7   86-7283
ISBN 1-55542-000-1 (alk. paper)

Manufactured in the United States of America

The paper in this book meets the guidelines for
permanence and durability of the Committee on
Production Guidelines for Book Longevity of the
Council on Library Resources.

JACKET DESIGN BY WILLI BAUM

FIRST EDITION

Code 8622

▼▼▼▼▼▼▼▼▼▼▼

The Jossey-Bass
Management Series

▼▼▼▼▼▼▼▼▼▼▼▼▼

Preface

Improved technological leadership is an imperative of our times. As a nation, we Americans worry about slowed creativity and innovation, about international technological competition, about our negative balance of payments. We are fearful that we are losing our position of technical leadership in the world.

In the same way that we as a nation are concerned about our technological progress, managers of research and development (R & D) are deeply troubled about trends and events in their organizations. The core activity of a technologically driven, or high-technology, organization is in its R & D function. The R & D part of the organization provides the ideas, concepts, and thrust needed for progress to occur. Leader-managers in R & D worry about high turnover among young professionals, about how to motivate these professionals, about burnout and technical obsolescence, about energy wasted in conflict. Most professionals, especially those in R & D, worry about burnout and obsolescence, about their work being increasingly standardized and formatted, about continuing personal development and career growth, about their psychic income and the balance between work, play, and family.

When I visit with professionals at work, especially in research and development organizations, I am often overwhelmed by the feeling that I am seeing powerful people who, for some reason, feel powerless. What is it that sets the R & D function, and the people in it, apart from the other parts of the organization, seemingly creating a gulf in communication? Some of this gulf may be due to a highly vocal group in our society repeatedly espousing bias against change, against science, and against the application of technology. Or, it may be based on the recent revelations about the negative impact on our environment of past scientific progress. Perhaps we are just seeing today's version of C. P. Snow's "Two Cultures" (1959, p. 4): "I believe that the intellectual life of the whole of western society is increasingly being split into two polar groups." Whatever the cause, we need to understand the schism. We need to improve communication and let highly educated professionals participate in appropriate technical progress. We need to maximize the effectiveness of these people and create work environments where they can maintain and enhance their vitality. *Managing Professionals in Research and Development* can assist us in achieving these goals.

Research and development organizations are staffed primarily by professionals: people who have invested considerable time and energy in preparing for their careers. They are knowledge workers, and they bring unique values and expectations to the workplace. Professionals are frequently achievement-oriented individuals who seek motivation from the work itself. A high level of autonomy in managing their own work is important to them, and they are increasingly sensitive to the quality of the work environment, climate, and culture. As a result, they choose to work for organizations that offer them a high psychic income (satisfactions like learning, achievement, impact, and a sense of self-worth).

We know little about managing the professional. Management principles useful in other parts of the organization have had only minimal success when directly transplanted to R & D organizations. Often, it seems as though the absence of management is what the professional wants. Self-management has become almost synonymous with being a professional. Thus, when leader-managers, even those who are former scientists, engineers, and programmers, try to apply ideas learned in conventional management development, they often meet with failure. By some managers, salaried professionals in organizations (engineers, scientists, and programmers) are considered unmanageable. This book lays the groundwork for increasing the effectiveness (productivity) of R & D organizations by helping the manager to understand the values, expectations, and goals of these professionals, to develop an experimental outlook and a participative style of management, and to explore specific techniques for improving his or her management style.

Management as well as nonmanagement professionals, human resource specialists, consultants, researchers specializing in R & D organizations, and professors and graduate students in the fields of organizational behavior and design will find this book useful. The strategies discussed here can also be applied to the management of professionals who are not in R & D organizations. Ideas about the importance of mission will probably be most useful to top management and to scholars studying organizations, while the specific use of vitality and effectiveness as goals will probably be most useful to R & D directors and line managers of organizations composed of professionals. The discussion of how environment, climate, and culture contribute to productivity and of how the manager bears responsibility for the design of environments should be helpful to managers at all levels in the hierarchy. The line manager will also find that the chapter on recruiting, selecting, and training brings these human resource functions into fresh focus. The professional can gain an understanding of how managerial functions are, and should be, shared by the nonmanager and manager in the chapters concerned with matching people and work and with managing performance. When decisions about person-job matching and work goals are left to management alone, leadership will be ineffective and the professional will feel powerless, uncomfortable at work, and deprived of psychic income.

Managing Professionals in Research and Development can be used in several ways. It can function as a text in management development programs that assist the professional turned manager to develop an initial understanding of the role and in programs that focus on developing management skills on an ongoing basis. It can also be used as a text for independent study by leaders and managers in technological organizations faced with having to improve the effectiveness (productivity) of professionals. Advocates of change will be able to use it to challenge individuals and groups with the concept that changes in environment, structure, and process can make their organizations better places to work thus increasing psychic income and morale. Finally, this book will provide ongoing service as a desk reference for all these groups of readers.

Overview of the Contents

Managing Professionals in Research and Development will provide the reader with useful perspectives and some new tools for managing professionals, especially scientists, engineers, programmers, and others engaged in R & D activities. It offers many suggestions and concepts for improving the effectiveness (productivity) and vitality of technical organizations as well as ideas for implementing change in organizations.

Part One sets the stage by discussing the challenge, characteristics, people, climate, and culture of R & D organizations. Chapter One describes the challenges facing managers of R & D organizations. It presents the root causes for the unique demands that are placed on leaders, primarily through realistic anecdotal stories that enliven the narrative. This chapter also evaluates the historical changes in the nature of R & D that make it imperative to improve management at this time and presents initial suggestions concerning what needs to be changed now.

Chapter Two presents several perspectives on the characteristics of R & D organizations and challenges the reader to develop a personal view. Presented first is the often critical view of R & D held by many people in other parts of the organization: that R & D is special and is allowed to operate free of rules and constraints. The contrasting view of those who work in R & D organizations—that these special needs are required to support creativity and innovation—is presented next. These views are followed by a discussion of both generic R & D characteristics that should not be changed and those characteristics that are legitimate candidates for change.

Chapter Three builds a foundation for understanding the expectations and needs that the professional brings to work. The needs discussed include the special importance of psychic income for the professional, partly a product of an extensive educational preparation, as well as the need for autonomy (self-management), for contribution beyond the organization (to the profession), for collegial support, and for continued development as a professional.

Part Two focuses on inspiring professionals by encouraging participation and open communication. Chapter Four discusses the conflict between managing technology and managing people, enabling the reader to gain some insight into the fundamentals of managing R & D. The need for constructive disturbance to maintain the productivity of a group, the need for an experimental outlook in management, and the concept that even the pursuit of an unfruitful project often results in a contribution to long-term success—all form part of the challenge of managing technology and people at the same time.

Chapter Five deals specifically with the need for a mission supported by exciting goals. Because much of the work of R & D is uncharted and often unpredictable, the professional relies on mission and goals to provide the raison d'être for the work. Participation by nonmanagerial professionals in establishing the mission and goals is offered as a way of encouraging the members of the organization to own and understand the organization's goals and, in the long run, to achieve congruence between their own goals and those of the organization.

Chapter Six proposes that the goals of vitality and effectiveness be promoted in conjunction with the more common management goal of results. In R & D the ability to be successful tomorrow depends on choosing tasks today that contribute to a gain in capability and knowledge in spite of the fast pace of change.

Chapter Seven presents environment, climate, and culture as tools for managing; explores the manager's role as designer of environments; and demonstrates how this activity can improve effectiveness. Differences between the company's culture and R & D's culture are discussed as a means of illustrating

some of the communication difficulties. Specific elements of
the environment, such as the emotional bond an individual may
have with his or her work, the human resource policy and program base, and reward and recognition practices are evaluated
as means of improving effectiveness.

Style is the topic of Chapter Eight. The professional
turned manager needs to understand the positive and negative
potential that is embedded in the way two individuals communicate and relate to one another. This chapter provides information on the origins of style, the impact of personal and organizational values on style, classical theory about managerial style,
ways to inspire others (by example and through personal chemistry), and several factors that affect creativity and can be used
by the manager. It concludes with a discussion of the leader's
need for control.

Part Three sets forth the concepts the reader can use to
improve the performance of an R & D unit by effectively building
and developing a team of professionals. Chapter Nine shows
how the initial psychological work contract, virtually never
documented and often inadequately discussed, shapes the relationship between the individual and the organization. Managers
are assisted in understanding the basics of effective and honest
recruiting. Continued development of both managers and nonmanagerial professionals is particularly critical in rapidly changing, technologically driven organizations, and the reader is
introduced to ways in which the organization and the individual
can interact to ensure that this development is timely and effective, especially in terms of avoiding or correcting burnout and
obsolescence. Suggestions for improving the crucial and difficult transition from nonmanagerial professional to manager are
also presented.

A thorough discussion of performance management in
Chapter Ten helps the reader to conceive of this process in new
and more positive terms. Specifications for an improved performance management system for R & D organizations are given to
enable the manager to evaluate the organization's current program and perhaps redesign it.

In Chapter Eleven organizational design is presented as a

tool the leader-manager can use to provide the stimulation necessary to ensure vitality as well as provide a sharp focus on goals. Concepts such as critical mass in groups (the number required for the creative process to be self-enhancing) and temporary systems or groups (which improve the organization's adaptive capabilities) are discussed along with the need for the manager's outlook toward organizational design to be experimental.

Chapter Twelve discusses the manager's most important function: matching people and work, matching the needs and capabilities of the organization with those of individuals. In R & D this must be a process in which the individual professional is involved. Job elements are described, and a framework that can be used to determine which factors are causing discomfort, and are thus candidates for redesign, is provided.

Chapter Thirteen ties all these ideas together and presents suggestions for implementing appropriate changes in the reader's organization. Since changes must fit the culture of each organization, there is no specific prescription. Instead, the reader is guided along a route that will help the leader-manager implement those changes that will improve effectiveness and vitality in his or her organization.

Acknowledgments

I want to thank my wife Fran for many hours of patient support, provided even when the going was rough because the computer failed or the creative writing energies were missing. Early in the process, she also contributed suggestions for readability and appropriate gentle nudging.

I want to thank all my friends, associates, and clients who, over the years, have contributed to the understandings that I have tried to shape for transmission to leader-managers and professionals for their personal use. While these people were not intimately involved in the creation of this book, they forced me to discover what I knew and did not know and to refine what I did know so I could tell it to someone else.

Some of my friends' situations are described in these pages. Their stories are so disguised, however, that even they

may not recognize themselves. Others will think they have
found the story of someone they know or an incident they were
part of, but most probably they will be wrong. We all tend to
think of these anecdotal stories as applying only to us, when in
actuality they are much more universal than that. In many
cases, they are today's equivalent of the wares of the ancient
storytellers.

My special and most sincere thanks go to several individuals who volunteered to read the manuscript in detail and to
provide the constructive comments that made this a better
book. These people made many suggestions for refinement,
caught ideas I had missed, and suggested the inclusion of ex-
planatory material. They include Richard Haglund, of the Department of Physics and Astronomy at Vanderbilt University;
Siegfried S. Hecker, director of the Los Alamos National Laboratory, who read the manuscript while he was chairman of the
laboratory's Center for Materials Science and Technology; and
John H. Brownell, an associate group leader at Los Alamos National Laboratory. William A. Weimer, a former colleague at
IBM, provided valuable assistance, as he has on previous books.
Two reviewers chosen by Jossey-Bass were especially helpful:
James A. Bixby, president of Brooktree Corporation, and Mary
Ann Von Glinow, associate professor of management and or-
ganization at the University of Southern California.

Saratoga, California   Donald Britton Miller
June 1986

▼▼▼▼▼▼▼▼▼▼▼▼

Contents

Dominant and Unique Value Set • High-Technology R & D
and the Professional • Self-Management, Autonomy, and
Control • Expectations: The Psychological Work Contract
• Needs for Contributions Beyond the Organization • Grow-
ing Professionally and/or into Management • Difficulties in
Achieving Collegial Support • Summary

Managing People and Technology: The Challenge • Conflicts and Problems • The Roles of the Manager • The Project Cycle • Negotiating for Scarce Resources • Disturbances
and Their Effects on Creativity and Innovation • The Experimental Outlook • Managing Useful Waste in Pursuing
Innovation • Effective Manager-Employee Ratios and Other
Ratios • Changing Organizational Structure • Audit Approaches and Teams • Sampling Attitudes and Opinions •
Financial Plans and Controls • Management-Leadership
Styles • Techniques Appropriate for Stable Versus Growing
Organizations • Leadership: Creating the Values • Summary

The Importance of a Mission • The Need for Excitement •
Creating Excitement • The Need to Belong • The Need for
Meaning and Importance • The Dream: Communicating the
Mission • Motivation Through Owning the Goals • Partici-
pation, the Vehicle for Achieving Ownership • Goal Con-
gruence Between Individual and Organizational Goals •
Summary

The Power of a Goal as a Reference for Direction • Throw-
ing Out Old, Nonworking Goals • The Crisis • Vitality in
Organizations: A Definition • The Relationship Between
Vital People and Vital Organizations • Measuring Vitality
• Defining Effectiveness • Measuring Effectiveness • The
Relationship Between Effectiveness and Vitality • How a
Vitality-Effectiveness Strategy Can Affect R & D • Specifi-
cations for a Vital and Effective Research Organization •
Specifications for a Vital and Effective Development Or-
ganization • Blocks to Creating Vital and Effective Organi-
zations • How Management Creates Vitality • Summary

Contents

The Dream Factor • Communicating the Dream Through Participation • The Necessity for Individuals to Buy In • Team Building and Planning Retreats: An Implementing Tactic • The Action Plan • Measuring, Benchmarking, and Feedback as Factors • The Recognition Factor in Managing Change • Course Correction for Enhancement of the Benefits • The Messages of This Book • Making This Book Work for You • Summary

▼▼▼▼▼▼▼▼▼▼▼▼

The Author

Donald Britton Miller is an independent management consultant who specializes in assisting organizations with significant groups of professional employees to increase their effectiveness (productivity) and vitality. He received his B.S. degree (1943) in mechanical engineering from the University of Rochester and his M.B.A. degree (1948) from the Graduate School of Business at Columbia University.

Miller's main interests and experiences involve the human resource aspects of managing professionals, especially scientists and engineers. These interests were kindled on his first assignment as an engineer when he found that good technical solutions were unappreciated in other parts of the organization and that professionals were not affecting decision making as he thought they should. At IBM in the late fifties, he pursued some of the earliest studies on the obsolescence of engineers, and he chaired a task force to study this phenomenon and recommend solutions. This was a period of major technological change— from vacuum tubes to transistors. The task force discovered that the company was expecting engineers to design components using a technology with which they were insufficiently familiar. At that time the solutions were direct and simple, and they emphasized the need for organizational support of continuing education; education had to be made part of work, not just preparation for it. In the seventies, while still at IBM, Miller felt the need to broaden the original solution to include design of work environments, mission and goal-setting practices, organizational design, and the process of matching people and work. As a result, he is credited with the development of the concept of vitality for individuals and organizations.

Miller worked as a designer and engineer at the Stromberg Carlson Company during World War II. From 1948 to 1952, he was assistant to the dean at the School of Engineering at Columbia University. After retiring from almost twenty-six years with IBM, he established his own consulting practice, focusing on environmental, climate, and organizational design; management and professional development; career development; and the creation of effectiveness and vitality. Many, though not all, of his clients work for research and development organizations. In 1978, he received the Distinguished Service Award from the Continuing Professional Development Division of the American Society for Engineering Education. He is the 1983 recipient of the Human Relations Award from the Society for Advancement of Management. Miller's earlier books include *Personal Vitality* (1977), *Personal Vitality Workbook* (1977), *Working with People: Human Resource Management in Action* (1979), and *Careers '80/'81* (1980).

▼▼▼▼▼▼▼▼▼▼▼▼

Managing Professionals
in Research and Development

*A Guide for Improving
Productivity and
Organizational Effectiveness*

PART I
▼▼▼▼▼▼▼

Special Challenges
of R & D Management

Managing R & D is one of the most challenging leadership assignments. It requires understanding the unique nature of the R & D mission and culture. It requires maintaining this uniqueness in organizations where others may be pursuing conflicting goals and may be supported by cultures with different values. To do this, the manager must be able to communicate effectively with organizational leaders who have different educational backgrounds, different interests, and different goals. The leader must also have a keen awareness of the need to balance a scientific and technical emphasis with a capacity for understanding and nurturing people. To do this the manager must communicate openly with nonmanagement professionals and must retain their respect. This requires understanding the values, motivations, and needs of the professional and involves managing in a way that supports credibility and trust. The manager must create an environment where the professional can be motivated by the challenge of the work and has the autonomy to be self-managing. Yet the manager must still find a way to exert leadership influence.

1

Chapter 1

Why Managing
R & D Is Different

The terms generally used to describe that segment of a high-technology organization (or of any organization) in which the creative and innovative work is done are *research* and *development* (R & D). Under the best of conditions, R & D departments are exciting places to work. Under the worst, however, they can sap the individual's energies in nonproductive activity.

Since people generally think of R & D in terms of cars, computers, space vehicles, satellites, and similar products, it is normal to use the terms *scientist* and *engineer* in describing the professionals of these organizations, but it is equally true that these organizations include other professionals: programmers, who can make the computers do our bidding; psychologists, whose work helps us to relate to and use computers; accountants, who calculate costs; personnel professionals, who design work environments; writers, who create instructions for the eventual user; artists, who work on creative packaging and make the product esthetically appealing; and many others. These are people who, in the right work environment, can and want to be self-motivating and self-managing. They want to be excited by their work. They are achievement-oriented and want to contribute. They should be the driving force for progress, generators of creative ideas. In general, they can be described as knowledge workers—people whose work is with ideas, concepts, and techni-

3

cal information specific to their role—yet by talking of them as a class, I am in danger of giving the impression that they all desire the same elements in a quality work environment. They do not, for quality is in the eyes of the individual beholders and thus has many definitions. This individuality in needs is one of the challenges of managing R & D.

These professionals of R & D organizations are those referred to in the title of this book. They are people who use their extensive educational preparation in their work—not as sole practitioners, but as members of an organization. It is our goal to help them be more effective for the organization by increasing their satisfactions from work. I believe that by improving the management of people, managers can increase the probability of reaching the technical and other goals of the organization.

The purpose of Chapter One is to establish a common basis for understanding the challenge of managing research and/or development. The challenge is to increase individual and organizational vitality and effectiveness (productivity) and thereby to increase the useful output from R & D professionals. I will share with you some of my reasons for the view that change is needed in the way we manage R & D. I will also share my excitement concerning ideas for an improved work climate (discussed in Chapter Seven). Some of the information in this chapter describes characteristics generic to the functions of R & D; an example would be the necessity to insulate the researcher, the inventor or creator of ideas, from some of the activities of the organization. I argue that insulation is necessary in order to provide a supportive environment for creativity, yet we know that creativity requires some disturbance, not just quiet. This is one of the exciting conflicts in design requirements for environments which support creativity and innovation. Other information in this chapter is conjectural, based on my experience in observing and analyzing technical organizational environments.

In this chapter, I shall describe the challenge in several ways. It is this complex and multifaceted challenge that creates the need for this book and for changes in our perspectives and in our styles of management-leadership in R & D. I hope you will be able to integrate these statements and anecdotal stories into a personal definition of the challenge as you see it; this integrated challenge should be the one that you wish to meet after having gained some ideas from this book. In addition, you should be able from your own experience to round out and extend the description of the challenge. One specific challenge that I see is to make leading and managing fun for the professional who is promoted into a leadership position. The necessary fun is included in my term *psychic income,* which is the group of satisfactions that provide the basis for motivation to manage and to lead. These satisfactions include helping someone else to learn, personal growth, achievement, a feeling of having made an impact, and a sense of personal worth.

The first several chapters endeavor to distinguish the real and the necessary understanding about what makes R & D different. For example, it is necessary to understand that some statements about these unique R & D organizations are folklore, such as the belief that the professional is unmanageable, and I cannot agree with that idea. This type of clarification is essential in order to separate the useful from the nonuseful myths and thus to achieve the necessary understanding on which to base improvement of R & D management. Understanding is difficult to achieve because some attributes of R & D lead to ineffectiveness, while others are vital to managing R & D. Whenever we consider making changes we must be able to make these distinctions to avoid changing necessary attributes.

Needs for Improving Leadership-Management in R & D

Leaders in R & D are usually chosen because they are technically competent and stand out in their technical contributions. It naturally follows that, as managers, their emphasis is not on managing people but on managing the technical aspects, the things with which they are familiar. For them to pay attention to managing people requires that they be shown the need by their leaders and that they be trained and measured on their people-management activities. Thus, as I see it, warm, caring leadership is not generally characteristic of research or development organizations unless some leader has established policy and practice that support this need.

It takes a very special person to lead such an organization. It takes a person who enjoys and is knowledgeable about science and technology and thus gains the respect of those to be led; it also takes a person who enjoys interpersonal relations and is knowledgeable about people and how to lead them. This combination is rare in R & D professionals because the second requirement is not normally supported by their education and because they most often work for someone who emphasizes technical aspects. Consequently, while all organizations may suffer from a lack of leadership and effective managership, R & D organizations probably have a larger deficiency in the people-understanding aspects of leadership than do others. The fact that it is rare to find a person in R & D who has balanced people and technical capabilities may be a result of some of the unique characteristics of the R & D environment; alternatively, it may be a result of the educational base, or it may be that the education tends to screen out those with a strong interest in people. Whatever the cause, there is a general lack of people-management and -leadership capability in R & D. The impact of this lack is serious because these engineers, scientists, and programmers are the principals, along with those they lead, on whom we rely for the new ideas, systems, processes, and products to improve our world. It follows that if you and I can improve the quality of the leadership and management of people in R & D organizations, a tremendous reserve power trapped in these talented people will be unleashed.

This book is dedicated to improving the ability of the manager-leader in R & D to manage and to lead. It is dedicated to helping the manager design quality work environments in which individuals gain the satisfactions that motivate them to work. It is designed to help the professional relate to the organization in a meaningful and satisfying way and to change R & D environments so that they support this goal. It provides ideas that will improve the ability of the R & D manager to work with individuals in other parts of the organization. This book is also dedicated to assisting managers in other parts of the organization to understand, communicate with, and work with managers and professionals in R & D organizations.

There are, of course, good manager-leaders in R & D who do demonstrate a balance between technical and people emphases. I have personally known and worked with many outstanding and inspiring ones. One of my managers, a talented electrical engineer, had a way of causing people to rise above themselves. He was unique, so much so that some engineers did not think of him as an engineer; it was as if they felt that in becoming a good people manager, he had deserted the technical profession. But he was a good coach. He helped people reach new heights of accomplishment. Where did his winning way with people come from? I suspect that it resulted from attitudes and interests developed outside his formal education. If we can capture some of the experiences and ideas that create such good leaders and pass them on to others, we will have a positive impact on improving R & D. If we can change R & D environments so that being a good manager of people is not only accepted but valued, we will amplify our positive impact.

In writing about why technical managers fail, Badaway (1978, p. 25) says: "The major cause of managerial failure among engineers and scientists is poor interpersonal skills. Many technologists are more comfortable dealing with matters in the laboratory than they are dealing with people. Because most of them are loners, they are used to doing things for themselves. Once promoted to management, however, they have to delegate responsibility to others. They often find this extremely difficult, especially if they have less than complete confidence in their subordinates' abilities. As a result, many technologists find that their advancement—and their managerial careers—are limited more by human factors than by technical ability."

Causes for the Unique Leadership and Organizational Characteristics of R & D

There are several root causes for the unique leadership needs in research and/or development organizations and for the differences in outlook and expectations of the people who populate them. Here are some:

- *Autonomy versus control.* The expectations of the scientist in research are for significant autonomy in deciding what to do and how to do it. There is also some of this feeling from the engineer in development, but the engineer has a greater tendency to accept the goals of the organization; the engineer's emphasis on freedom tends to center on how to do the job. These expectations, reinforced by educational preparation and often by the promise of unrealistic freedom at the time of recruitment, set up a fundamental conflict. It is a conflict between individual expectations and those organizational expectations which must be carried out by the manager. This subject is thoroughly discussed from several authors' perspectives in a special issue of *Human Resource Management* (Bailyn, 1985; Raelin, 1985; Von Glinow, 1985).

- *Conflict between the pursuit of knowledge and its application.* Along the continuum that starts in research and ends in the release of a product, there are many different appropriate balances between the pursuit of knowledge and its application. The appropriate balance at the research end, where invention or the conception of an idea occurs, is closer to the pursuit of knowledge, but it cannot be totally pure (as it might be in a university) if it is supported by a business that produces products. At the development end, the engineer will often argue that if everything concerning which technology to use and how to use it is known, it is not true development. Technical managers generally agree that innovation takes place at the product development end where the commercialization of the idea is accomplished. Since managers must meet the goals of the organization for results (commercialization), there is a natural conflict between leader, who tends to emphasize application, and professional, who tends to emphasize pursuit.

- *Protection and special rules versus the rules of the organization.* One of the struggles between management and the professional stems from the belief that the creative-innovative process is fragile and must be protected from the harsh reality of schedules, budgets, and bureaucratic controls. This is the basis of another, often more serious conflict between the managers of R & D and the managers of other parts of the organization. Much of the difficulty in leading R & D is re-

lated to how special R & D is and how much protection the
idea-creating process needs.

- *Development of managerial interest and capability.* The
  knowledge base and experiences that precede becoming a
  manager-leader in R & D are different from those in other parts
  of the organization. Scientific knowledge and ability, which
  are the attributes that cause the individual to be considered
  for management, are necessary but not sufficient for leadership. The experience gained as a professional does not expose the individual to the knowledge and outlooks needed in
  order to be a leader. It is probable that those who choose science and engineering as a career are not primarily people-
  oriented. This does not mean that scientific managers are
  antipeople; rather, it means that their outlooks and emphases are not on people. An excellent discussion of the effect
  of personality on what is the right job for a technologist with
  certain characteristics can be found in *The Engineer in Society* (Mills, 1946, chap. 2).
- *Facts versus feelings.* The training that technical people get
  in their formal education stresses paying attention to facts,
  not feelings; therefore, they tend to deny feelings as legitimate input. This creates problems in interpersonal communication because important cues to meaning are left out.
  This may be a basis for some of the problems that technically trained people have as managers in understanding those
  they lead. Both the leader and the professional fail to pay attention to tone of voice, body language, and other cues to
  meaning. Conducting an interview in a technical organization, I detected a lack of trust and openness in communication; when I said that people in the organization evidently
  did not share their feelings, the interviewee said, "Right, we
  don't even share facts!"
- *Management is not an honorable profession.* Most scientists,
  and some engineers, look at management as administration
  or paperwork and thereby devalue management as a role.
  Francis (1977, p. 15) says: "To some, the designation manager suggests one who acts as a caretaker of assets (people,
  money, and things) and who makes decisions regarding their

disposition. However, in today's dynamic and aggressive technological environment much more is expected of the R & D manager than simply to act as an organization caretaker; the term *administrator* more appropriately characterizes that function." Because of this view, those nonmanagerial R & D professionals who do not consider management an honorable profession often distrust all management intentions and actions. Consequently, R & D professionals promoted to a managerial role are likely to feel uncomfortable; often with good reason, as they begin to understand the role's broader requirements and understand that their subordinates condemn them for having deserted the profession.

- *Specialization versus the general management view.* The culture of the scientist and engineer, built during education and supported by peer interaction, reinforces the view that success means knowing a lot about a very narrow subject. The very existence of R & D as a separate function, together with the aforementioned belief that creativity must be protected, sets up an inherent conflict with management. Higher levels of management must take more than technical factors into account in decision making, such as financial, marketing, and manufacturing needs and even organizational politics. This tends to establish another dimension of conflict between the professional and management. It is the conflict between the view of the specialist and the view of general management, the conflict over which view represents success, that supports a lack of trust between the professional and management. In commenting on this, Riggs (1983) suggests that improvement in organizational success requires that the technical view must be represented in the top councils of management and that the scientist and engineer must in turn develop the general management view.

- *Individuality in specifying quality work environments.* The image of the classical research person is that of one who desires to find the characteristics of the university environment in industry. While this is true of some research people, others are frustrated because their activities seem unconnected to the purposes of the organization, and yet others are uncomfortable because their leaders are not telling them what needs to be done. The R & D leader is thus challenged by the need to satisfy many different expectations, all within the context of the organization's goals.

- *Planned versus nonplanned activity.* There has been a fundamental belief structure among scientists and engineers that supports the idea that R & D cannot and should not be planned, managed, and measured. They have recently accepted the idea of planning, but not of scheduling innovation, and remain fearful of being micromanaged. There is little doubt in my mind that the influence of the business schools on the management of technology has come dangerously close to causing business leaders to kill the goose that lays the golden egg—the creativity of individuals. This negative impact results from overly tight management and financial control of the front end of the creative process. There is room for compromise on this issue, and designing appropriate controls can lead to improved output. The challenge is to acknowledge that there is a conflict of values and to manage in such a way that this conflict does not have a negative impact on innovation.
- *Independent versus team activity.* The image of R & D fostered by the professionals' training in the academic world is that of the dedicated, talented individual working alone. This creates two conflicts, or management difficulties. First, it leads to technical managers feeling that their employees, being people of high technical competence, are independent people who cannot possibly need personal attention, coaching, and a pat on the back. This is wrong, for even the Ph.D. is human. Second, it creates a conflict between the actual work environment and the individual's image of career and reward, for the team projects that represent much of today's technological work do not meet the expectations of the individual.

Lest I give you the impression that the task of managing R & D is impossible, I will stop listing these root causes. Some of them tend to have a negative overtone, but this is part of the nature of describing a problem, or challenge. It is a way of defining the "hurt" that provides the motivation for organizational and personal change. Such negatives will be offset by the positive ideas of this book. The above list of root causes is not complete, but it should be sufficient to transmit the message—which is that there are causal bases, both positive and negative, for the unique aspects of R & D organizations and the challenge of managing them.

The Challenge Through Anecdotal Stories

Toward communicating clearly the nature of the multifaceted challenge of improving the effectiveness of R & D, I shall try another approach—describing aspects of the challenge through several anecdotal stories drawn from my experiences in working with professionals, managers, and leaders in R & D.

One day I was invited to visit an organizational unit that had a large population of technical professionals; it was similar to a laboratory. I talked about things that other organizations were doing to improve the probability of individual growth in capability. I tried to show them how to develop vitality, productivity, and effectiveness rather than to encourage obsolescence, or decline, over time. In the morning, I addressed an audience of over one hundred professionals and managers; in the afternoon, the same. By the end of the day, I had talked to about one-half of the technical professionals in the organization. As I was closing out my visit, I had a conversation with the director of the operation.

"I am very pleased you came," the director said. "I have talked to some of the people who heard you, and they are excited about the message you brought."

I responded that I, too, had talked with some of these people. Then I asked the director, "What are you going to do differently?"

His jaw dropped. He asked what I meant.

"The people tell me that 100 percent of the time in your office is spent on technical matters," I said, "and that if you are

not going to change this and put some of your attention on people issues, nothing will happen as a result of today's discussions." I also explained that if he did nothing new to support individual development, his professionals might never again believe
that he was really interested in them.

This leader did not understand that his behavior shaped
part of the culture, climate, and environment that supported, or
in this case failed to support, improvement in the capabilities of
people. He did not grasp the need to change his own behavior.
(Chapter Four, which discusses the conflict between managing
technology and managing people, should help managers achieve
an improved balance and not make the mistake this director
did.)

Another time, I was visiting a leading, scientifically driven
organization, by which I mean that the activities of the organization were built around a technology and its development.
Along with me, several others had been invited to talk about the
organization's need to provide support in career management
and development for individuals, especially the technical professionals.

In the afternoon, a group of managers, directors, vice
presidents, and scientists were sitting and talking with us about
what to do. Repeatedly, members of this group spoke up and
said that they had not had to manage their careers; as they re-
called it, they had been pushed up to their present positions of
scientific management or leadership strictly by reason of having
done their work well. They did not understand that the era in
which they had gained these positions was one of numerical
growth in R & D (1948 to 1968 was a period in which the portion of the gross national product related to R & D grew ten-
fold, but that portion has not changed substantially since 1968).
They did not understand that organizational growth had affected their own growth and that such organizational growth
was no longer occurring. Nor did they understand that organizational complexities, team projects, and the pervasive change of
technology had changed the world of work. Consequently, they
did not understand the impacts that these changes were having

on those who were following them—those who were intent on learning, growing, and developing their careers in today's world.

They did not listen to themselves that afternoon in their coffee-break conversations about head-count reductions and workforce limitations. Listening would have helped them understand one reason why it is more difficult than before to try to develop one's career in this changed work environment. Most of all, they did not realize how these changes necessitated more active career management on the part of the individual and thus, correspondingly, required management to support this process.

What was it that caused these intelligent leaders to miss such an important aspect of managerial perspective? They were in the middle of this "changed world" without acknowledging the change and the necessity for changed managerial style and emphasis. I suspect that they were too intent on managing the technology and had failed to listen to their employees' needs. (The discussions in following chapters about obsolescence, vitality, meaningful conversations between manager and professional, and the need for career management should help avoid this type of problem.)

Several of the organizations with which I work are trying to improve their performance management and appraisal systems to make them more useful, reliable, and credible. Many types of organizations do poorly with this necessary part of managing people, and R & D organizations are no exception.

In part, this probably stems from the belief that the scientist's creative work cannot be measured. In part, too, it occurs because the leader who is a scientist or engineer assumes that appraisals constitute a personnel function rather than an integral and required part of the manager's role. This may result from a past use of appraisal systems for ancillary purposes. Since other uses of the systems are not generally explained or understood in the beginning, people lose faith in management's positive intent.

Part of this problem can also be attributed to the focus on rating scales, filling out forms, and paper handling rather than on process. I remember one group of engineers who designed their own appraisal scale and form. While this was good in that they owned the system, it was bad because they came up with a scale that had two decimal places beyond the significant figure of the rating. This gave them the impression of accuracy in a field in which judgments about another person are usually accurate to plus or minus a whole point.

Technical leaders tend to fail to understand the dynamics of the process wherein the manager and employee talk meaningfully about performance improvement, about measurement, and about how the individual can grow in his or her capability and career. Creating clear understandings about what is expected, explaining how performance will be measured, and providing feedback help individuals know where they stand. This information is essential in the management of people. All individuals need to be measured. If management does not measure what the individual does, the individual tends to feel that what is done is not important—but one of the necessary psychic incomes for the individual is a sense of impact and/or a feeling that what is done is important to the organization. In organizations, importance is signaled by measurement, reporting, and attention. Evaluation is most important in R & D today because of team activities and long innovation cycles. An effective appraisal system—one that is well-understood, and well-supported —is a vital part of a quality work environment for the professional. (Chapter Ten provides new ways of looking at and implementing performance appraisal systems.)

One scientist leader-manager I was privileged to assist was struggling with an individual who was not performing adequately. No previous manager had faced up to the inadequate performance of this individual. In fact, quite typically, those managers had been unconvinced that they had a role in correcting behavior; moreover, they were afraid of the confrontation. This manager had decided that things had gone too far; not only was this individual not performing, but his lack of performance was negatively affecting others in the group.

I coached this manager to realize that improvement must

start with a clear understanding of what she required. She then clarified her expectations, even to the extent of writing out the requirements, an action which met with strong resistance from the individual. The individual took the position that the scientist, not the manager, was best able to determine what should be done and what was right. This is an example of the classical conflict between the professional's beliefs and the reality of organizations (it will be covered more fully in Chapter Three).

The manager stuck with her task, working to gain understanding on the part of the individual. She kept emphasizing that there were organizational as well as individual goals of value. After a couple of months, she realized that this process was taking almost two-thirds of her managerial effort. She was not devoting attention to science, but to a person. This felt and seemed wrong to her as a scientist turned manager, for she felt that managerial time should be devoted to science. Yet for the first time in the relationship with this individual, a scientific manager was doing the right thing—focusing on the person. She was focusing on matching the needs and capabilities of the individual with the needs and capabilities of the organization. Unfortunately, in this case, this attention came too late in the relationship of the individual to the organization, and the organization and the individual had to separate. Had it come earlier in his work experience, it might well have met with success.

The important message here is that an ongoing appraisal and counseling program, supported by a culture that supported management's emphasis on managing people, might well have created improvement and growth rather than failure. It should not take the intervention of an outsider, the consultant, to bolster the system. (Chapter Ten, on appraisal, will provide some answers to the dilemma posed by an unsupportive culture.)

One scientific leader-manager whom I coach is having difficulty getting people actually to do what they say in the manager's office that they will do. I have tried various techniques to get this manager to understand the power of his position and the ways to make it work in support of, rather than against, his organization's goals.

I have talked with him, for instance, about the "magic" of the office doorway. People who go through the manager's doorway understand that they can get away with saying almost anything they like about what happened inside the office. People who have a particular perspective to put forth will use a visit to the manager's office to create the image of support, whether or not support was given. People who hear the manager ask a casual question or express a wish that something would happen will go forth and say that the boss said, "Do this."

This manager tends to focus on the content of the message rather than on the feeling conveyed in the message. He also fails to use the simple follow-up technique of asking the person to feed back what was heard, or agreed upon, in order to ensure that a correct message got through. He fails to understand the power of the office and use it in a positive way. Why is this so and what can be done about it?

I believe it is so because of the bias of technically trained people against management (which I listed above as a root cause). In this case, it worked to keep the scientist turned manager from accepting, learning, and using the management understanding that he needed. It can be overcome by restructuring management development for the scientist (as discussed in Chapter Nine).

An outstanding engineer was promoted to a position of leadership because of his technical brilliance. Like all leaders moving from science, from being a doer of the work, this person needed to change the sources and desired kinds of psychic income that he gained from work. Rather than getting his kicks from doing science, this manager needed to shift to getting them from leading—from the growth and accomplishments of others. It is necessary for every leader to get some satisfactions "secondhand." As in the case of the teacher, success for the manager comes from knowing that his or her personal support, encouragement, and leadership helped someone else to be successful.

Unfortunately, this engineer turned manager could not make the shift. He continued to design, depriving the group and the individual professionals of the opportunity to contribute and to grow through contribution. He would tell people how to do things in such detail that they were "turned off" and stifled. Such a manager fails to develop a true understanding of personal leadership power and how to use it for the inspiration, growth, and development of others. This type of manager exemplifies another of the fundamental managerial challenges in R & D. There is a strong need to improve the choice of leaders, improve their training for the position, and improve their understanding of the role.

Many years ago, I convinced my boss, a division president, of the importance of the manager's role as a cultivator and developer of people. The president wrote a letter to each of the laboratory directors in the organization, some fifteen in all, asking that they recognize and reward a manager who had done an outstanding job of developing people. Out of the fifteen, only one director could find such a person. No one had bothered to keep track of this important part of managerial performance. Because it was not measured, it was not important. Even today, I know of no personnel data system that keeps track of the manager's performance in developing people.

This story emphasizes the great importance of shifting the emphasis in technical management away from overemphasis of the technical and toward increased emphasis on managing people, which is the goal of this book.

One last story. Contrast the stories you have just read with one about a group of scientists that was ineffective because of internal bickering, excessive interpersonal competition, and lack of team effort. An outsider called in to help the group interviewed each person and amassed a list of organization problems from their comments. The group then took several days to discuss the problems, sort out those that were serious, and plan to do something about them. The outsider, serving as a catalyst for the process, kept the group's members focused on attacking the problems rather than each other. The outsider helped them set up a team learning situation. Improvement started with little changes that they decided they could implement. As a follow-up to the group process, both the group's leader and the outsider reinforced the improvements with positive feedback to group members. A few months later, the group had become a team and was acknowledged by the organization as effective.

This is an example of management ideas that can make a difference in effectiveness. This one, team building, is described in Chapter Thirteen on managing change.

What Has Changed That Makes It Vital to Change R & D Now

One can easily argue that the root causes and the anecdotal stories talk about challenges and problems that must have been present in R & D organizations all along. What has changed? Why is it important to modify the R & D environment and to change management's emphasis now? Several things have changed, and looking at them can intensify our motivation to do something different now. Here are some of the changes:

1. The "golden era" when there were seemingly unlimited funds for research is gone. General management, the government, and the public no longer buy research on faith; in fact, many people question the positive nature of the outcomes of technological progress. This means that it has become necessary to "sell" people on the need for support of research. This need to sell has increased dramatically, and it requires different outlooks and different training of research people. It requires that research activities and research people be demystified in the eyes of others in and out of the organization.
2. A larger portion of the total cost of creating a product or service is now in R & D than it was in the past. This means that there is strong pressure for making the R & D process more effective. Some of the management attention that used to be focused on manufacturing as a place to reduce cost is now focused on R & D because management leverage seems greater here than on other parts of the cycle. It is

therefore necessary for the managers of R & D to gain an improved understanding of the process and what they can do to affect productivity.

3. Interdisciplinary approaches are necessary in order to solve the difficult R & D problems of our era. This puts significantly increased emphasis on management and requires improved managerial skills and understanding. Success is often dependent on the quality of communication, interpersonal relationships, and teamwork.

4. Competition in R & D has increased on several fronts. There is increased competition both between projects within the organization and between organizations. Competition has also increased on the international front. Competition also increases the pressures for improved managership and leadership.

5. There is increased emphasis on the translation of research discoveries into useful products and systems. The ability of an organization to accomplish this transition smoothly and quickly can make the difference between success and failure, especially where the competitive edge lasts but a short time. A review of the history of the rapid improvement in the hand-held calculator shows that the lead of one company with a particular product was very short. Thus, rapid rates of change require increased emphasis on improving the management of R & D.

The Need for the Manager-Leader
to Gain Psychic Income

I have discussed some of the problems, or challenges, facing those who manage R & D. These challenges certainly point to the need for a change, but they do it primarily from the perspective of upper management and the organization's goals. Let us look now at the individual as a leader.

Are the individuals who are leaders in R & D gaining all the necessary satisfactions from their roles? I suspect that many are not. If this is so, it further supports the need for changes in perspective, emphasis, and style in managing R & D. The challenge can be seen from this quotation from Katz and Kahn (1978, p. 407): "Self-expression and self-determination are the basis for *identification with the job,* that is, for satisfactions deriving directly from the role performance. The scientist derives gratification from scientific inquiry, the musical composer from creating a symphony, the craftsman from the exercise of skill in a job well done." A successful scientist, and that is usually the one picked to be the leader, was originally attracted to the work by the opportunity to pursue scientific inquiry and/or has learned to gain satisfaction from scientific inquiry. The scientist turned manager, put into a role devoid of that type of satisfaction, immediately feels the loss of intrinsic satisfactions from the work. For the engineer turned manager, the loss is slightly different, but the effect is the same. The engineer loses the opportunity to apply technology to the solution of problems and to create devices and systems. For other professionals, there are similar losses. For the programmer, there is no longer the opportunity to create programs that others can use to solve problems. For the doctor, who becomes the chief or manager of a hospital function, there is loss of the opportunity for direct personal service to the patient.

In each case, through promotion to a managerial role, the organization has taken an individual away from a role in which he or she was gaining psychic income and presumably having fun. Neither management nor the individual knows at the time of role change whether there will be psychic income and fun in the new role. No one helps the individual to find the different types of satisfaction from the new role. No one knows whether the substitution of satisfactions will provide the individual what the individual needs to be motivated by the new work of managing. Some individuals make the transition and find that they enjoy management. Others, however, find that the role does not meet their needs for psychic income.

Management will be disappointed if it expects these latter individuals to be motivated to carry out the new role with excellence. Such individuals learn from this experience that management presumably feels that it is all right to take psychic income away from a person. We must therefore expect that the manager will not be sensitive to the psychic income needs of those who are to be to be managed. It certainly must appear to be acceptable in this work environment to take away job satisfactions. When this same manager is later told that managers should be sensitive to employees' needs for satisfaction and that managers should work to achieve a good match between the individual and the job, which message is believable? Generally, the message based on action will be stronger than the one delivered in words.

The challenge is to find a way to select people who will have fun in the managerial role and to support these individuals in the transition to manager. It is to do this in a way that helps the individual find psychic income in the new role.

Some observers have suggested that the solution to this challenge is to pick from among the technical professionals a person who is not necessarily the best scientist or engineer. Presumably, this saves the organization from losing the technical work of the top technical professional, but there is no guarantee that this will mean getting a good manager, especially one who can gain satisfactions from managing. Since the authority to lead a technical function comes more from the technical reputation of and respect for the individual than from the position or role, promoting the lesser technologist may mean that the person is not respected by those to be led.

In the past, some organizations have tried coleaders, but this has not generally worked any better than coconsuls worked in Roman times. For this organizational technique to work, there must be a special chemistry, a special compatibility and sharing, which is neither easily found between two people nor easily accepted and respected by the people who are to be led.

Most technical organizations use the approach of assigning the leader an assistant who takes on a lesser role, usually encompassing the administrative part of managing. This is supposed to leave the leader free to continue technical activities. It actually tends to reinforce the belief among scientists that management is merely an administrative function and is of a lower value than anything technical. It reinforces the wrong image of the manager's role. This approach probably helps the leader to miss and undervalue the real essence of management, the interpersonal relationships. The essence of management should be to assist another person or a team to reach greater heights of achievement.

Some organizations have set up centralized functions to handle part of the managerial role. This happens most often as a result of finding that scientists and engineers dislike or are poor at some aspects of managing. An example is to set up a career counseling center, given that managers tend to feel ill-prepared and noncompatible with the role of counselor, but this allows the manager to abdicate an important role. It is bad, too, for the individual who is being led, for the technique has the effect of splitting the management function, multiplying the number of managers to whom the individual must relate.

This centralized arrangement is not the only way that upper management misdirects the manager. Some organizations have measurement systems that reinforce the wrong goal. For example, many organizations consider the number of people being managed as a factor in determining the manager's pay. Larger numbers to lead mean more pay. If this factor weighs too heavily in an organization, the ambitious manager will try to gain functions in order to increase the size of the organization. This can also have the effect of encouraging the manager to hoard human resources, holding on to underutilized people or to those for whom a career move is desirable. Peter Drucker (1974) suggests that the most serious force for misdirection of the manager is the compensation system. Through compensation schemes, upper management tends to emphasize certain managerial functions over others and often provides the wrong cues about expectations.

None of the above options addresses the basic challenge, which is to help the manager gain satisfactions from managerial duties so that they are handled well.

This book takes three basic approaches to the challenge of making it fun to be a manager and thus of gaining better leadership. These approaches differ from those just discussed in that they try to capture the interest of the technical leader in the challenging activities that are part of the management role.

The first is to improve everyone's understanding of the environment, climate, and culture of R & D. This has the advantage of making expectations more realistic and helping the individual learn how to get the most from the job and organization. The second is to improve the selection of leaders, clarify the expectations of managers, and provide the manager with assistance in gaining new and satisfying psychic income from the managerial role. The third is to provide those organizational and managerial concepts and techniques which help to shift the focus from an "all technical" to a balanced view, putting increased emphasis on the leadership of both individual professionals and groups of professionals. This has the effect of increasing the probability that everyone will gain satisfactions from their work.

What Needs to Be Changed

There is a need to improve the productive output and/or effectiveness of professionals in organizations. Along with this need comes the need to improve the quality of work life for the professional so that we ensure that the professional gains psychic income from work.

The key to improving the performance of professionals lies in improved human resource management. The scientific capability is there; the leader-manager, and management in general, must be catalytic, nurturing, and supportive. The talent is there; managers must bring it out and let it flower. In the words of Dowling and Sayles (1978, p. 276): "The effective supervisor is the man or woman whose presence makes a positive difference. Who a person is and what that person does contributes to satisfactory morale and productivity. The task is formidable. The supervisor must determine the behavior that is appropriate to the situation—and remember, no two situations are exactly alike."

To be effective, leader-managers must not only meet Dowling and Sayles's requirements but must also design and implement improved work environments to support a better matching of people and work, especially for professionals. This means designing environments that support continued improvement in human capability and vitality rather than using up these resources in obsolescence and burnout. It means designing environments that support improved achievement. It means designing environments that help improve self-motivation by making it possible for the individual to achieve personal goals within the goals of the organization.

Managers must meet the challenges documented in this chapter, for we live in an era of changed values. For example, our era is one in which the historical motivation to climb some hierarchical ladder has become less dominant than before. Managers must learn to manage professionals who are primarily inner-directed (seeking intrinsic rewards) rather than outer-directed (seeking extrinsic rewards). One of the results of achieving this focus will be that it "releases a greater potential for commitment to organizational goals and creative effort in the pursuit of those goals" (Schein, 1978, p. 67). Managers must manage in an era in which the ability to fulfill the individual's goals within a larger support system requires managerial creativity and innovation far surpassing the requirements of the past.

As reinforced by their education, the natural tendencies of engineers and scientists bias them against some of the activities necessary for success in this demanding and changing management world. As indicated in *Authentic Management* (Herman and Korenich, 1977, p. 219): "We who have been raised in Western cultural and educational traditions have learned to depend on rationality, logic, and theorizing in our dealings with people and situations. As a result of this bias, we have developed magnificent processes for handling complex data in orderly ways. However, in our exclusive devotion to the logical, rational, and theoretical we have cut ourselves off from a great deal by blocking out much of our access to intuition, inspiration, and other noncognitive resources in our lives." For scientists and engineers, even more than for the general population, education has emphasized the left-hemisphere-of-the-brain type of activity; this is the analytical, rational, and/or sequential type of thinking. In the same way, it has deemphasized the humane, emotional, and/or imaginative activity of the right hemisphere of the brain. Improvement in the effectiveness of R & D organizations requires that professionals and managers work with the whole brain. The most creative scientists and engineers have achieved the ability to use both hemispheres effectively. Using both hemispheres appears to be one of the necessary ingredients in the creative moment.

For all R & D personnel and managers, a better balance can best be brought about by environmental redesign, by policies that support the new culture, by appropriate new management concepts and emphases, and by new forms of reward and recognition. To bring new management approaches into being requires new conceptual frameworks and improved managerial training, and this book provides the ideas on which you can build the necessary improvement.

Summary

- Managing R & D is a unique challenge because of the conflict between the need for freedom on the part of the research scientist and the engineer and the need for control on the part of the organization. Improved management must be based on an understanding of the unique characteristics, conflicts, and requirements in the R & D functions.

- Improving the effectiveness of R & D organizations (or of R & D units within organizations) is the primary challenge. Improved effectiveness requires improved understanding of the function's characteristics, the needs of individuals, and improved communication between professionals and managers. It requires managerial ingenuity by way of providing individuals with the psychic incomes that will motivate them to meet the goals of the organization. Manager-to-manager communication, both inside and outside of R & D, is another necessary component of increased effectiveness.

- Leader-managers of R & D, because of their training and interests, tend to emphasize technical matters, sometimes even at the expense of human matters. Because of this lack of attention to human resource management, some productive efforts of the professional are lost to the organization, and the professional's psychic income and vitality are less than they should be. Improvement in effectiveness will require a new balance between the emphasis on technology and the emphasis on people, with a shift toward more emphasis on people.

• Several things have changed in R & D that support the need for improved management in the current time frame. There is a dramatically increased need to sell research. Gone are the unlimited funds and the support of research on faith that we had in the past. A larger part of the total cost of a product is tied up in R & D costs than in manufacturing. In addition, organizations seem to be having difficulties in translating research into useful products. All these changes tend to make the need for improved management more severe.

• One reason for the lack of good management in R & D is the loss of psychic income experienced by the leader-manager in the transition to management. Ways must be found to assist the manager in the transition from "bench scientist" to manager. New psychic incomes replacing those that were lost can help motivate the engineer or scientist who is assigned to important managerial tasks. Ways must be found to make managing fun. Failure to do so lets the manager continue old behavior patterns and continue seeking the old psychic incomes, and such behavior depresses the creativity and motivations of those whom the manager leads.

• For maximum individual development and growth, as well as for appraising the work of creative people, there is a need to find new ways of planning, measuring, coaching, and leading. Finding these new ways will unleash new inventive and innovative power. The task at hand is to improve the professional's growth in capability, the professional's output for the organization, the organization's effectiveness and vitality, and the psychic income (or satisfactions) for the individual.

• The leaders and other people in a scientifically driven organization must put new emphasis on understanding and improving interpersonal communication. This improvement is much needed between the leaders and those whom they lead and between the leaders and those others in the organization with whom they must interact in order to carry out the organization's mission.

• Managers must understand their impact on the growth and development of people. Only by making the positive aspects of this role a better-understood, -accepted, and -practiced part of managership will we reduce the negative effects of work and increase its positive payout for the individual workers.

Chapter 2

Understanding
the R & D Culture

When C. E. Kenneth Mees was hired by George Eastman in 1912 to start a research function, he told George not to expect a usable, commercial idea for five years. Mees knew that the research organization he was hired to create could be destroyed by improper management expectations even before it got started. Research and/or development are fragile functions that are often misunderstood, and sometimes envied and disliked, by others in an organization.

Good R & D organizations are ad-hocracies. As Alvin Toffler (1970, p. 122) says: "The more rapidly the environment changes, the shorter the life span of organizational forms. In administrative structures, just as in an architectural structure, we are moving from long-enduring to temporary forms, from permanence to transience. We are moving from bureaucracy to Adhocracy." An ad-hocracy is characterized not by a rigid structure but by adaptability; it is characterized by task groups and temporary organizations. It increases the probability of invention and innovation because it decreases the organization's cultural support of those who would customarily seek to hide behind rules or otherwise defend their organizational boundaries, thus impeding change. In short, rather than wasting the energies that a conventional organization uses to support its bureaucracy,

an ad-hocracy frees these energies for creativity. This does not
mean that ad-hocratic organizations are without structure; it
means that, unlike many other organizations, their structure
and culture make it possible for people to break the bounds of
their jobs. In fact, if the activities represent true research or true
development, these activities should not be totally predictable.
A good R & D organization is one in which management has
chosen to accept the waste of unpredictability and of actions
later determined to be counterproductive in order to achieve
creativity. From these few thoughts come many of the problems of understanding, communicating with, and managing R &
D organizations. They are founded on values different from
those of the parent organization—and value differences can lead
to conflict.

       In this chapter, I will describe R & D organizations from
the perspectives of various observers and participants, thereby
differentiating the fundamental, or generic (and probably unchangeable), organizational characteristics from those which are
under management's control. The purpose of identifying the
characteristics that specific managers can change and control is
to clarify the scope of the opportunities we have to make organizations more productive. (Since no two organizations operate
under identical conditions or malfunction in exactly the same
ways, it will of course be up to you to take the broad perspective of this chapter and tailor it to your own organization.)
When management focuses its efforts on changing only those
things which can and should be changed, then change can re-
vitalize the organization and improve both the quality and the
effectiveness of work. Consequently, the manageable characteristics that help create this vitality will be my reference points
for the concepts and suggestions presented throughout the remainder of this book. If Chapter One has already convinced you
of the need to change and if you feel quite familiar with the
various ways that R & D is viewed in your organization and
have a clear picture of what needs to be changed in your organization, then you might skip this chapter until a later time.
Otherwise, read on.

Characteristics of R & D: As Seen by Outsiders

Top management of organizations should have an overall focus, one that takes in the many separate priorities of the sub-units and integrates them. Managers in particular functions should emphasize their function's unique attributes and goals. The managers at each of these two levels, when looking at R & D from the outside, will see a slightly different organization. Each will perceive research and/or development differently, based on their educational specialties and on their functional outlooks and goals. For example, a member of marketing sees R & D as a source of new products and services to meet customer needs. A member of accounting sees R & D as an expense (or overhead) that must be supported. A member of personnel probably sees R & D as a source of personnel challenges and as a group of nonconformists. In a sense, each view is right. In a sense, each view is also wrong.

Not all the views I am about to discuss apply equally or even accurately to all organizations, and certainly no one person believes them all, yet if we are to manage R & D effectively, we must understand and deal with the perceptions of people outside of R & D. The following are some of the typical views I have heard expressed by general managers as well as by managers in marketing, finance, and other parts of the organization (which I shall describe as if it were, in a sense, a "person"). Our purpose in sorting through these views is to discover together the "real" R & D organization.

1. R & D organizations are expensive luxuries. At random, and unpredictably, they can—but often do not—produce usable ideas that can be turned into profitable products, services, and systems. They are primarily public relations vehicles, and they must be limited to an arbitrary size and budget.

2. The members of R & D seem to take great pleasure in not conforming to the rules, practices, and policies of the organization as a whole. Their behavior, when viewed from

the perspective of other functions, is often seen as self-centered and perhaps even counterproductive. I remember some programmers, for example, who had just had a new building constructed for them and who were assigned to offices in accordance with their organization's planning principles—but rather than being happy, the programmers were upset. They wanted individual cubicles, with sound-proof insulation, whereas other professionals in the organization were housed two to an office, with only seven-foot partitions. Management had to struggle for over a year to deal with the programmers' strongly presented special needs—needs that ran counter to organizational principles. Others believed their demands to be unnecessary, even inspired by a desire for status, and a lot of managerial energy was used up on the issue.

3. In terms of the standards used in other parts of the business, R & D organizations are poorly managed. For example, R & D characteristically seems to have budget over-runs, missed schedules, and more than the normal number of personnel problems.

4. Managers and members of R & D organizations often seem to portray themselves, by virtue of their creative activities, as being special. For example, they often do not want to use the same performance management and appraisal systems or the same budget forms or to conform to the same work schedules that others do. Some non-R & D managers see them as special in a different way—as childish and immature.

5. In general, the members of R & D organizations have more formal education than do others in the organization. They have often tried to transplant the university environment into the business world in ways that make no sense to the others. They sometimes seem snobbish and remote, even unconnected to the organization as a whole.

6. It is difficult to communicate with R & D people. It is hard to get them to hear and understand the needs of other parts of the business, and it is hard for others to understand them. They seem to support and respond to different

values. Others may feel that R & D people simply march to
a different drummer and will never be understood. In an
early study of managing scientists, Hower and Orth (1963,
p. 36) report that there is general agreement that "scientific investigation must be autonomous—'free' in that the
investigator is not subject to religious, political, or economic constraints in his choice of problems or in the way
which he pursues his investigations." The struggle to achieve
enough but not too much autonomy—to attain an elusive
balance—tends to set up and continually reinforce these
communication difficulties.

7. R & D managers often appear not to be result-oriented.
    They seem to stray from the key purposes of the enter-
    prise and seem actually to avoid managing their operations.
    They seem to have less control over their employees than
    managers in other parts of the organization have over their
    employees.

8. Outsiders often feel as if they are being "blackmailed" by
    R & D leaders. R & D managers make their pleas for sup-
    port in such a way as to imply that if other managers do
    not back them, they will go somewhere else with their good
    ideas; they do not understand that upper management can-
    not back every idea. They also seem unwilling to share the
    burden of cutting some part of their organization when the
    rest of the organization has to cut back; in fact, they al-
    ways have large wish lists, with which they try to intimidate
    other managers. The threat of taking their ideas elsewhere
    is real, for many start-up high-technology organizations have
    been formed as a result of systems people, programmers,
    scientists, engineers, and technical managers having walked
    out of more mature organizations in which they felt frus-
    trated.

9. If left alone and not pushed by others, inventive and inno-
    vative technologists will go on polishing their idea or prod-
    uct and never release it to manufacturing and the world.
    They seek an unnecessary level of perfection and seem not
    to feel the pressure of the marketplace for solutions and the
    pressures of management for product leadership and profit.

This list could go on and on, but let us see how we can use these perceptions. The natural reaction of the research or development manager is that these do not represent a true view of R & D organizations and people, yet one of my reviewers reacted that the list really represented reality from the other's point of view. Thus, two kinds of action are necessary. First, the creative organizations have a large gap in understanding to overcome through improved relations with other parts of the organization; we must demystify R & D by letting others see the high energy and hard work that goes into invention and innovation. Second, we must pursue the intent of this chapter to find the necessary differences, the key to the management process in R & D. Presumably this should help by preventing R & D managers and professionals from pursuing unnecessary differences, differences which appear to others to be created just for the sake of creating a special class.

Characteristics of R & D: As Seen by Insiders

Next, it is desirable to look at the R & D organization from the perspective of the insider, the research and/or development professional or manager. As in the previous section, not all of these statements or viewpoints are held by any one person. Furthermore, while some of the views may be true, they may or may not be necessary characteristics, and others may just be folklore that impedes effectiveness. Our objective is to choose candidates for change.

Before looking at the list, one should ask why the insider views R & D differently than the outsider does and whether the characteristics are more true because they represent the insider's viewpoint. As in the case of outsiders, an insider's perspective reflects that individual's goals, education, personality, and values. Thus, a scientist who is trying to push back the frontiers of knowledge will view the organization's needs and necessary characteristics in terms of how they assist the scientist. Those organizational characteristics which block goal achievement will be bad, and those which facilitate goal achievement will be good. Generally, even though we tend to characterize people by their educational background, an individual's perspective is most closely related to pursued goals. An engineer, trying to perfect a new product, will judge organizational characteristics with respect to that goal, and a programmer will want the organization to be ideal relative to the programmer's goals. Personality also affects one's perspective. An individual who needs much managerial support and a high level of reinforcement (positive feedback) will judge management and the organization from that perspective, but one who has a strong ego and a high level of self-reinforcement will be less critical if such support is lacking. Meeting every individual's criteria for the right organization is impossible, of course, yet understanding the different perspectives is essential.

Here are some characteristics, as seen from the perspective of insiders:

1. Pushing back scientific and technological frontiers by invention and innovation is necessary for man's progress. Much of it is—and should be—carried out in special organizations, which must operate with special rules. Galbraith (1982, p. 15) states that "Invention occurs best when initial efforts are separated from the operating organization and its controls—because innovating and operating are fundamentally opposing logics." Thus, these are places where people can be free from many of the normal organizational restraints in order to pursue directions and ideas that may look useless and may indeed not yield useful ideas or concepts. These special places are R & D organizations—and they must be led by managers who are themselves expert in the field of endeavor in which the professionals are working. This latter view is held so strongly that I have known biologists who felt that a manager several levels above them could not possibly be a good leader because that general manager was a physicist. I have known programmers who felt similarly about a general manager several levels removed who was a marketing professional.

2. R & D must be supported on faith by the other parts of the organization. Other managers should not judge us R & D

people by their criteria; at the same time, they should be generous in their praise, recognition, and rewards when we do produce a useful output. Their support is best measured in increased financial support, freedom to accomplish a task in our own way, and increased faith that we will succeed even after the last deadline has long passed. (Note that this perspective is in a way a denial of the increased need to sell R & D to others, as mentioned in Chapter One.)

3. Research work cannot be planned; if it can be planned, it is not research. Since development largely depends on using the new and unpredictable, it cannot be planned and scheduled completely, either, and is thus like research; still, most of us would generally accept the desirability and necessity of planning the development program. What others see as wasteful in the process is viewed by us R & D people as activities essential to pursue in order to find the new. The search is what is fun, and most important.

4. The time scale of R & D activities transcends the budget year; consequently, R & D ought to have stable funding and not have to go through an annual rebudgeting iteration. Much of the financial planning that we are asked to do takes us away from meaningful and important work.

5. We must have a way of recognizing scientific and technical prowess that does not require us to promote our people into management. Although we surely need the "dual ladder" concept, it has been managed by managers, and they do not appreciate the proper values. As a result, many people on the technical side of the ladder are not competent scientists; they are people who failed as managers. It should not be easier to get pay and promotions just because you are in management, but that seems to be the case.

6. The professional performs the core and most valuable functions. All others should support the physicist, biologist, chemist, programmer, or engineer. I find that this tends to set up classes of citizenry and thus to make support people, even those with Ph.D.'s in their fields, feel like second-class citizens. Generally, the professional sees this distinction as appropriate and the individual in the support function (pro-

fessional or not) sees it as unfair discrimination. I believe that it does interfere with the effectiveness of organizations, yet I know of no laboratory where it does not exist to some extent.

Our goal in reviewing these snapshots is to find the "real," or "true," R & D organization. After presenting one more perspective, I will try to sort out those characteristics which should be maintained from those which are candidates for change.

Characteristics of R & D: As Seen by the Author-Consultant

As a result of many years of working in R & D organizations and, more recently, of consulting with them, I offer the following observations for your consideration:

1. Research organizations tend to have rather stable structures, with few organizational changes. While this is true of many research organizations, it is not true of all; research in new fields that are in foment (as biotechnology is now) are not necessarily represented by a stable organizational structure. Development organizations tend to change form and leaders more often, usually in response to the development cycles of the product. Mixed R & D organizations tend toward the structural stability of research rather than toward development's model of change. Change of structure is a managerial tool that should be used.

2. In industry, the life of a leader-director as the head of a laboratory tends to be about three years. In national laboratories connected with universities and independent research organizations, the cycle of leadership is longer. This difference has both good and bad effects; these effects tend to reflect the personalities of the individual leader and that individual's understanding of when to stir things up and when to put the hands behind the back. I found in

my own management that I was better at fixing a mal-
functioning organization or establishing a new one than I
was at running a stable one.

3. R & D organizations that operate under contract to the
    government or are government-owned and -operated have
    unique characteristics. For example, their structure often
    reflects the current interests of Congress, especially since
    they must sell to get support. One source of the differ-
    ences is accountability; the government contractor is not
    only accountable to stockholders but also to the govern-
    ment. This often means different rules of behavior, such
    as reflected in congressional stories about one-hundred-dol-
    lar screws. The government-supported laboratory has a
    different relationship with the customer than does the
    commercial laboratory, and this can affect its goal-setting
    process, its staffing, its control, and its reporting empha-
    sis. Some of these things increase the difficulty of creating
    the necessary climate of freedom.

4. Leader-managers are picked from the ranks of the profes-
    sional community, usually based on outstanding perfor-
    mance in their technical area. Seldom is the choice based
    on inherent or demonstrated leader-manager characteris-
    tics. This comes about for several reasons:
    a. The job requires technical expertise as well as man-
        agerial capability.
    b. The authority in such an organization is that of re-
        spect, not of position, and thus flows from acknowl-
        edgment of the individual leader's technical exper-
        tise.
    c. Few if any R & D organizations have established cri-
        teria for managership. They have no specifications for
        the type of person who is successful. So the choice is
        often a reflection of personal relationships or senior-
        ity, or sometimes even of availability.

5. Much leadership performance is dependent on personality.
    Leaders thus build followings and territories. Turf battles
    (arguments over territorial rights) are frequent in R & D
    organizations. Even in a multidisciplinary laboratory,

where interdisciplinary synergism is desired, organizational borders are a problem in achieving total effectiveness.
Turf battles can be made even worse by a competitive
budgeting process.

6. In organizations that are self-standing (that is, not part of
a large industrial organization) and in those which are tied
to universities, there has been little attention paid to the
training and development of managers. In part, this is because administration is looked down on as an activity—
and all management is seen as "administration." In part,
it is because of a lack of understanding of the need for
trained leaders. And in part, it is because the people tend
not to be motivated to study management; they do not
view it as an activity of high value.

7. Budget impositions and annual financial iterations have
had negative effects on R & D. These controls were
brought on by large overruns and (some believed) a waste
of financial resources in the 1950s and 1960s. In general,
overly tight controls have been imposed as a result. Early
in the cycle of innovation, tight controls, which might be
appropriate later, tend to stifle experimentation, suppress
new ideas, and kill some of the creative thrust.

8. In recent poor economic times, the financially motivated,
result-oriented, short-term focus of top management has
caused many organizations to lay off professionals. This
professional group, which prior to the 1970s had considered itself a part of the "management team," has thus become increasingly alienated. For one thing, this has led to
pressure on professional societies to set up standards of
employment and to become much more active in the protection of the professional. For another, the unexpected
layoffs have sparked feelings of insecurity among the professionals and encouraged them increasingly to question
top management's views regarding the importance of their
work. Furthermore, insecure people do not take risks—yet
risk taking is an essential part of the innovative process.
This change in practice has also exacerbated the powerlessness felt by professionals.

9.   There are conflicts in values, thinking, and priorities be-
     tween non-R & D management and R & D management
     that can cause real difficulties: For example, the non-R &
     D manager tends to feel that more money and more peo-
     ple will shorten the cycle to a successful answer. After one
     reaches the critical mass of dollars and people necessary
     for success, however, R & D cannot usually be sped up
     with more money and people. Many of the differences of
     opinion stem from not really knowing what the necessary
     critical mass is.

10. Even within the R & D community, the person who was a
     professional yesterday and has been moved to manage-
     ment today loses credibility. The distrust of management
     is so deep that even one of their own is spoiled by "cross-
     ing over." When you combine this natural phenomenon
     with the feelings expressed in item 8, it suggests that there
     is much to be done to help the professional and manage-
     ment feel that they are once again on the same team.

11. Many subunits within R & D organizations are most effec-
     tive when formed around a task for a short period. Some
     of the important breakthroughs occur when several people
     with different backgrounds are brought together by a
     common problem. This means that authority in such an
     organization flows not from the conventional position on
     the organization chart but rather from being in on the
     definition of the problem and its answer. The task group,
     characteristic of an ad-hocratic organization, is often an
     agent for change and the center of power for a short peri-
     od. Interestingly, it is also an underutilized place for en-
     hancing the development of individuals.

12. Much of the time of the R & D manager is spent negotiat-
     ing for scarce resources. These resources may represent
     needs for people with special skills, needs for equipment
     and facilities, increased dollars, work-flow modifications,
     or service support or time, as in a schedule change (Sayles,
     1964).

13. The true scientist believes that one responds to an ethical-
     ly right way, which scientists usually associate with the

profession, and that when management's directions go against this, one has the right not to follow the leader. This leads to an undermining of upper management's direction, to different subunits doing different things, and thus to ineffectiveness and often apparent unfairness. There is a time for a manager to argue upward to assure that a perspective is understood, and there is a time for the manager to support upper management's decision as if it were one the manager made.

14. Some of the conflicts between nondevelopment management and development management are the least severe during the early days of a high-technology organization. This seems to be because the founder-inventor is the center of the activity and is imprinting his or her values on the organization. During this period, R & D deviance is tolerated and sometimes admired and valued. As the organization becomes successful and matures, however, the tolerance of R & D deviance usually declines. One question we should face is whether we can achieve in a mature organization the support inherent in a start-up organization.

The preceding three sections do not list all the characteristics seen by the non-R & D manager, the member of the professional group, or the trained consultant, but they do provide the necessary insights for us to establish the basic (or generic) aspects of R & D organizations and to sort out some characteristics that, if changed, may cause improvement in effectiveness and vitality.

Differences Between Research and Development

Although I have been using the term *R & D* as if research and development were the same, they are not. There is no universally accepted definition of the differences, given that the functions covered, the expectations, and the modes of operation vary from one organization to another. For example, some organizations combine the two functions in one laboratory; Bell Laboratories represented this type of structure. IBM Research, on the other hand, represents more nearly pure research because development is carried on in many separate laboratories, but even in this case some research projects are nearer than others to commercialization and thus appear more applied.

We therefore come to the first basic difference: *Research* is generally thought to be broader, more basic (closer to pure science), and less applied than development is. People in research tend to think of themselves as scientists when talking about the behavior of materials. Those who are software-oriented in research think of themselves as working on systems architecture. The creativity in research can be thought of as invention; it is the activity in which ideas and concepts or new discoveries about the behavior of materials are the product. *Development,* as a term, is most often used when a product or service, rather than a concept, is the expected output. People in development are thought of as programmers and engineers. Development takes place where the idea is taking commercial form and the activity can be thought of as innovation; in contrast to research, there are usually fewer unknowns and the process is usually more predictable as to time, results, and budget. I can think of specific examples, however, where development teams were pushing the state of the art and it took considerably longer, with much more staffing and budget, than predicted. Programming development has been especially difficult to predict. Fred Brooks (1975) wrote a book entitled *The Mythical Man Month,* in which he talks about the man-month of effort used as a planning unit and the difficulty of predicting what programming effort is really needed for a development project.

From this short discussion it can be seen why there is no hard, accepted, and defensible definition of the differences between research and development. In this book, where there are no differences that affect the topic, I will use *R & D.* Where there are differences that do seem to affect the topic, I will either speak of *research* and *development* separately or draw attention to the differences.

For example, there are significant differences in how one recruits Ph.D. scientists for research and how one recruits

M.S. engineers for development. In general, the Ph.D. candidate is first contacted long before the receipt of the degree, and then cultivated and followed over several years; research organizations work very hard to develop an early collegial relationship between someone in the organization and the potential recruit. B.S. and M.S. graduates are more normally contacted in the last year before the degree, invited to the work site, and made offers a couple of months before graduation.

The second basic difference concerns how managers set goals and objectives when one expected result is to add to the basic store of knowledge and the other is to produce a new machine or system. It is this difference which has caused many research managers to resist performance planning and appraisal processes. Research managers claim, because of the unpredictability of results, that individuals who do not meet their results objectives may still be performing outstandingly. Thus, there are also differences between research and development in terms of how one sets objectives and appraises performance, since the results are usually more measurable in development.

Furthermore, people in research generally have different priorities for specific psychic incomes from work than do people in development. For example, a research professional properly matched with the work would probably be more comfortable with a lack of concrete results than would a development professional. The researcher may also need more peer recognition from outside the organization than may the development professional. There is normally a greater need for titles and structure in the development organization because its people have much greater needs to negotiate with and communicate with other parts of the organization than do their friends in research. When one negotiates, one needs to know who is sitting across the table and what power that person has in negotiation.

These examples of differences should be sufficient to demonstrate to the reader who is not familiar with these borders between creative activities that the management approach in research must sometimes be different from that in development.

Fundamental R & D Characteristics: Generic

When one considers changing organizational climates, structures, and management styles, it is necessary to sort out those aspects which one should keep from those which one should change. Many organizational changes are conceived and discussed but never implemented because of a fear of changing something that is fundamental to success. Some organizational changes bring about unexpected behavior because the managers who implemented them had not carefully analyzed the pressures and rewards that currently guide R & D behavior. Or perhaps they had failed to study and understand those structural supports in the current organization which have kept things from being even worse—the classical case of which occurs when management decides on a matrix form and usually greatly underestimates the numbers of people needed to provide the project and program leadership that was previously supplied in the functional line-management structure (as discussed in Chapter Eleven). For now, our task is to take from the several viewpoints that we have looked at those few fundamental characteristics which must be kept in mind as necessities when making other changes in organizations.

No characteristic of R & D organizations should be discarded that supports the work process, makes the work easier, and/or increases the probability of success. In fact, if one can discover new characteristics (such as ad-hocratic forms of organization) that accomplish these purposes, one should *add* them.

The following are examples of characteristics *not* to be changed because they support the inventive and innovative work. They are necessarily broad, and so you will have to find the particular equivalents in your own organization. You should therefore read this list with several questions in mind: What aspects of our culture or environment support the need inherent in this characteristic? What policies and practices support this need? Is this characteristic as strongly supported as it should be in our current environment and policy structure?

We should not change:

- *Those organizational design aspects which contribute to the professional's and/or to the group's perception that the need for autonomy is understood and supported, both in policy and in management actions.* Autonomy is not a single-dimensional factor. The two components are the freedom to decide what to do and the freedom to decide how to do it. The first is exemplified by participation in choosing strategy and goals. The second is exemplified by being free to establish schedules and to choose the means of achieving the goals; this factor is important in the individual's sense of power or powerlessness, which (as I indicated in the Preface) is a pervasive problem in R & D. An exciting and enlightening discussion of these dimensions and differences in autonomy, in context of R & D, is presented by Bailyn (1985).

- *Those policies, programs, and cultural elements which support the continued development of the individual's knowledge and capability.* Support can range from those policies and programs which provide additional technical, professional, and managerial education to those which assure that the work itself causes the need for personal development. A good match, with the right kind of work, fosters an increase in capability. Both are necessary in a quality work environment for professionals. (Chapters Seven, Nine, and Twelve discuss this type of support further.) A quick overview of some things one organization did can be found in Miller (1977b).

- *Those organizational aspects which increase the probability of building bridges between ideas, concepts, and technology.* Much creativity occurs when two previously unassociated ideas are brought together and thus provide us with a way to do something we could not do before. Arieti (1976, p. 271) suggests that "many scientific discoveries are the result of individualizing a common characteristic or connection between things that were deemed dissimilar or unrelated before. But of course the observation of similarity is not enough. . . . when Newton saw this similarity between the apple and the moon, *a new class was formed,* to which an indefinite number of members could be added thereafter. . . . The discovery of this class revealed a new way of looking at the universe." It is important to invent and innovate with respect to those aspects of culture, organization, and/or facilities design which improve the probability of creating synergism between those working in the same and different areas. Thus, this dimension can be affected by a culture that supports open communication, the sharing of ideas, and significant communication between professionals rather than the protection of one's personal work project. It can also be affected by so designing buildings as to facilitate face-to-face contact.

• *Those aspects of an organization which support the free communication of ideas and concepts from the place where they are created to the people who can apply them to needs and create commercial products.* This dimension should be thought of both in the sense of flow inside the organization and flow from outside the organization. No organization can create all the breakthroughs it needs; it must be aware of those things happening outside which can be used.

• *Those aspects of policy, program, and structure which provide for a flow of information about needs of the world that fall within the mission of the organization, either today or within the long-term strategy for development of the business.* This is the informational flow that assists the organization in determining which products to develop. For example, in writing about high technology, Riggs (1983) suggests that customers can also be sources of innovation, thus underlining the importance of open informational flow.

• *Those aspects of environment, mission, and policy which make the organization attractive to the types of creative and innovative professionals needed to pursue the mission and goals of the organization.* It is necessary both to attract them to come and then to provide the environment and work that will give them sufficient satisfactions to stay.

• *Those aspects of the work environment and organization of work which provide psychic income—the satisfactions from work that give the individual and the team the return on their investments of energy.* Chapter Seven on the designing of environments and Chapter Twelve on the creative matching of people and work will discuss these characteristics. In *Improving Life at Work,* Hackman and Suttle (1977, p. 9) reinforce this by saying: "The quality of an individual's work life has been shown to affect many of his responses to his job. Improvements in quality of work life might lead, for example, to more positive feelings toward one's self (greater self-esteem), toward one's job (improved job satisfaction and involvement), and toward the organization (stronger commitment to the organization's goals)."

• *Those things which attract individuals to the work and/or are generic to the work itself.* These include:

- The intellectual and technical challenge in the work.
- The potential for impact on the improvement of life.
- The potential for a breakthrough and the resulting collegial, management, and public acclaim.
- The technological cycles inherent in the field. (Short cycles attract some people and long ones are more attractive to others.)
- Those top-management beliefs and policies which create an exciting and attractive environment and demonstrate a high level of support.
- Those aspects which assist the individual to build an emotional connection to the work and its result (ownership).

• *Those aspects of environment or style which support openness to the creation of new organizational designs.* These include experimentation with new ways of doing things and the use of temporary systems with ad hoc groups and task teams.

Each of these aspects, which are undoubtedly not all the characteristics that we should resist changing, should cause you to think of others in your organization. On the other side of the coin, let us now look for candidates for change. By looking at both sides, we should be able to sharpen our ability to make judgments. Having ideas about what to change and what not to change in broad perspective can assist in reading the following chapters, which present specific ideas and suggestions.

Candidates for Change

Candidates for change include:
• *Methods of control of dollars, facilities, people, and*

time that are time- and energy-consuming irritants to the creative professional, inhibit the creative process, and are not absolutely necessary for the survival of the business. For instance, these include the extremely repetitive cycles of the budgeting process and multiple managerial signatures on the expenditure of small amounts of money.

• *University-related practices that, although they seem to be desired by some professionals and may create comfort for some highly educated professionals, are not useful and supportable in the industrial world.* Examples might include the encouragement of patents, papers, and speeches widely divergent from the possible interests of the company. I remember one professional who complained to management about his lack of promotion and of increased pay. He supported his eligibility with stacks of papers and patents but he was unable to demonstrate that he had accomplished anything that contributed to the goals of the company. Perhaps the organization had given him the wrong cues, but it is more likely that he chose to hear what he wanted to hear. Another example might be work assignments that respond to status differences rather than to expertise or to need to develop and grow.

• *Communications impediments.* These include status separations, a poor physical relationship between groups whose work is related, organizational boundaries that are unnecessarily polarized, and, in an effort to protect secrets or proprietary information, overly tight interpretations of the need to know. All these things can block that creativity which occurs when people are free to contact each other and share. Special attention must be given to (1) the flow of information about needs and problems from the field to the creators and (2) the flow of data for production and use from the inventors and innovators.

• *The ways in which we measure and reward results and accomplishment, for both individuals and teams.* Special emphasis should be given to improving the balance between measurement and reward for short- and long-term goals. Much current emphasis is too heavy on the short-term goals. For example, managers are rewarded more often for meeting schedules and budgets in the short term than they are for the long-term goal of developing people. Special emphasis should be given to the recognition of teams. As of today, our increasingly team-oriented work arrangements have not been matched with innovative rewards and recognition for teams.

• *Practices and policies that are nonsupportive of the individual in increasing the individual's capabilities and knowledge.* This does not mean that an emphasis on measuring results should be eliminated; it means that there should be some measurement and recognition of the development of people, not just lip service to that goal. Over and over, I have had managers tell me that no one has ever commented on or recognized as proper anything they did to help people to grow. This bias must be changed.

• *Policies or practices which contribute to a feeling of insecurity and which thus inhibit the risk taking necessary for progress.* The individual must understand what is at risk when taking an aggressive action that may be wrong. Does the person risk loss of job? Does the person risk simply the particular assignment? Some form of personal security, knowing the rewards and the limits of the punishment, is necessary in order for the individual to take the risks necessary for progress. I do not mean that penalties for failure should be eliminated, but I do mean that the emphasis should be on the positive—how one can improve. On another aspect of security, I have seen organizations of thousands where everyone became insecure because of a reduction in funding that meant the loss of support for a few. Such a change can and should be handled in a way that limits the impact to the small number where the impact will be felt.

• *The selection, training, and support of manager-leaders, the clarification of management expectations of managers, and the definition of and understanding of their roles.* Few R & D organizations have set up criteria for the selection of managers. Management development has in general been borrowed from programs designed to provide other managers in other parts of the organization what they need, not developed for these managers facing special demands. This is an area for much needed work, and Chapter Nine provides some suggestions. In the broader context, this book is a management-development tool for R & D managers.

• *The knowledge about and understanding of R & D by*

managers and others in other functional parts of the organization. As indicated by the first listing of perspectives in this chapter, there is much misunderstanding and misinterpretation of R & D. A massive communications effort accompanied by actual improvement in the quality of management in R & D can go a long way to assist in the several parts of organizations working together.

• *Human resource policies and practices.* What is needed is the creation of new human resource policies and practices that better match the needs of professionals and are not built on the idea of the nonexempt worker as the typical employee. New policies must provide improved support for the effective matching of people and work—and for creating quality work environments which attempt to meet some of the professionals' expectations and which recognize the new work modes. For example, the advent of computers has brought a new work mode and has meant that the work of professionals, who previously were free to decide how to do the work, has now been formatted.

• *Concepts and definitions of growth and career opportunities for the professional.* Gone are the days when hierarchical promotion was desired by almost everyone. Yet few organizations have developed cultures which support the idea that being able to do something tomorrow you can not do today is growth. Even fewer have found ways to recognize and reward this growth. Current environments seem to put far too much emphasis on growth into management. Dual ladders, while holding potential for improvement of this situation, are themselves in need of overhaul.

• *Those classical ways of designing organizations which impede creative thinking about organizational structure, policies, and practices and reduce the freedom to experiment.* In most organizations, the organizational structure is considered to be fixed or permanent and there is a lot of trauma surrounding a change in structure. Yet other fast-moving and effective organizations have been making increasing use of the temporary organization, which brings emphasis and multidisciplinary knowledge to bear on a problem. This is but one way to experiment.

• *Practices that support turf restrictions, defensiveness, and destructive competition.* Over and over in the pursuit of invention and innovation, the real breakthroughs have come at the interstices, the boundaries between previous fields or organizational functions. New ways must be found to provide sufficient definition of function for focus—but not so much restriction as to keep people from exploring the boundaries.

With this background, it is now possible for you to assess the performance of an organization against these suggestions of things to change and not change. You can also measure the performance of this book in providing suggestions for the areas where change is needed. As you read on, you can ask: Does this book assist you, the manager or professional, in changing those things in which change has an opportunity to improve effectiveness and vitality? Does it discourage tampering with those things which should not be changed? Does it provide a conceptual framework for inventive and innovative thinking about the leadership of R & D?

Summary

• The nature of the work and the training of the people who populate R & D organizations establishes some differences in values that make it hard for the non-R & D manager and some others in R & D to communicate with, understand, and work with each other. Generally, people outside R & D question the need for special rules and special treatment in R & D. Communication has not been sufficient to build an understanding that supports the differences.

• Some of the characteristics that set R & D apart are primarily in the eyes of the beholder and are based on folklore or on a misunderstanding of the requirements for the inventive and innovative processes. Therefore, it is very important to look at R & D from different perspectives and to find out which of the characteristics are generic or vital and which are really unsupported.

• Some of the characteristics that set R & D apart are generic to the work itself, necessary and supportive of the special aspects of the work process. There is, for example, a need for freedom—and it may be strategic freedom or operational freedom or both. It is important to understand which freedom is needed to support the creative process.

• In some ways, research and development organizations differ. While definitions are difficult because they reflect the particular organization, research is generally closer to invention, the creation of an idea, and development is generally closer to innovation, the commercialization of an idea. When it is important to understand the differences, the terms will be differentiated in this book; otherwise, research and development will be spoken of as one.

• Some of the characteristics that set R & D apart are candidates for change because they impede the work and make goal achievement difficult. These were listed as candidates for change; they include: improving security for individual risk taking; selection, support, and training of managers; and new human resource policy support for improved matching of people and work.

• Enlightened leader-managers have a real creative opportunity to experiment with new policies, environment designs, structures, management styles, and outlooks as means for improving R & D effectiveness and vitality. All the required creativity is not in technological areas!

Chapter 3

Values and Needs
of R & D Professionals

Generally speaking, more professionals are found in R & D than in other parts of an organization, but this is not to say that they are found only in organizations that have research and/or development divisions. Social service, technical service, and educational organizations have a great need for professionals. Similarly, high-technology organizations require professionals in manufacturing, sales, and other functions.

People classified as *professionals* typically include scientists (in both the hard and soft sciences), engineers, economists, accountants, doctors, lawyers, programmers, and business majors. Unlike liberal arts majors, they have pursued a college degree with the specific intent that it would prepare them for a career. Because professionals invest more time and energy in educational preparation for their work than do most other employees, they bring higher and more specific expectations to work. They expect their work assignments to relate to their education and prior experience; consequently, when their initial assignments fall short of their high level of preparedness (as is often the case), they feel shocked and disappointed, making for a bad start in the world of work. Since their achievement orientation is usually very strong, professionals expect to be able to use their expertise to the full and thus to make an impact.

In a study of professionals at work, Kerr, Von Glinow,

53

and Schriesheim (1977) have identified six characteristics of professionals. In addition to expertise, these are: autonomy, ethics, commitment to a calling, identification with the profession or fellow professionals, and collegial maintenance of standards. Although other employees may also share them, these six characteristics are generally more descriptive of professionals or of greater importance in describing them.

Every person needs some feeling of autonomy in managing work, but for the professional this need to control one's own work takes on high importance. Some observers argue that the engineer is but a quasi professional (Raelin, 1984); however, my work with both scientists and engineers on the need to control what they do indicates that this need is strong for both. It becomes one of the definitions of being professional, especially when one works for an organization. (Note that for our purposes in this book, I consider engineers, programmers, accountants, and others to be *professionals*; when my experience suggests that a differentiation should be made, I will make it.)

The professional's long training, especially for the Ph.D., usually helps build a strong value set. Here, the indoctrination of the scientist appears to be stronger than for the B.S. or M.S. engineer; that is, the scientist usually has well-defined values and feels clearer about what is important than do engineers. In a review of creative talent and its characteristics, Cole (1980) finds that professionals have strong esthetic and theoretical values and weak economic values. These characteristics may well set up the potential for conflict over values, goals, means, and ends between the technical professional and the profit-making business. This makes it important for management to find ways to get the professional to "buy in" to the organization's goals and policies.

Challenging work and the status of colleagues are also important factors. Scientists most often choose where they will work and what work they will undertake based on the importance of the work to them. Professionals assess the reputations of those already working there in making their choice of which organization to join; they know that their potential for success is related in part to the quality of those with whom they work.

As members of a profession, scientists usually wish to contribute beyond the needs of the organization; although engineers generally show less of this desire, I feel this is changing. Increasingly, engineers are building stronger ties to their professions.

Despite our ability to identify the characteristics of professionals, determining who is a professional requires looking at the individual. Not all people who have these characteristics will act like professionals; and by the same token, some who do not meet the educational specifications will act like professionals.

Given the strong characteristics of professionals managing them requires special knowledge, techniques, and style. The professional's need for autonomy usually means a higher need for participation in goal setting and decision making. To support participation, the professional expects high levels of information about mission, goals, and management's intentions. The professional also generally resents the feeling of being managed, accords authority only to a manager who can be respected, considers it a responsibility to challenge a manager's decisions, and expects candid discussion. These characteristics and behaviors are the basis for the professional's expectation of shaping a work environment and work relationships different from those more generally experienced by others at work.

In summary, the point is that as individual professionals and as leaders, we need to understand the values, characteristics, behavior, and expectations of the professional. The ability of professionals to see a way to match their personal characteristics, values, and expectations with their work, their colleagues, and their organization's environment, behavioral norms, and management style is the key. The quality of the match determines whether they join, whether they achieve and gain psychic income, and whether they stay; it affects the quality of their commitment and is basic to their motivation. In other words, building a quality work environment for professionals is the key to their effectiveness and satisfaction. For productivity, therefore, a *quality professional life* (*QPL*) is our goal. Like the more general term, *quality of work life* (*QWL*), it identifies factors in the eyes of the beholder that contribute to a good match of the professional's needs and capabilities with those of the organization.

The Effects of Extensive Preparation for Work Life

One of the things that differentiates the professional from others is the length, narrowness, and applied nature of school preparation, and often internship, before one becomes a professional. Normally, we think of internship with respect to medicine, because it is formal, yet the scientist or engineer usually works in an organization two years before being acknowledged as a professional.

This investment shapes, perhaps even warps, the professional's personality, outlook, and expectations. When the typical (if there is one) young professional to be graduates from the university, that person has a pent-up desire to achieve, to use this preparation. The professional to be often graduates with a financial debt for the costs of preparation, and this individual has probably postponed many of the enjoyments of life and so has a pent-up desire to live, to have fun. This is particularly true of engineers, whose study has been so prescribed that electives have been limited to one or two and so intense that they have accumulated thirty (or so) more credits than the typical bachelor's degree graduate. It is also true of the doctor, who has virtually denied normal life in order to get through study and internship, and of the lawyer, who often starts for less money after having graduated from law school than does the typical high school graduate.

Professionals usually have a clear, though perhaps unrealistic, picture of what they want to do to achieve, and their job search is an attempt to match that expectation. It is possible that some may feel that society, industry, or the organization owes them something for their investment in preparation. They are in a hurry, expecting quick recognition and promotions. Although no one individual expresses all these expectations, the professional's outlook is shaped to some extent by feelings like these.

Differences Between Professionals and the Effects on R & D

The many professionals in an R & D organization bring different educational backgrounds to it. The core group generally consists of those whose education is closest to the technology on which the unique activities of the organization are based. In computer research and development, the core group of professionals consists of electrical engineers and computer science majors; when nuclear science is the basis of the business, physicists, astrophysicists, chemists, and materials science majors tend to make up the core group, with appropriate engineers to implement the ideas. In every R & D organization, the work of core groups must be complemented, supplemented, enhanced, and supported by others, many of whom are also professionals in their own areas. Unfortunately, professionals not in the core activity tend to be thought of as, to think of themselves as, and often to be treated as second-class citizens. This organizational phenomenon leads to many of the difficulties of designing and managing a productive R & D organization.

Despite the fact that all professionals share the characteristic of extensive investment in education that can lead to similarities of attitudes and expectations, the choice of education and work creates differences. For example, differences in personality are believed to influence career choice and to make some careers better choices for individuals with particular personalities. Allowing personality to affect career choice is desirable because congruence of personality and career leads to career satisfaction. John Holland (1973) associated personality with careers and developed a six-personality-type scale that is used in assisting people in career choice. Since personalities influence career choice, each professional field tends to have members whose personality profiles differ from those of professionals in other fields. This, in turn, leads to differences in behavior patterns in organizations and to the issue of an individual's compatibility with the resulting different environments. Edgar Schein (1978) has developed the career anchor theory, which provides five classifications that reflect major interest, activity, and capability themes; the five are technical-functional, managerial, security, autonomy, and creativity. From these titles, one can see that people responding to them will exhibit differences in values and behavior. These differences will be reflected in the types of psychic income which motivate these professionals and which represent work satisfactions for them. In turn, different career anchors affect how professionals communicate with and relate to other members of the organization and augur for different managerial approaches from those who lead them.

Because the professionals differ in their work functions, management will normally differentiate between them in terms of their value to the organization, which is reflected in pay and may thus set up status differences. Some organizations, for example, have different pay hierarchies for technical professionals than for administrative professionals. This can be further reflected in perceived and actual career growth possibilities, or growth limitations, for the particular professional. Thus, an administrative professional in a technical laboratory does not usually have the possibility of achieving as high a managerial level as the technical professional. These things further reinforce the second-class citizenry dichotomy.

One of the realities of organizations is that different professionals behave differently, based on their personalities, values, career interests, and functional responsibilities. Their perceived worth (resulting from their core or noncore activities) and their behavior cause these different groups to be treated differently both by management and by others in the organization. As I write this, I recall the case of a technical professional who had worked in the core activity of the organization and who was offered and took a promotion into a noncore activity; within a year the individual was unhappy. The individual's perception was that attention, interest in the work, caring, interest in the individual, recognition, and pay had all been lost by the move. This type of occurrence in turn reinforces, or exaggerates, differences in behavior and status. It is also reflected in the status of the functions of whole subsections of the organization. Status differences affect all employees. A nonprofessional working in an organization with a function dominated by professionals who reflect second-class status becomes third-class. In actuality and/or in their perceptions, they are being valued differently from nonprofessionals in the primary function of the organization. This can have a profound affect on morale and sometimes leads to such negative feelings that it is a causative factor in unionization activities.

Those who study organizations may well report that differences in status occur in all organizations, not just in R & D, but my thesis is that the effect is more severe in R & D. It is more severe because the functions of the organization are more closely related to the interests, education, and values of the individual professionals. These differences have a profound effect on the culture of the R & D organization. Finding ways to have all professionals and all nonprofessionals in R & D feel that they are valued for their contributions is a major challenge in R & D management. It needs to be done in a way that moves in the direction of minimizing (although they can probably never be totally eliminated) the effects and feelings of second- and third-class citizenry.

Psychic Income: Nonmonetary Gain from the Work

Research into the relationship of the individual to work indicates that the best match, the one which leads to effectiveness and productivity, occurs when one gains psychic income from work. As Hackman and Suttle (1977, p. 129) write: "Internal rewards are obtained by an individual when he *learns* (knowledge of results) that he *personally* (experienced responsibility) has performed well on a task that he *cares about* (experienced meaningfulness). These internal rewards are reinforcing to the individual and serve as incentives for continued efforts to perform well in the future."

Psychic income is the term I use to encompass all the gains that the individual feels are received from investing energy in a work activity. One extreme includes peer recognition outside the organization and the feeling of serving humanity and the profession by pushing back the frontiers of knowledge; this is the global aspect of psychic income. The middle ground includes a sense of accomplishment, a sense of making an impact on the organization, an increase in capability, and evidence of personal worth. The other extreme includes little things like being noticed, being asked, an occasional thank you, and just feeling good about some small accomplishment; this is the microaspect of psychic income. In all three categories, some gains can be established by the individual's relation to the work itself—intrinsic work motivations. An example would be feeling good about creating a formula that expresses an experimental phenomenon. There are also gains that require responses from others—feedback and recognition—and these are extrinsic, but also related to the work. An example would be acknowledgment from a colleague that a piece of work was a real contribution.

When I say that the professional brings higher expectations to work than others do, I am indicating that the professional puts a high value on psychic income. And it may be true that the professional brings higher monetary expectations as well. The challenge for the leader is to match people with the right work, the right environment, and the right recognition so that these gains are reinvested in the work and the organization gains effectiveness (productivity). This challenge must be met within the mission and goals of the organization and within the support that can be allocated to a specific function. Meeting it is difficult because all of the work does not provide psychic income, yet it must be done. It is difficult because it requires frank disclosure of needs and capabilities between leader and individual. It is also difficult because much work is teamwork, not something the individual can do alone. In this regard, it is important to note that the loss of psychic income from satisfying work is one of several things contributing to the difficulty that many professionals have when moving into management.

Dominant and Unique Value Set

Professionals who devote long periods to preparation for work must have strong values in order to resist the many temptations to deviate from the goal. Some values are shaped in early family life, and some are shaped later by peer interaction and education. Values are "the stuff of which motivations are made." Individuals take risks to achieve what they consider to be important value-based goals. They make decisions with respect to values. But often they are unaware of or unable to identify their values. The evidence of a value is behavior, and from it we infer values. Values shaped early in life tend to remain relatively constant, yet individuals who determine that they wish to change values or who join environments with different values can change them.

Understanding how to manage one's own life and career as a professional or how to lead other professionals requires an understanding of values. Although the value set of a particular professional is as individual as a fingerprint, some generalizations can be helpful (keeping in mind that in describing professionals' values, one must resist the danger of assuming that all professionals are alike). Here are a few generalized organizational and work values:

- A future payoff warrants an investment of energy, time, and money today. This is exemplified by the professional's investment in education and by those who work in research, where the payoff is in the future, if at all. It is true, too, for the professional in development, although the future in this case is shorter-term. This willingness to accept delayed reward has historically shaped the professional's career expectations, although today's professional seems to expect a more immediate recognition.

- Professionals feel that they have a moral and ethical right not to follow the direction of management when it goes against their principles. As I write this, I am studying a research group with poor morale; it has many complaints about management, and some members feel that this justifies not following the manager. For the organization, this is a problem, but what if the manager is really wrong? Should we not expect professionals to make legitimate complaints? This is one of the conflict areas in which the pursuit of a value can create both good and bad effects.

- The absence of a feeling of being directed is the desirable type of management-leadership. Feeling self-managed is part of being a professional. Professionals' pride in their professional status is linked to feeling that they are not being managed. Feeling overmanaged leads to a sense of powerlessness.

- Being critical of management is a professional responsibility. Despite wanting minimal management, they see it as their "right" to blame all kinds of failure on management. They often interpret nonsupport by management as arbitrary—as giving in to politics or to bad technical judgment by an obsolete technical manager. They are more willing to tolerate differences of opinion from another professional than from a professional turned manager.

• Individualism is strong among professionals. They feel that they are entitled to be treated as individuals, not as part of a class or group. Typical professionals are quick to resent appearances of being classed as a group, especially if it is for administrative effectiveness. In one organization, professionals have rejected the idea of a summary statement, or number, at the end of a performance evaluation; apparently, they feel that rejecting it on principle is more important than providing management with an analytical tool for establishing fairness in salary administration, or perhaps they feel that it is a gross sort of data bank about people. Yet, professionals are usually quick to blame management for not keeping salaries in what they feel to be a proper relationship.

• The goal of good science for the scientist—or of a powerful and effective program for the programmer—is often more important than, and transcends, organizational goals in the eyes of the professional. This value is often at the base of conflicts with management over short-term goals. Thus, meeting the schedule is not as important as doing the job right. A scientific or technical compromise to achieve a product goal can be the source of deep hurts.

• To the extent that the professional applies personal knowledge in a creative way while working alone (or working with a team on an identifiable part), there is usually a strong emotional bonding with the work output. This can be good because it supports a drive for quality and perfection. But it can be bad, for when the results are defective, it can lead the individual to feel personally defective; in programming, there has been interest in egoless programming because of this problem (Weinberg, 1971).

• Professionals put a high value on the honesty, precision, and congruence of messages from management to them and to others. They enjoy identifying "bullshit." It is defined as

"Managers' statements that can be disproved by management's actions or by facts." They see as political any emphasis on or shading of data by management in upward-selling communication. They are upset when they perceive what they feel to be a misuse of their data.

These few samples are sufficient to demonstrate the potential for conflict with management and the difficulties of leading the professional. View them as representative of the kinds of values that may be behind difficulties in your organization. All professionals do not exhibit these specific values, and I have exaggerated them to some extent to sharpen the picture of the issues.

High-Technology R & D and the Professional

Is there a difference between professionals in nontechnology-driven enterprises, low-technology enterprises, and high-technology enterprises? Earlier discussion has provided some clues. High-technology professionals, those who are frontier persons, seem to demonstrate more characteristics that have effects like "religious fervor" than do those farther from the frontier. This tends to make the distance between them and their management greater. A professional in a product-development area who has accepted the realism of the product goals of the company will often appear more compatible with the organization than will a frontier scientist. Scientists and engineers in an older and more stable organization will also, from a technological point of view, appear to be more compatible with management. The professional in a defined field, such as automotive engineering, will generally buy in to management's goals more often than will the professional who is working to understand the physics of controlled nuclear reactions. The closer one gets to the situation where the professionals can, in their minds, justify the phrase "I know and you don't," the greater the dichotomy.

Disputes arise over values (principles). Managing is also affected by the difficulty of measuring accomplishment. Measuring the output of a theoretician is almost impossible. Measuring the output of a programmer or design engineer is somewhat easier.

Thus, leading a group of nuclear scientists is more difficult than managing a group of microchip designers, for both the values and the unknown component of the work create difficulties. The professionals' position is strengthened by the cases they can cite of how some scientist fought management and was later proved right. It seems as though every laboratory has such a story.

Self-Management, Autonomy, and Control

My work has convinced me that of all the characteristics that contribute to a match between professionals and their work, the sense of self-management is the most significant and powerful. It seems to be the one psychic income that professionals value most highly and even equate with being a professional when working for an organization. Yet even if it is high, it does not follow that professionals will be happy in their work or be happy with a specific work climate.

In two different projects involving professionals, I discovered the sense of personal control to be high, yet there were effectiveness issues, questions of trust, and differences with management. If the need for autonomy and control is so important, why is it that satisfying this requirement does not override other mismatches and dissatisfactions? In the one project, I was working with a group of educators; in the other, with a group of scientists in physics. Here are some common characteristics of the two situations that may give some clue as to why the satisfaction of this dominant work expectation for autonomy and control was not enough:

• In both cases, negative public attitudes about the work, its value, and the competence of those pursuing it have at times been expressed by a small but vocal public group. In both cases, the individual professionals, for a variety of different reasons, felt that internal approval was insufficient. One can theorize that a lack of external approval raises the need for internal approval.

• In both cases, the last several decades have witnessed an increase in the management hierarchy above the individual professional. The working professionals see this as overhead, as negative, and as symbolic of placing a low value on and a low trust in the professional. They reason that this has devalued their contributions.

• Even the lower-level managers in both groups are frustrated. They feel ineffective, and in some sense, powerless. While satisfied with operational autonomy, they speak of a lack of strategic autonomy (Bailyn, 1985). That is, they feel that the big decisions are made without their input or ignoring their input. The clue may be in an imbalance of these two dimensions of autonomy.

• In both cases, the professionals report confused messages about the importance of their function. They feel undervalued in pay, in facilities support, and in top-management attention and interest. Their feeling of being undervalued seems to be an important cause of dissatisfaction.

The important message in understanding the professional is that, however powerful one factor in the work/person match may be, one positive factor is not necessarily enough to override other negatives. Yet I have often heard a manager say of an individual, "I don't understand why that person's unhappy; he's getting more recognition than anyone else." For recognition, you can substitute any single factor. There must be a balanced set of positive factors. Matching people and work is a key managerial responsibility and a vital element in achieving effectiveness. (It will be more thoroughly discussed in Chapter Twelve.)

Expectations: The Psychological Work Contract

Attitudes are closely related to the special value set. Each individual creates a psychological work "contract," specifying expectations brought to work, the desired work environment, and what he or she expects to carry away from work. This psychological work contract, important for all who work, is extremely important for professionals, who are quick to generate negative attitudes if they feel that management has abrogated it.

Unfortunately, communication about this contract is generally incomplete, and often the parties to it have heard differ-

ent things. It is rarely documented. With scientists, the difference is often about how much freedom individuals will have to
pursue their own personal research interests. For engineers, the
important issue can be whether or not they get assigned to the
"hot" project where visibility and the potential for success are
high. With programmers a key issue is often the balance of creative to boring and repetitive work.

I remember one professional who, in the hiring interview, asked many questions about the company's policies in
support of continuing education. The interviewing manager responded with all the positives. The employee later filed a griev-
ance, for the employee had understood that one could come to
work and spend full time studying. The manager, and the company, expected some work—with only part of the time devoted
to study. This distortion was extreme, but it is typical of the
fact that both sides, to some extent, hear what they wish to
hear. Clarifying the psychological work contract is essential in
establishing a good working relationship—one that can lead to
productivity and psychic income.

Here, from the individual's perspective, are some typical
expectations that make up the psychological work contract.
The individual professional expects:

A Professional Organization of Professionals. Because
professionals feel that their contributions to the organization
are unique and because they feel that they are different from
other employees, they expect the organization to accept their
values and to relate to them as professionals, not as it relates to
others. For example, their desire for autonomy suggests that
they expect to be more independent and less dependent than
other employees. This factor can reflect a difference in expectations about status and pay because of their education and
knowledge. It can reflect an expectation for a more participatory management style. Participation in role definition, in decisions about goals, and in the means of achieving goals is part of
this expectation.

Leadership-Management Quality. Professionals feel that
they are qualified to judge the quality of leaders and managers.
If they feel that management chooses people for managership
who they feel are less than the best, this will establish a negative

climate. Leaders will be judged on whether they act as professionals in what they do and say. Leaders will be judged for both their technical and their managerial competence. Gaining technical respect is critical for R & D managers, for in leading professionals, the authority accorded the manager is the authority of knowledge and experience, not the authority of position. Some organizations, in recognition of this, have created professional development programs that expose all professionals to management issues and challenges and raise the general level of management understanding. Some have experimented with promotion review boards to make promotions more fair and more professional; these seem to be of mixed value. Some have experimented with new techniques of career support and selection, such as assessment centers. *Assessment centers* are places where individuals go through a set of structured exercises that simulate the management role with intense one-on-one observation, assessment, and feedback by an experienced manager. Forward-looking organizations, understanding this expectation and their need for improved managerial capability, invest in continual and extensive training of managers.

Freedom-Conformity Balance. The professional wants to be self-managing and judges QPL on the basis of evidence that management trusts professionals and gives them freedom to manage themselves. Freedom at all levels—in decision making, conduct of work, and expression—is the underlying expectation of the professional. The balance expected between conformity— the requirement to do it the company's or the manager's way— and freedom is individual. Some need more rules and limits than others. Autonomy, the freedom to be self-managing, has both strategic and operational dimensions, and again the need is personal.

Opportunity to Achieve. A useful assumption in managing professionals is that the professional has high achievement motivation. Professionals need to feel that they have been provided with the opportunity to achieve. This means assigning tasks which fit their risk-tolerance range, which have a probability of success, fitting their needs but requiring stretching to achieve, and which have an identifiable end result.

Team Spirit. While professionals are individualists, some

recognize that many activities today are team activities. They look for an environment in which team formation is encouraged, in which teams thrive, and in which the synergism of different knowledge and experience bases is utilized. Organizations, recognizing this need, have experimented with team-development programs. A *team-development program* is one in which, after data has been collected via questionnaires and/or via interviews about problems, the organizational family group spends several days in group problem solving. They learn about learning together and working together to achieve effectiveness and make work more fun.

Minimal Rules, Restrictions, and Limits. Organizations become vital by doing things that enhance vitality and/or eliminating things that erode or destroy vitality. The professional generally views rule-bound behavior on the part of others in the organization, especially management, as inhibiting creativity and individual vitality. If management allows its service functions to become primarily control-oriented and control-driven, then the professional will react negatively.

Job-Change and Career-Change Freedom. The force of technological change affects professionals directly and means they get beyond their knowledge base or run out of stimulation and learning on a particular job or career in a short period (three to seven years). Management that creates QPL understands this and makes job rotation and career change a supported and encouraged process for the enhancement of vitality and learning. There are times when, and particular assignments for which, the organization must require the professional to stay beyond what would be the natural time to change, because losing the professional would mean a loss of organizational memory. This can cause a narrowing of career options and technical obsolescence for the individual. A good organization compensates for this by supporting the individual in a later transition to a new assignment with education and refurbishment.

Many of the most significant human resource management actions affecting the professional are starting to take place in this area. Organizations are training managers as career coaches and counselors and are setting up information and career centers to provide support in improving the job/person match on a continuing basis. Organizations are also stepping up the intensity of support for continuing education, emphasizing individual development, and finding ways to allow and encourage job rotation for broadening.

Open Communications. The professional expects to be a participant in the management process and to be informed about strategy, plans, and objectives. The professional is especially sensitive to being left out of communications.

One way that organizations have responded to this need is by having annual reviews of the state of technology, technical plans, and organizational changes. These are meetings attended by all professionals, with professionals as speakers. Topics include past accomplishments, organizational goals, and plans for the future of technology.

Recognition of Career and Work Realities. Despite the professionals' negative reaction to budgets and program plans, some are necessary. Creative managers find ways to offset the negatives of these processes. I remember one director of development who understood this and found a way to emphasize the importance of the unplanned programs. He gave the under-the-table activities his interest and attention, thereby validating their existence.

Challenge. Challenge is in the eyes of the beholder, yet all professionals judge work environments and organizations on this factor. It is of prime importance in creating a good work environment, a QPL. For example, attitude surveys among professionals usually indicate that they want more challenge. They are almost chronically discontent with this factor. Years ago, when IBM had its first opinion survey of professionals working in a development laboratory, on one question about 24 percent responded that they wanted more work. Upper management questioned this response because they took it literally and felt that it meant underutilization. I was asked to help study the issue, and what we discovered was a relationship between basic discontent and this factor of challenge.

An organization desiring to establish a good work environment, or QPL, for professionals should ensure that professionals are used as professionals and not used to an excessive extent at lower-level tasks. Managers should ensure that professionals are required to apply their expertise and are required to stretch in order to succeed.

Armed with these understandings, but recognizing that each individual will interpret these needs differently and put different priorities on them, the manager has some of the elements necessary for managing the professional.

Needs for Contributions Beyond the Organization

The professional is, in part, identified by a strong internal need to make a significant contribution. *Significant* is usually defined in a broader contextual framework than the particular organization; that is, it means contributing to the data bank of knowledge and to the profession, not just to the organization's goals of product, systems, or service. This is one of the dimensions used by some (Raelin, 1984) to differentiate between scientists and other professionals. Engineers and others seen as quasi professionals are believed to think more in terms of contribution within the framework of the company. There is a difference in the degree to which this need to contribute beyond the organization is felt by different individuals. For the manager of the professional, this desire to contribute beyond the organization presents a golden opportunity to harness the interests, talents, and dedication of the professional. By finding the right balance between the internal needs and the individual's motivation in the larger context, the leader can gain significant contributions from the individual.

For some professionals, contributing beyond the organization is relatively easy since the character of their work opens the opportunity for creative contribution and for communicating about the work. For others it is more difficult, either because their work is not creative in the sense of adding knowledge to the field or because of communication restrictions, and it is in these assignments, where there is no basic demand for creation and innovation, that the manager can make a difference: It is possible to expand these assignments so that they include the discovery of something to talk about. Writing papers and making presentations is sometimes circumscribed or limited by the needs of the organization to protect proprietary information, but even these restrictions usually do not mean that the information can never be talked about; rather, it means that there needs to be a delay in communication. In the case of work related to national defense, individuals are further limited in communication by national security requirements. Because of defense considerations and other limits on talking about work, individuals inside the organization select work assignments based on their personal need to make this broader contribution, to be recognized in the world beyond the organization. Those who feel the need strongly tend toward the more open activities. Those who do not may be attracted by the excitement of the more closed activities; in fact, some seek the comfort of escape from the publish-or-perish environment, which they equate with the world of the professional in academe and which is sometimes duplicated in industrial research organizations. Others are torn by the conflict between the excitement of the secret work and their need to contribute broadly and gain peer acknowledgment. There is also a career effect of working on things that one cannot talk about, for it tends to narrow one's career options as one works longer in a restricted area.

Growing Professionally and/or into Management

I can remember several friends who were never comfortable with their decision to accept a managerial role. They continued a personal debate for their entire working lives.

Our society has put a high value on being a manager. If I describe two people as identical in all respects and I give a group of people only one difference—the fact that one is a manager—they will feel that the manager is more important. Professionals come into the work world with a bias that favors getting into management. Most organizations intensify this because they have a culture in which the image of getting ahead is to become a manager. Many organizations have salary and recognition systems that seem to reward managers more than nonmanagerial professionals. The perceived desirability of management seems to exist even where a dual ladder (alternate promotional paths) is used; dual ladders were devised to address this imbalance and to make it clear that there can be professional growth. Scientists leave their science for the status and pay of the managerial position even though they dislike the management role. Programmers and engineers leave the activities they like for the status of the managerial position. Some organizations dilute the meaning of the managerial role by assigning managerial titles to those who do not manage. All these things are going on today despite the fact that the historical advantages of being a manager have been eroded by an increased management hierarchy and a change in culture. One young professional turned manager commented that managers used to have power, but not after she was promoted.

This bias in favor of management causes many a professional to aspire to and try management for the wrong reasons. It results in many people entering management ranks and giving up the fun and the psychic incomes of their profession. The loss of their former psychic income sometimes causes them to try to replace it in the wrong ways. Few really understand the new kinds of psychic income associated with managing. In the early stages, this often means that they continue to do what they did before—but now as managers. It often means that they rob those whom they lead of their appropriate activities. It sometimes means that they emphasize power and become tyrants in the management role.

This difficult transition or transformation, successfully achieved by but a few, is one of the root causes of poor R & D management. The transition is little understood, and organizations have generally not found out how to help individuals who try. Even worse is the social cost of admitting the mistake and returning to their professional role, for it is seen as a public admission of failure. The longer that the admission of a wrong career turn is delayed, the greater the cost—and usually the greater the damage—to the individual and the organization.

Difficulties in Achieving Collegial Support

The need for collegial support was cited earlier, but it is important to discuss it more thoroughly in context of describing the professional.

The people we work with are important in building a positive bond with our work and the organization. Einar Thorsrud, once the head of the Work Research Institute in Oslo, Norway, found social support to be one of the six desirable components of jobs (Rosow, 1974). For the professional, this means finding co-workers in one's field and related fields who are stimulating and supportive as well as fun to work with. Support networks go beyond the walls of a given organization and sometimes beyond the physical space of the group. I remember an IBM engineer in Germany who talked of this as one of the strengths of the IBM technical organization. He pointed to his phone and indicated that he could pick up that instrument and call another technical person in any IBM organization and have an open, unrestricted sharing of information.

In some sense, many professionals are snobs. It relates to their large investment in preparation. Their own self-respect requires that they value that investment highly, so they choose to work in groups and with people who also value it highly. Thus, Ph.D.'s will judge the suitability of colleagues in terms of whether they hold a Ph.D. and, if so, what university granted the degree; they will value a Ph.D. from certain universities, representing work with certain professors, more highly than others. But the technical leader must set up an environment which breaks down such barriers if effectiveness is to be achieved. Professionals will often make choices about relating or not relating to colleagues on their use of language, their speed of comprehension, and their thinking modes. They will choose to work with leaders in their profession, such as Nobel laureates. They will also discriminate according to field of study; thus, in the eyes of the scientist, a Ph.D. in electrical engineering is not as good as one in physics. The ability to create collegial support is thus affected by the personalities and values of the professional.

The building of a collegial-support network, which is necessary for a sense of a quality work environment and for effectiveness, is further complicated by the nature and level of interpersonal competition. The natural potential for interpersonal competition is high among bright, ambitious people with strong egos; these are the ones whom organizations work hard to hire. Competition can cause insecurity for those with less inner strength. If people are insecure because of business pressures, an inadequate budget, or a lack of technical progress on a project, this can lead to competition. They may compete for attention as a means of acquiring some sense of security. Insecurity leads to a lower level of risk taking, and the creative process requires risk taking. Competition also means that people will not share data and knowledge, and this has a negative impact on effectiveness. Some leaders deliberately set up situations and work environments that encourage interpersonal competition, feeling that this will assure better solutions. Some competition is probably desirable, but too much makes collegial support difficult; it creates a closed rather than an open organization.

Thus, having the right colleague in the organization does not assure collegial support. The environment, or climate, must be designed to create a sense of security that will make the risk of sharing worthwhile yet gain the motivation that comes from appropriate competition. This is a tough balancing act because these are perceptions that are difficult to communicate and understand.

Summary

• The professionals in the title of this book are people whose work is built on a university degree, or its equivalent, and who work for a salary in an organization. They are scientists, engineers, programmers, biologists, and others. Beyond this, the professional is usually defined in the context of the role the organization expects the individual to fill. There is no universally agreed-upon definition.

• Because professionals have invested large amounts of

time, energy, and money in preparing for professional work life, this investment shapes their values, attitudes, and expectations. It affects how they are hired, their relationships to the organization, and usually where they work within the organization. It tends to create a pent-up desire for achievement and recognition.

- In some sense, all professionals share similar characteristics, but those whose education matches the technology of the organization tend to become the core group in the R & D organization. This has the effect of establishing classes of society—status differences—that affect the culture, feelings, and effectiveness of both professionals and nonprofessionals in the organization.

- Psychic income, the nonmonetary gains that the individual wants to take home from work, is particularly important to the professional. This probably results from the bonding of the individual and work. It puts a premium on individual self-understanding and on the leader understanding the needs and capabilities of those being led. The effective matching of people and work is the key to professional productivity.

- The values held by professionals are descriptive of their work needs and expectations. The unique role of the salaried professional sets up the potential for conflict with the organization. In general, professionals exhibit a strong need for self-management, and it is therefore critical to understand both the strategic and the operational dimensions of the desired autonomy.

- Measurement of the professional's accomplishment is most difficult at the theoretical end of the work continuum and easier at the applied end. Thus, the work of the scientist is more difficult to measure than that of the programmer working on a program product.

- Individuals create a psychological work contract. It describes the needs and capabilities they bring to the organization, their expectations of the work environment, and what they wish to take home as psychic income. This contract is seldom written and often differently understood by professional and manager. Clarifying it can improve effectiveness and work attitudes.

• Professionals vary in their individual need to contribute beyond the organization. It is generally felt that the scientist has the strongest need for this type of contribution. The creative manager can gain significant contributions by properly balancing this need with internal needs. Failing to achieve the right balance between the individual and the organization can set up potential for conflict.

• Collegial support is important to the professional. Creative leaders need to find the way to create a productive balance between interpersonal competition and collegial support.

▼▼▼▼▼▼▼

Getting the Best from People

Because of interests, education, and goals, the R & D manager tends to emphasize the technical rather than the human resource aspects of management. In this part, the reader is given guidance in achieving a balance between technical and people management. One approach is to create ways for the nonmanagement professional to actively participate in setting goals and thus gain a sense of strategic autonomy. Leaders are encouraged to equate the goals of increasing vitality and effectiveness with the goal of improving results. Encompassing these new goals becomes one of the keys to creating an environment that enhances creativity, and this is a central task of the R & D leader.

Chapter 4

Managing People and Technology

Achieving a Healthy Balance

Professionals, scientists, programmers, and engineers push back the frontiers, discover new technologies, and provide the driving force for a technology-based high-technology organization. The leader of an R & D organization has a dual challenge, having to manage both the technical thrust and the people who create it. These two challenges require different knowledge, different emphases, different perspectives about management, and different styles of management.

While in some sense all managers experience a conflict between managing people and managing a function, this challenge is most taxing in R & D. Some of the reasons for this stress were covered in earlier chapters in discussing the unique values and expectations of the professional. In this chapter, the focus will be on balancing the conflicting demands of the technical and human managerial roles. The emphasis will also shift from the description of challenges to suggestions for solutions. My bias is to urge more emphasis on managing people and less on managing technology; I urge this because I believe that technically trained people naturally favor the technical aspects of management. I will discuss some perspectives or discoveries which I have made or which others have uncovered—ideas and processes that have been and/or may be useful in improving R & D effectiveness and vitality.

There are several useful management perspectives that can increase effectiveness. One is to assist the manager in uncovering or creating a personal image of managerial roles and in learning how this affects what happens—such as learning how temporary systems can be used to emphasize a particular perspective and to ensure that directed energy is applied to a specific issue. Thus, if the leader wishes to emphasize the need to apply solid-state devices where they have not been used, a task group focusing on increasing solid-state device application might be set up. Understanding when it is appropriate to use temporary organizations is a key skill necessary for managing fast-moving, adaptive R & D organizations. For effective leadership, it is also necessary to understand program and project cycles and the different approaches required in different phases. These cycles are unique to R & D and affect organizational structure as well as management style.

It is necessary, too, to understand how changes in organizational size and structure also alter the management challenges and the balance of emphasis needed on technical and human resource issues. In other parts of the organization, it is often effective to have but one manager per fifteen or more people. In R & D, the most normal ratio becomes one to seven, in part because of the need to manage both technology and people.

Learning what research or development managers actually do, as compared with what the textbooks say is done, is another part of building an effective management perspective. For example, observers have found that books overemphasize decision making and underemphasize negotiation for scarce resources. It is often necessary to ask managers to keep a time-oriented diary of activities for weeks in order to find out, and to help them understand, what they really do. What they do also changes with the phase of the program, and an activity that is emphasized in one phase must be downplayed in another phase. It is important for the manager to know when and how to use audits. The use of technical and/or human resource audits, properly staffed and timed, can make the difference between success and failure. Sometimes reviews by outsiders can strengthen the manager's leadership. One type of general audit, although not generally seen as an audit, is the periodic opinion survey, or attitude survey. Through this process, it is possible to take the organizational temperature and determine possible discomforts that call for change. All audit processes provide the leader-manager with the necessary feedback on which to base strategy, directional decisions, and tactics.

A key challenge in the management of R & D comes from the fact that most members of upper management today grew up during the growth phase of the organization. What they learned through experience generally works with a growing organization. For example, in a growing organization little emphasis is put on weeding out inadequate performers; the prime emphasis is on adding people, even warm bodies. Yet many of these managers are today managing stable or declining organizations. In such an organization it is vitally important to put emphasis on weeding out inadequate performers. Since the leaders' experiences have not prepared them for the changed emphasis, it is necessary for them to gain the understanding in another way. It can be gained through reading, through new experiences, through management development, or through the catalytic assistance of a consultant.

Top management must create enterprise strategies. In this chapter, I will use stories of some R & D leaders to demonstrate the importance of this leadership outlook; an organization and its members will normally pay attention to those things which the leader demonstrates are important. I will also emphasize the necessity to make innovation in management and in other organizational aspects a way of life, not just to think of innovation as a technical project goal.

Managing People and Technology: The Challenge

Managing another person requires matching that person with appropriate work. It is a process of influencing behavior in creative ways that help the person to become productive, develop capability, become self-managing, be an effective team member, and learn how to gain psychic income.

How a manager does this is strongly influenced by that leader's self-image. Thus, if the manager's self-image is one of teacher, the emphasis will be on coaching and learning. If the manager's image is one of information processor and communicator, the emphasis will be on data and how to communicate it. Many managers think of themselves primarily as decision makers and thus emphasize decision making. No manager has a purely singular (one-function) self-image as a manager, so leaders have a high probability of presenting a confusing picture to those being managed. How one relates to another individual is also governed by one's empathy, which is a combination of the ability to listen actively to the other person and to feel what another person is feeling; only through this process can the leader be responsive to the other's needs. These requirements make it evident that leaders need skills that are not taught or developed through scientific or technical training.

Success in assisting another person by being a catalyst and a coach is thus highly dependent on self-image, interpersonal communication skills, and the chemistry of the relationship. By contrast, for the technically educated person, the ability to manage technology is more directly related to education and to technical experience as a professional. This seems self-evident, but the important point is that it creates a preferred way of looking at the world.

In the management of technology, the leader must first become sensitive to the various possible technical paths, learn how to assess the potential for payoff, and establish a direction. Next, the manager must estimate the time, people, and activities necessary to pursue the defined goals and must sell the plan to higher management. Having gained higher management's approval, the leader then has to recruit the people and find the facilities and technological capability necessary to achieve the goals. It is only at this point in the process that the leader arrives at the need to manage people. But arriving at this stage does not mean that one can leave the technical decisions behind because there will continue to be iterative technical decisions, as well as business- and people-related decisions, in the pursuit of the goals.

The leader's challenge is to combine these two necessary perspectives—the technical and the human—into a balanced outlook that enhances effectiveness in the scientific and/or technical environment. Unfortunately, few organizations provide guidance or real help for the manager in developing this balanced perspective of the roles of a leader. Some organizations provide manuals describing the process and rules for project or program management, but the content tends to emphasize administration, not the technical or human aspects discussed here. Some organizations provide project management courses, others depend on the manager's immediate manager to provide guidance. In either case the emphasis is on the technical or functional aspects of the management process. Management-development programs, where they exist, tend to provide descriptions of general management duties; they teach how to get certain administrative things done, like processing a pay raise or making up a budget, and these processes are usually supported by a manual; additionally training indoctrinates the leader in the philosophies and policies of the organization (this representing the limited coverage of the people side of the process). These supports do not help the individual create a conceptual framework for managing, nor do they help in achieving a balance between technical and people emphases. They do not help the individual understand the personal changes necessary to become a manager. The transformation from professional to manager is usually a personal and private experience negotiated in a trial-and-error fashion, with little guidance or assistance from others.

For specific insights, let us look at a stereotypical transition to management: Carol has been a productive technical professional. She has worked hard, learned how to get things done in the organization, and made significant technical contributions to projects important to the organization. She is seen as technically knowledgeable, as witnessed by the fact that others come to her for advice. There is an opening for a manager, and she is chosen because of her technical competence. After the congratulations are over, she sits alone at her desk and tries to figure out what she is supposed to do. The first sensation is probably loneliness, since others see her as different. The first event is probably someone coming to her to tell her that he is upset because he really wanted the job she got or in some other way feels underrecognized. This is her first need to be a people manager. Next, someone comes with a technical problem and she feels at home. She digs in and works with the person to help solve the problem, or perhaps draws from her experience to suggest the answer. Her most natural tendency will be to fall back and do it as she would have done it as a professional. She does not yet understand her role change. On the way home that night, she muses about what technical leadership is and how one becomes a manager. By the end of the next day, she finds that her time has been taken up by others and by meetings and that she has become a response mechanism. Maybe later she will awaken to the fact that the job is running her, not vice versa. Perhaps even later she will go to a management-development program, but if she is the typical professional turned manager, she will react that all this is administration (the usual reaction) and somehow less important than the technical part of her job.

Keep in mind when reading this chapter that, like Carol, the novice leader-manager normally starts with a poor managerial foundation, an unclear picture of roles, and a lack of clarity about upper management's expectations.

Balanced emphasis on the two aspects of managing—technology and people—requires understanding their differences and developing a conceptual framework for managing. It requires the individual to recognize personal predispositions or biases in emphasis. It requires the individual to study human resource management and to establish some techniques for getting that feedback about their personal impact on other people which is necessary to learn leadership skills. The appropriate balance varies with function and varies with the culture of the organization in which the leader works. The manager will have achieved the appropriate balance when managing becomes fun, the group being led becomes productive, and the individuals in the group gain the necessary satisfactions from their work contributions.

Conflicts and Problems

A young MIT graduate joined one of IBM's laboratories where disk files are designed and produced. He was assigned to learn about the design of magnetic heads. This is a complex technical design because the head literally flies over the disk and there are aerodynamic problems to solve. It is also complex because it involves designing a magnet that can be pulsed to record discrete readable magnetic images on the disk. The design challenge is further compounded by the goal of increased density (more lines to the inch), which requires that the magnetic head be closer to the disk. He learned quickly and soon became a good designer.

His reward for a successful design was to be given another head to design—one with tighter and more difficult technical specifications. This reward, which is typical of managerial response in technical organizations, has both good and bad aspects. It is good because it recognizes achievement with a greater challenge; this is positive psychic income. It is bad because it begins a specialization route and a narrowing, which, if carried too far, will deplete vitality. After a couple of designs, he asked his manager if he could do something else. His manager agreed to keep it in mind, but right now he had another design project with a short time schedule. Schedule pressure biased the manager in the direction of using the person who already knew how to design magnetic heads—in this case, our young man, whose learning rate will drop as he does the same thing over. The story was repeated until the young professional resigned because he was never given the opportunity to do anything different.

A talented professional was lost because the manager was not convinced of the need to listen and adapt to people needs. The manager was caught between the conflicting goals of (1) being seen as successful in meeting project deadlines and (2) providing the employee with the opportunity to discover what he really wanted to do and/or with the variety necessary to maintain technical competence. This is a classical conflict between short- and long-term goals—between technical and people-oriented goals—and is the first of the conflicts listed below.

What follows is a brief list of the conflicts faced by the research or development manager in a technological area. These are conflicts between focuses on technology and on people, between what feels right and what the managerial role seems to require, and between technological and business goals.

- Conflict between the pursuit of the technical, project, and/or business goals and what is right for the development of the capabilities of the people and/or for the continued motivation of the people. This can be a conflict both between short- and long-term goals and between people-related and business goals (as in the preceding story).
- Conflict between short- and long-term goals in the technology. The need to get a product out on schedule, for example, conflicts with the scientific desire either to take the time to do the research necessary to understand thoroughly what is happening or perhaps to refine the development to make the resultant product better. Product planners and marketing people always feel that they have to force the technical person to come to closure, believing that unless they snatch the product, it will never be released.
- Conflict between the nonrational nature of some management decisions and the need to provide those working in the organization with rational, understandable bases for decisions and goal selection. Often the manager is not told why the decision was made, but just told to go and do. The first-line manager is then caught with no explanation for the professional.
- Conflict between the need to fight upward to assure that one's point of view is considered in the decision-making process and the need to implement a decision that one fought against as if it were one's own. The transparent manager, seeking support from the people the manager leads, will go to them and say, "I do not agree with this decision, but I am forced by upper management to carry it out." Even worse, some technical managers who were participants in the decision making will insist that it is their professional right not to carry out decisions with which they do not agree.

- Conflict between the necessity to carry out economically driven business decisions (such as staff reductions) and the negative effects this action will have on the productivity and psychic income for the group. In times of staff reductions, the professional's autonomy is reduced (Marcus, 1985), and this sets up negative, nonproductive responses from the professional.
- Conflict between letting the individuals in the group change, grow, and move on and the need for a sufficient work force to perform the function. An example would be the conflict between letting a person leave for a higher-priority need or for a promotional opportunity and blocking that move because the individual is indispensable. One action is good for the individual, and the other preserves the manager's performance capability. Replacing someone lost to the group usually means diminished response capability, at least for the hiring and training time. This is the conflict which causes many managers to keep people, sometimes underutilized as a sort of reserve power, so that they can be heroes and respond when asked.
- Conflict between maintaining the manager's psychic income, which may come more from activities associated with the former professional role than with the managerial role, and the need to provide the opportunity for psychic income for others. When the manager continues as a researcher or continues to design and thus robs those being led from the fun of design, the manager is deciding in favor of personal psychic income rather than psychic income for those being led.

These are but some of the conflicts faced by the manager-leader in the technical world. They have been discussed by way of supporting the need for some of the suggestions that follow. Without acceptance, guidance, and support from upper management, the individual leader will find some of these suggestions difficult to implement. The difficulty will have its base in the conflicts we have just reviewed. The remainder of this chapter presents a series of concepts and ideas that I have collected from my years of working with the management of technology in search of ways to create vitality and effectiveness. As in the case of other lists of suggestions in this book, do keep in mind that the success or failure of each of these ideas depends on the acceptance of a need for change, on the culture of the organization in which it is implemented, and on the approach taken by the person trying to introduce the change. Like garden plants, all good ideas are not universally transplantable, for the transplant may not be compatible with the new environment.

The Roles of the Manager

For many years, management-development literature and programs tried to sell the idea that managers planned, organized, directed, controlled, and communicated. These role identifications are the result of rational thinking about the process of management rather than of observing managers at work. They are possibly useful concepts, but knowing the list never helped me manage. Mintzberg (1973) actually observed what managers did and came up with a different perspective on managerial activities. He suggests that there are ten roles common to all managers and that they can be classified in three groups: *interpersonal roles, informational roles,* and *decisional roles.* Another researcher (Strauss, 1977) suggests that managerial roles can be broken into *consideration* (psychological support), *facilitation,* and *participation* (managing in a participatory way). This is not the place to debate the various views; rather, understanding that all these views are legitimate, the points to be made here are that managers in an organization need (1) to develop a personal concept of managing, a perspective, (2) to find a part of the organization where that concept is compatible with organizational culture, and (3) to understand that consistency of perspective or image can make the manager more effective.

Within this overall concept of the need for a perspective, it must be understood that there is a need for different emphases with different people, different emphases at different times, and different emphases at different levels of management. The first-line manager, the person leading the professional nonmanagers, needs to emphasize the technical aspects, one-on-one relationships, and small-group or team issues. The manager of that manager should probably give less attention to technical matters and more to broad human resource and conceptual functions. In the higher levels of management, the emphasis should shift toward a greater attention to conceptual functions, such as environment design, goal setting, and policy determination, and an even greater attention to broad-scale human resource issues, such as personnel policy. The top-level manager should pay attention to strategic technical issues and should therefore appear to put less overall emphasis on technical issues than managers at lower organizational levels.

The Project Cycle

In a development laboratory where products are created, a close observer will discover a project (or program) cycle. In some sense this is also true in research laboratories, but it is usually less dramatic since the cycles are longer. The cycle affects the nature of the team interaction, changes the skills needed, creates a need for altered structure of the organization, affects the size of the organization, and changes the type of leadership needed. Understanding cycles is important if one is to understand leadership in development organizations. The project cycle has the following phases: inception, planning, early development, midperiod development, final development, transfer to a producing organization, and (in the long run) maintenance.

Laboratories that develop different kinds of products and use different technologies have these same phases, but the time periods vary. In a computer-development laboratory, for example, the product cycle has historically been about three years, at the end of which the project enters the maintenance period. In some heavy-equipment industries, such as those which develop steam turbine power generation systems, the cycle, up to the maintenance phase, is probably more like eight years. The length of the cycle depends on the rate of movement of the technology, the documentation system, and the period of time required for manufacturing or construction.

At the beginning of the cycle, the inception phase, the numbers of people needed are very small. The leadership need is for a person able to define the product and sell the program to management. For this phase, the organization needs a leader who can articulate a dream. In the second phase, planning, the organization needs a leader who can translate the dream into the numbers and kinds of people needed and into financial plans or budgets, one who can organize the function and set up a schedule for the several phases. This person must also convince management that the program plan is viable and gain management support. In these first two phases, the numbers of people involved are small and the people-management skills needed are minimal. The needs for understanding the technology, for competence at presentation, and for organizing skills are high. All this changes in the execution of the early development phase. Now the leader must attract other leader-managers, attract professionals with the necessary skills, and start managing them toward a time-constrained goal. In the design of a new computer, I have seen this phase take the organization from a dozen people to several hundred.

Thus, one of the challenges of managing development is that different phases and different sizes of organization require entirely different capabilities from the leader. Often the leader who conceived and sold the program proves to have the wrong personality for leading development, but the transition to a new leader at that point is a sensitive and difficult process, with high potential for negative effects on the project, so most often the one selected is a compromise between the different skill needs. The negative effects when a leader is changed can include delayed decisions, loss of team spirit, increase in individual insecurity, and even the loss of key individuals who came to work with the first leader.

In the midperiod development phase, the organization reaches its maximum numbers and complexity. By the final development (execution or transfer) phase, the problems are again different. In this phase, the major task is to document the information and transfer the product to another organization for manufacture. Here the emphasis is on data, on redesign to make manufacturing practical, and on the initial phasedown of the development organization. Choosing those members of the team who should move on to another project at this point or at a later time is a difficult task, requiring yet another set of skills from the manager. The leader must keep motivation high for those who continue on the project, and schedule pressure is normally at its peak, yet the attention of the professionals is on their careers and how to gain the next challenging assignment.

The final phase, maintenance, requires a small group of professionals who provide answers to the field, make minor modifications in design in response to sales and service organizations' requests, and support manufacturing with engineering backup. The leader who started the program, and/or the manager who managed the large, complex organization, is almost certainly not the right person to manage the maintenance phase. Motivating people for the less exciting tasks of maintenance and maintaining an effective service posture are entirely different from the challenges of the early creative period. The nonmanagement professionals for maintenance must also have different skills and outlooks from those who developed the product.

These phase changes make the challenge of selecting and training managers even more difficult and exacerbate the problems previously described. Since the skill and perspective required of the leader changes with time, the training of the leader must enhance adaptability. Unlike the organizations of manufacturing or sales, the organizations of the development laboratory exhibit birth, growth, and death in a relatively short time period. Each of these phases requires different capabilities from the leader.

Negotiating for Scarce Resources

Many years ago I invited Professor Leonard Sayles, of Columbia University's Graduate School of Business, to study an IBM laboratory. His approach was like that of an anthropologist visiting a strange culture. He included the results of this study in *Managerial Behavior: Administration in Complex Organizations* (Sayles, 1964). A significant finding was that the managers in the IBM laboratory were spending a major part of their time and energy *negotiating* for scarce resources. The importance of this activity had escaped the attention and understanding of the management of the laboratory. Negotiation was necessary because managers did not have, under their personal control, the resources necessary to carry out their responsibilities. They had to convince other managers to dedicate their resources and support. In turn, those managers they asked to support their program had to resolve conflicting requirements from different managers. Negotiation had never been taught in any management-development program. Never had laboratory management considered negotiating skills as a selection criterion for managers.

I suspect that in every R & D organization there are unrecognized requirements falling on the shoulders of leaders. Managers are facing responsibilities that neither they nor others thought of or discussed when they took the assignment. They are facing skill or perspective requirements that have not been discussed in any management training which they have received. Because the requirements have not been recognized, their performance is being measured against incomplete and perhaps ill-defined criteria.

Disturbances and Their Effects
on Creativity and Innovation

Donald C. Pelz of the Institute for Social Research at the University of Michigan studied the productivity of development teams. He reported his work in Pelz and Andrews (1966). One of his discoveries that adds to our understanding of the management of R & D is that *teams need a constructive disturbance in order to be creative over extended periods.* He calls this disturbance the dither factor. It took some time to discover this factor because the need for it was masked by the continual growth of R & D. When new professionals were regularly being added to teams, their questions (arising from their lack of having shared the experience of the group) provided the necessary disturbance. In a stable organization, one which is not growing in numbers, the manager must either provide the disturbance or find some alternate controllable source.

Pelz's findings demonstrate that a development team left together without change of personnel and without change in goals, technology, or direction for eighteen months begins to decline in productivity. Too much disturbance, such as a change of direction and goals every few weeks or months, destroys effectiveness—but too little disturbance also destroys effectiveness. The change in balance is unique to each team's personality and the technology being pursued. Disturbance management is yet another complexity and another understanding required of leaders who manage in R & D.

The Experimental Outlook

Scientists and engineers are experimental in their technical work, for that is the process they use to push back frontiers, yet often they fail to think in terms of work-process, organizational, and managerial experimentation. The Hawthorne Studies (Morris, 1975) demonstrated to all managers that experimentation in working conditions and management styles has a measurable effect on productivity. The studies were focused on production workers, but it is fair to suggest that the principle holds for any group of people and thus for R & D organizations.

The discovery was that productivity improved when conditions were improved and also improved when conditions were made worse. The effect is that the additional attention brought about by the experiment stimulates productivity. Morris (1975, p. 118) suggests that the principle of experimentation should be used by managers in all organizations: "In fact, the key to productivity improvement strategies lies in the skillful design of experiments. Experiments based on whatever experience may be available, but experiments designed to reduce our uncertainty about what might be the costs and benefits of various approaches to productivity growth." Changes in work flow, in working relationships, and in management style may also create an effect similar to the dither factor just discussed. Organizational changes can provide a constructive disturbance. Implementing changes and measuring their effects, although requiring more than the usual attention and interest from management, seem to have a positive effect on productivity (effectiveness) and vitality.

One of my recent consulting assignments required discovering reasons for poor morale and high discontent. The scientists in this group expressed the feeling that management did not appreciate the importance of their contributions. The discontent was based to a large extent on their feeling that management was not actively paying attention to them and their work. One of the several solutions implemented was a deliberate plan of management attention. This was an attempt to use the Hawthorne effect by getting upper and ancillary management to be part of an experiment designed to improve morale and effectiveness. Unfortunately, although there was an improvement, management's attention was short-lived. As is often the case when experimenting in the real world, there was no closure, no proof.

Managing Useful Waste in Pursuing Innovation

Basic research activities and some development activities, as I have previously stated, cannot be totally planned because by their very nature they involve the mastering of unknowns. Katz and Kahn (1978, p. 176) explain it this way: "It is difficult to institutionalize basic research since it deals with yet undiscovered areas of knowledge. An organizational framework, with its role prescriptions and control devices, is based on existing knowledge." Processes involving unknowns require the pursuit of paths which do not lead to technical discovery, which turn out to be solutions that are too costly, which yield solutions too difficult to manufacture, or which for some other reason prove undesirable. The managerial challenge is to achieve the right balance between pursuing useful and nonuseful paths when the area is unknown and the paths are not preidentified. It was for this reason that I created the concept of necessary, constructive, or useful waste. Some waste is necessary if the pursuit of the unknown is to be sufficiently aggressive.

Managers need to learn how to identify and use those types of waste that contribute to creating the best work climate. Choosing research and development paths that, even if the objectives are not attained, will contribute to the increase of knowledge and the ability to make other paths successful is the management art that can make the difference between success and failure in achieving overall technical goals. For example, in the early days of data processing, IBM laboratory management made the decision to pursue ideas to the *plate model* level (which means building an experimental machine). The experimental model proved the concept. Many product concepts were pursued, but only some were released to manufacturing and the marketplace; the remainder ended up in the "product morgue." For that period, one could judge useful waste by the percentage of projects that ended up in the morgue. The managers decided how many alternate approaches to pursue and thus managed the application of people to problems. Often the model that was not released to production contributed to the ultimate product and thus, in having made that contribution, identified itself as useful waste.

One of the problems in R & D management is that general management tries to eliminate all waste through tight controls and predetermined solutions. Some managers fail to learn and understand that some effort, which may later appear to have been misdirected, is a necessary part of the discovery process. Commenting on how to maintain inventiveness, R & D managers have made the point this way (Harris, 1985, p. 213): "Avoid the M.B.A. syndrome of trying to minimize risk by betting on only that which seems a sure thing and economically feasible."

In today's world, the equivalent of building multiple plate models (which all organizations did in the past) is the simulation of a proposed solution, in a manner similar to having a current computer work as the proposed computer is to work. The key is to make the organization open to experimentation up to the point where an intelligent decision can be made about its potential in the marketplace. This means not forcing too early a decision, which might impede creativity, and not delaying the decision until the wrong idea has been pursued too long, which might turn *useful waste* into a misuse of people, facilities, and funds. Thus, for example, it is possible to understand *use-*

ful waste in the following ways or combinations of the several ways:

- Internal pursuit of competitive approaches
- Longer research or development cycles to allow exploration of alternatives and thus contribute to greater learning
- The use of more people-intensive approaches, thus providing opportunities for more employees to learn
- Duplication of effort, or redundancy
- Freedom for individuals to pursue nonplanned activities that offset the negatives of formatted or tightly specified efforts
- Inclusion of education, training, and technical refurbishment time in the planned time for the pursuit of the project
- Making broader efforts to assign a person to a task that requires learning rather than to one already mastered
- Organizational experimentation and change
- Audits and reviews
- Boundary defense and turf battles (usually a negative choice)

In each organization, the character of the technology and the type of process help define the range of possible choices of useful waste. In the absence of technical leadership, waste will take place, but its contribution to technical progress will rest on chance. In the presence of technical leadership, waste will be taken in the most useful ways, ones fitting the state of the technology, the ancillary goal needs, and the culture of the organization. For example, in an organization in which one of the key goals is to avoid or overcome obsolescence, appropriate management decisions would emphasize the enhancement of learning. The time spent in continued learning might seem wasteful to some general manager, but in context of the management of R & D, it would be appropriate, useful, and necessary activity even if it were not associated with the immediate goal.

Effective Manager-Employee Ratios and Other Ratios

If you are managing a group of people all of whom do essentially the same thing and whose work is not creative in nature, you can manage more people than you can when managing a group of individually creative people. The appropriate number to manage is inversely proportional to the need for one-on-one or one-on-small-group time. In my experience, most effective R & D organizations find the appropriate ratio to be one manager-leader to seven professionals. This ratio is most appropriate at the first level, where a manager manages people doing the work of the organization. In other words, while upper management can and should be counted when calculating the ratio of managers to employees, it is not appropriate to achieve a low ratio of managers to employees by adding an overwhelming structure of upper managers. The principle is that each employee is entitled to see, know, and have the opportunity for substantial contact with his or her manager—and to be clear about who that person is. The leader must not have so many people reporting in that the manager is unable to perform effective coaching, counseling, and nurturing functions. Appropriate one-on-one and one-on-small-group managerial functions also include knowing about and exhibiting an interest in what individuals and teams are doing.

In the late 1950s, R & D leaders spent a lot of time looking at the ratio of Ph.D. to M.S. to B.S. graduates in the professional population. There was an interlaboratory competition of sorts to beat the other laboratories by having more professionals with higher degrees. While it is still important to have a variety and to match the ratios in a gross sense to the state of the technological development, these ratios are not golden. It is especially important in rapidly moving technologies to have individuals with up-to-date knowledge. I suspect that the level of degree is far less important than is the time that has passed since exposure to formal education. In all technologies, after one has been out of the university for five years or so, the important criterion is what the individual can do for the organization, not what degree has been obtained. Failure to recognize this fact can reinforce class differences based on degrees and also usually contributes to the organization's ineffectiveness and to a poor quality of work life for some members.

Another ratio that has attracted the attention of R & D leaders is the ratio of professionals pursuing the core activity to support people. Support is sometimes defined as technicians and sometimes as technicians plus administrative people. For a while, leaders felt that effectiveness was enhanced by making each professional the virtual, if not the record, manager of a group of technicians. Others argued that the most effective organization was one almost totally made up of professionals. I understand that managers in the Soviet Union believe that a ratio of one professional to one technician is appropriate. Again, there is no golden ratio. The appropriate ratio is determined by function, culture, and capital equipment support. For example, the computer does for the engineer what technicians used to do. In some functions, a set of activities appropriate for technicians or a technician category, as opposed to a professional category, has not been defined or developed, in which case the professional carries on the technician's role part-time. This was true for many years in the programming profession.

Changing Organizational Structure

Organizational structure tends to fit yesterday's needs. There is a natural lag in adaptation of the structure to changing needs. Managers must identify the need to change the structure and then design the change to meet the need. I have already differentiated R & D from other parts of the organization by noting that the structure in technically creative and innovative units is less permanent. I now wish to suggest that, beyond the change forced by activity cycles, management should manage change in organizational structure. There are four fundamental reasons for changing structure.

The first reason is to heighten emphasis. This is done when an organization is formed for the purpose of paying attention to a specific activity or approach. In research, this is done by choosing a fundamental technical area, either a field of science or a technology specific to the business, and establishing a unit in that area. An example of a field of science would be a materials science section, department, or group; an example of a business-specific technology would be a storage technology group in a computer-creating organization. In development, the most normal organizational unit has either a project focus or a functional focus. Units built around a project have a life cycle characteristic of the industry; those around a function, such as engineering-change processing, usually have a continuing life.

The second reason for changing organizational structure is to eliminate the negative waste that occurs in boundary-defense and turf battles. I have seen organizations in which the manager's primary attention is on protecting boundaries, not on research. By changing boundaries, you can encourage members of the organization to establish their organizational relationship bond to the larger entity, not the subunit. This has been accomplished in IBM over the years by frequent and deliberate changes in divisional structure for effective focus on a goal, thus dispelling tendencies to build permanent bonds with small units. Consequently, people in IBM tend to relate to IBM or to a location unit, such as Poughkeepsie.

The third reason is to stimulate vitality. In this case, the change is stimulating because it accelerates new learning—as opposed to building protective boundaries of personal or organizational territory.

The fourth reason is to adapt to changing technological, business, and market needs. Organizations can be changed temporarily or permanently. Deliberate change of structure is an important tool in the hands of the leader.

(Chapter Eleven develops these four reasons more fully.)

Audit Approaches and Teams

The technical audit team is a useful tool for forcing review, for stimulating learning, and sometimes for making decisions about strategy, tactics, or organization. It is a way whereby management can ensure that the best available knowledge is brought to bear on decisions.

Generally, technical audit teams are composed of peers and managers drawn from other parts of the organization, people who by training and experience bring complementary knowledge and ask penetrating questions; in a multilaboratory organization, the team may be drawn from other laboratories. The approach varies from an unstructured review, in which the research or development group determines what is presented, to a highly structured review. When a structured review is used, the structure comes from using questions that have proven significant in past reviews and thus forcing every audit to require answers to a specific series of questions. Often the leader of a project requests the review, in which case it may strengthen managerial and technical understanding and be reassuring to the leader and the group. Sometimes upper management requests an audit because it has unanswered questions about direction or progress. Typical managerial goals in requesting an audit review are to:

- Force a decision about cancellation, acceleration, or change in emphasis.
- Fend off those criticisms which can erode credibility, lead to negative morale, and slow progress.
- Broaden the consideration of alternatives on the part of the project team.
- Reassure and support a project team that has become discouraged through its own activities.
- Support the leader in those decisions and goals which the leader wishes to implement.
- Provide necessary attention to and nurturing of a critical project.
- Spread the word about an otherwise unknown activity.

The timing of an audit is an art. The choice of auditors is an art. Time and team-composition choices are usually made in response to political forces, but they may be made in response to the need for decisions at a technical crossroad. The goals of the manager or of management (as listed above) may be different from the goals of the audit team. Considerable managerial expertise is required in order to make the goals of an independent team congruent with those of management. Decisions about the composition and leadership of the team can make congruence more or less probable. An example may clarify the use and characteristics of an audit: You are heading a project to develop a new calculator. You are at a point where an important decision must be made. One direction means staying with a known technology and meeting marketing requirements for quick release; another means changing to a new, untried, but potentially powerful technology, thereby delaying release. You have been unable to gain a consensus within your group or with your management and feel that you are stuck at a crossroad. You request an audit to assist you in gaining support for one of the choices. Choosing the audit team is a touchy matter because potential members are already polarized in favor of one direction or the other. You pick the team leader from within the organization because you feel that management will listen to this person. The choice of leader affects the choice of members, and choosing members is the next step. The audit team recommends one direction, and management supports that direction. This is a good scenario. A negative one would be that the audit team determines that the problem is with your leadership, and thus a new leader is picked. This is a typical risk faced by the manager.

Sometimes it is advantageous to choose an audit team outside the organization. In our example, this might be true if you could find no one inside the organization who can be sufficiently objective. The major difference between the use of an inside and an outside team is the nature of the technical impact. If, for example, the leadership determines that it is necessary to enhance external credibility, then an external team is used. Sometimes external audits are called in response to perceived public relations or marketing needs. Such would be the case in asking an outside group to review some research gem that has little probability of near-term application. While internal teams are often used when projects seem to be in trouble, outside teams are almost always used when things are going well. The audit's timing and the choice of members are, again, an art and depend strongly on what the leader is trying to accomplish through the use of the audit.

One variation is an audit in which human resource rather than technical issues are the prime focus. A manager might call for a human resource review when support is needed either for adding people or for taking people with specific talents from other projects—but if it is to be an example of creative leadership, a human resource review must above all be a management tool for assuring the maintenance and enhancement of vitality. A variety in one's work is necessary in order to maintain and extend one's vitality; as previously discussed, however, the manager's tendency is to keep the experienced person doing that work which the individual already knows how to do. Since utilizing the experienced person is the natural tendency and the shortest route to an answer, I recommend that a required annual review be conducted by the manager's manager to consider the future of each person in the group. In this review, the higher manager supports human resource goals by asking questions like:

- How long has each person been doing the same type of task? Has it been the right length of time for the individual and/or the organization? If it seems too long, what change is planned to enhance vitality?
- Has the manager been caring, nurturing, and rewarding in ways that improve performance?
- What has the manager done to encourage each specific person's learning and growth in technical capabilities?
- Has the manager had a career discussion with each person? What was the outcome? Have the employee and the manager jointly developed plans for the employee's career development?
- What has been the turnover of people in the function, and why has it occurred? Who has graduated from the group in the last year? Were these moves good for the individual or the organization, or both?
- Does the manager have any people on temporary assignments or rotations? What plans exist for using their new capability when they return?
- Has the manager any underutilized or unstretched people? Is there evidence of hoarding human resources?

By paying attention to these issues upper management tends to ensure that managers will also manage the long-range needs for human resource development. What management measures and reports becomes important to people in the organization.

Sampling Attitudes and Opinions

Another way of sampling, monitoring, and managing the human resource climate is through the use of attitude, or opinion, surveys. These are usually formal sets of questions about work climate, relations with managers, career needs, and one's relationships to work and to the organization. Large organizations often have internal professionals who design and execute such surveys; small organizations can hire outsiders. The purpose is to gain feedback on how management is doing in managing people and to provide a vehicle for communication between individuals and managers on these subjects. Using opinion surveys is an important part of maintaining a healthy environment. Progressive organizations do it on a cycle of once every year and a half, followed by feedback of data, extensive group discussion of issues, and creation of action plans.

An opinion survey is similar in function to a thermometer. When you take an individual's temperature, you can determine whether something abnormal is happening, but you cannot determine the cause by this measurement alone. This is also true with an attitude survey. The reasons for employee dissatisfaction are usually not evident from the survey; as a result, the most important aspects of a survey are the feedback and discussion. It is through open discussion that the causes of problems can be uncovered. This is also the source of solutions. Through discussion, organizational learning is enhanced.

Most opinion surveys contain general questions that apply to all organizations. Typical issues addressed in the general questions are:

1. Quality of communication with and relations with managers.
2. Salary in relationship to contribution and performance, as well as feelings about being ahead or behind what one could earn in another organization.

3. Clarity of understanding about and communications about missions and goals.
4. Fairness of assignments, fair distribution of work, and quality of appraisal and counseling.
5. Expectations about staying with the organization.

R & D organizations need to ask additional questions. Topics often included in R & D surveys are:

1. From both the technical and the human resource perspectives, is there a fair and respected process for selecting and training leaders?
2. Is there a quality work environment for professionals that helps the individual gain psychic income?
3. What is the nature and quality of collegial relations?
4. What is the nature and quality of technical decision making? Who is involved in the process?
5. Is there adequate support for continuing formal education? How about growth in capabilities through informal means and through the job itself?

Financial Plans and Controls

The financial planning and control process should be designed to support, not impede, the research or development process while providing the organization with the necessary information and controls. Unfortunately, financial control has been driven by the annual report and financial audit requirements, by the contractor's needs, and by the pervasiveness of an annual budget. As mentioned in Chapter Two, this means that financial systems seldom fit the cycles of work in R & D and often waste valuable professional time in planning and reporting. Creative R & D leaders need to find new ways to meet financial planning and control needs without destroying the creative environment, for it is important to understand that financial control is not an end in itself. The purpose of R & D is to create the ideas, products, systems, and services that will bring income to the organization.

Peter Carruthers (1984, p. 62), a Fellow at the Los Alamos National Laboratory, has been quoted as saying: "There's been an increasing trend to the illusion that you can manage science, whereas all you can really do, is to get good people who are interested in the subject you want to develop. Thus increasing accountability . . . exudes a cold air that dries out the kind of neurotic and creative people you need to make a breakthrough." I believe that one of the trends he is responding to is the drive for financial accountability.

Management-Leadership Styles

The appropriate management of research is leadership that does not feel like management to those who are being managed. It is not, however, the absence of managing or leadership (as a literal interpretation of Carruthers's comment might suggest). In managing a group of individualists, the leader must fit the style to the culture and to the specific conditions and individuals.

In recent interviews of research people, I quizzed them about how the manager ensured an appropriate match of people and work. They described an approach that seemed to give the individual a choice from among alternatives offered by the manager. They felt that no one had been assigned. For most, this was an appropriate level of freedom, but for some it represented a lack of leadership. Those who felt the lack wanted their manager to suggest assignments more strongly, based on the manager's broader view of the organization. The perception of being led is an individualized reaction. This example demonstrates but one aspect of the sensitivity of the balance between influencing a person and allowing that person to feel free, which is the desired characteristic of the research environment.

The manager's challenge is to establish a relationship that fits the unique needs and expectations both of the organization and of the individual. I remember a manager who had a unique style. When listening to a report or proposal, he had a way of causing the proposer to argue against the proposal within five minutes or so of starting the presentation. The manager judged the quality of the proposal by the proposer's demonstrated understanding of alternatives and the negatives. The approach was unnerving for the proposer, but it satisfied the organization's need for credible input to decision making.

Techniques Appropriate for Stable Versus Growing Organizations

Most of today's upper management of R & D organizations grew up in an era of R & D growth. This meant they learned how to manage growth—the recruiting and assimilation of new people, the management of ever larger organizations, the acquisition of new physical plants, and all the activities associated with growth. There was little emphasis on vitality during this period because growth brought sufficient change to keep the organizations stirred up and the people exposed to variety. During this growth era, there was little emphasis on effectiveness because the need for hands was so great. Less-than-adequate performance was tolerated, and getting on top of the challenge outweighed the need for creating effectiveness.

Today, however, many of these managers are managing stable or moderately declining organizations in terms of staffing and of organizational size. To be sure, managers of new technological organizations and even of some mature organizations still have to manage growth—but I want to emphasize the conflict between our past experience, which taught us to manage one type of situation, and our present need to manage another type. For example, the manager of a declining organization must learn how to assign duties (which were formerly delegated to others) back to the delegator and not have that person feel demotivated—or worse, demoted. The manager of a stable organization must create stimulation, which in the growing organization is provided by its very growth, and must aid people in growing new capabilities when the stimulation from the job has declined. This challenge is severe, for it is now often acceptable to admit stability and/or decline.

Leadership: Creating the Values

An important aspect of any organization is the set of values or beliefs that underlies its existence and purpose. These values embedded in the culture will grow without anyone deliberately creating them. However, as pointed out by Peters and Waterman (1982) and by me in *Working with People* (Miller, 1979), strong personalities can imprint values on an organization. Such was the case with Thomas J. Watson, who felt so strongly about the fact that the organization should respect the individual that he made it one of IBM's core beliefs. Thomas J. Watson, Jr., later captured the essence of his beliefs and stressed their importance in the company's success in *A Business and Its Beliefs: The Ideas That Helped Build IBM* (Watson, 1963). While these core values are important in any organization, they are even more important in R & D. One reason is the characteristic of the professional discussed in Chapter Three: One who has made beliefs central to preparation for life will seek an organization with an identifiable set of beliefs that the individual can buy and respect. In my consulting, I often see organizational difficulties that I believe can be traced to a loss of core beliefs or an erosion of their clarity. In order to understand the process better, here are some examples:

• *Enterprise strategy* can be defined as the overall set of goals and principles that guide the people of the organization toward some common course (Nash, 1983). An example of an enterprise strategy was the statement of C. E. Kenneth Mees quoted at the opening of Chapter Two. Mees's commitment to provide a commercial idea in return for freedom, when accepted by George Eastman and implemented, created organizational beliefs. The organization was committed to give research five years without any short-term pressure for results. The idea was accepted that a research environment was different, that it had to be protected from some business pressures in order to create the work climate necessary for discovery. In this statement, too, was a belief that research can pay off in a practical and applied sense and that it needs to be tied to the organization providing the facilities and money. This is how enterprise strategy is formed.

• A few years back, I was listening to the comments of a group of researchers from a top laboratory in the United States. They were questioning the purpose of research in that organization. One point of view they voiced was that the company kept them around for advertising purposes. This view was supported by the feeling that the company did not seem to want concepts or products as output. Some researchers felt that they were in an expensive sandbox. It was fun to play, but the play did not seem to be related to the business in a definable way. They were not happy with this feeling of being unnecessary. Yet this research laboratory had been the source of many profit-making breakthroughs! Something had been lost, and I feel that it was an understanding and acceptance of an enterprise strategy. "Research workers become accustomed early to the failure of hoped-for discoveries; to some extent they must become accustomed to the failure of discoveries to be utilized" (Katz and Kahn, 1978, p. 178). Leaders need to do more than enunciate the organization's principles, values, and goals; they must also work to communicate and maintain them through both word and deed.

• A belief in the *need for "wild ducks"* was one of Tom Watson, Jr.'s, contributions to values. He indicated that he felt that an organization with a goal of creativity and innovation needed to find ways to utilize the talents of people who are nonconformists. It is not an easy concept to implement because it requires a careful balancing act. If the wild duck becomes disruptive to the work of others, then the manager may have to sacrifice the creativity of the wild duck for the health and effectiveness of the group. But if the wild duck is forced to conform, then the manager may have killed the creative force. R & D leaders must decide how many wild ducks an organization can have and what kinds of wildness to tolerate, and they must learn to create safe places for these nonconformists to work. They need also to link these people with others who can make their ideas practical and to establish beliefs and a work climate that will support these individuals without destroying the culture positives for the non-wild duck.

• Leaders must learn how to *let go*. As indicated previously, different styles of leadership are required for different phases of the development cycle. The strong leader who can create the values and beliefs and translate them is usually a strong personality, with a strong ego. For the survival of the organization, it is necessary for these leaders to sense when they must let go and turn the leadership over to someone else more appropriate to the needs of the organization and the people. The literature is full of examples of leaders who held on too long, like Sewell Avery at Montgomery Ward, Nicholas Murray Butler at Columbia University, and Henry Ford at Ford. When the leader holds on too long, there is a risk of killing the organization with the leadership approach that was effective at an earlier stage. Gene Amdahl, a leader of technological enterprises, seems to understand this need to let go; he acted on it. I am sure there are some who will say that he was forced out of Amdahl, his company, but I believe that he set up the conditions for his own letting go with full knowledge of the need. It is not as clear that Steven Jobs, of Apple, understood the need to let go.

For the leader of R & D, it is important to know when to let go. But leaders are human, and creative ones become emotionally attached to their approach, to their organization. So the talented R & D leader must not only sense when to let go but must also design an organization and establish a climate in which other leaders in the organization will let go when needed and in which the trauma of doing so is minimized. It is to avoid this trauma that dual or triple ladders (discussed in Chapter Nine), fellow programs, and other techniques are devised.

• Edwin Land imprinted the concept of *innovation as the primary goal* on Polaroid. His life has been centered on creativity and innovation. He shaped his company in his image. He established a belief in and a high value for innovation. As a result, Polaroid made many breakthroughs. But this example is important mainly because it demonstrates that this important characteristic can be carried too far. He pushed Polaroid to develop an instant movie system at a time when video recording was available. It was a commercial flop. One should not follow a belief in a vacuum. The leader must be conscious of the advances in the world outside the organization.

Summary

• There is a difference between managing technology and managing people. The leader in R & D must somehow bridge this gap and be sensitive to the different needs. Technical education tends to cause technical leaders to emphasize technology and not human resource management.

• Managers should gain psychic income and have fun managing. For the professional turned manager, there must be a shift in satisfactions. This difficult personal transition is not generally well-supported by the organization.

• The R & D manager is faced with conflicts that make the leadership role very difficult. One conflict is the need to pursue short-term project goals and also support long-term goals for development of individuals.

• Managers are required to play multiple roles, such as providing consideration, facilitating the work of others, and doing this in a participatory way. It is necessary for the manager to develop a self-image that transmits role clarity to those being led and to adapt style to the situational demands. One useful outlook is the use of an experimental approach for its motivational impact.

• Development laboratories can be characterized by program or project cycles, which affect organizational structure and climate. Different phases require different skills of the leader.

• One of the underappreciated activities of the R & D manager is the need to negotiate for scarce resources. Another is the need to manage constructive disturbance to encourage creativity.

• Managing the necessary *useful waste* is an important part of managing creative and innovative activity. If all work is planned and controlled, creativity diminishes. Pursuit of the unknown requires the exploration of unfruitful routes. While this activity may appear to be waste to the business manager, the R & D manager knows that it is a necessary part of the process. Conflict with other managers over how much financial control is necessary is another part of this difference.

• While there is no golden ratio of managers to nonmanagers in R & D, successful laboratories seem to approximate an overall ratio of one to seven.

• Deliberate change of organizational structure allows the manager to focus energy on goals and to reduce the energy lost in turf battles. The goal is to have the individual create a bond with a larger unit.

● Effective management requires feedback to improve results. Audit approaches were suggested as viable techniques for clarifying decision making. The human resource review was proposed as a way to avoid obsolescence, improve employee development, and create vitality. Opinion surveys were described as another feedback technique.

● Ideal management in R & D does not feel like management to those being led, but it is not the absence of leadership. Leadership needs vary between growing and stable organizations. One of the functions of leadership is the creation of values that improve the focus on goals.

Chapter 5

Involving Professionals in Developing Exciting Missions and Goals

The mission of an organization is the raison d'être, the purpose, around which the members of the organization come together. Missions provide the base for a rallying call, for the generation of interest, excitement, and commitment to the strategies and goals that support the mission. As Schein (1985, p. 52) writes: "Every new group or organization must develop a shared concept of its *ultimate survival problem,* from which is usually derived its most basic sense of core mission, or 'reason to be.' In most business organizations this shared definition revolves around the issue of economic survival and growth, which, in turn, involves the delivery of a necessary product or service to customers." A good mission is one which is easily communicated and which is attractive to the people with the skills and knowledge necessary to pursue the goals that define the means for achieving the mission. It is also one which attracts the financial support necessary to put the people to work and which can be explained to the public in ways that will cause them to see that achieving the mission is of high value, so that they will grant the organization the right to exist. One of the problems in our world today is that some missions of importance to the country or for the overall good of a significant subgroup are not bought

112

by some segment, who actively blocks achievement of the goal that supports the mission. An example might be the environmentalists, who, however desirable their goals may be, have had the net effect of raising the consumer's cost for electric power unnecessarily and without achieving their goals. A well-articulated mission, bought by those who must commit themselves to achieve the goals that support the mission, is a key element in the effective management of an organization. It is particularly important in R & D organizations because of the inability to define all the necessary activities when pursuing the unknown. The mission can act as the reason even though more specific statements of goals cannot be made.

A person who has invested much of life, twenty years or more, in extensive preparation to do something important generally builds up a strong need for achievement relative to that goal. For the salaried professional, achievement is not just doing something about which only the individual cares. Achievement usually requires a larger context and means being part of a larger purpose, a field of endeavor, a profession and/or an organization. The feeling of achievement is also associated with a strong need for exciting and meaningful work. Meaningfulness is in the mind of the professional. It is defined by the individual, although there are some generally accepted criteria during a given era. For example, in the public view it is now thought to be more meaningful to work on space vehicles than automobiles. In any era, there are "in" things to do, influenced both by societal values and by the newsworthiness of the technology and the attraction of the goal. The investment in preparation came about because the individual made a commitment. Fruition, making it all worthwhile, requires a new commitment to work that provides the individual with a return for the preparation commitment and the investment of time and energy. One return is the feeling of accomplishment, which is part of my term *psychic income*. Accomplishment generally requires the opportunity to apply oneself, to use one's skills and knowledge; support from management and colleagues; and acceptance of, use of, and recognition for the results by the organization and the profession. For most, although some professionals operate alone, it is the marriage of the individual and the organization that makes accomplishment possible. It is the organization that provides the mission or purpose, the equipment, the fellow professionals, and the dollars, all of which set the stage for individual accomplishment.

Missions and goals which we participate in setting and which we "buy" provide the bond between us and the organization. In discussing how to manage the performance of the organization, Nash (1983, p. 272) states it in this way: "The idea is to be very clear about the overall strategy and goals of the corporation and then to involve everyone—at least at the management and professional level but preferably all employees—in the process of implementing that strategy by division and function and by individual position." Goal congruence, compatibility, and overlap between the goals of the organization and those of the individual should be the result of the participative goal-setting process. Congruence makes it possible to achieve our personal goals in the process of achieving those of the organization. Congruence is desirable for both the individual and the organization. Goal congruence contributes to individual motivation and psychic income since accomplishment for the organization and personal achievement become synonymous. It is the glue for a bond between the individual and the organization. If we are turned on by the work itself and our work fits in the context of the organization's mission, it takes on greater meaning. This is the basis of today's equivalent of missionary zeal, evident when you talk to a committed and enthusiastic professional. This is the desirable source of today's calling for the professional. Achieving goal congruence is a core concept in building a productive and vital research and/or development organization.

The Importance of a Mission

People who work in a hospital, almost regardless of their job and even if they are volunteers, gain a sense of worth in their personal activities because of the mission of the hospital, restoring health and saving lives. Raelin, Sholl, and Leonard

(1985, pp. 29-30) say: "Certain types of industries and organizations are more or less responsive to professionals. Greater professional identification is likely to be found in such organizations as universities, hospitals, government agencies, and certain professional service organizations (such as public accounting firms) than in most industrial organizations." This quotation not only provides an insight, over and above the nature of the mission, as to why identification through mission varies from organization to organization but also provides a clue to one of the functions of a mission—it is to support the individual's sense of meaningfulness, of personal worth and of importance. It is probably this factor that helps to attract individuals with talent and skill to join the organization and/or to choose not to join the organization. A clear mission contributes to the recruiting process, to the initial sorting out of people who will be compatible or noncompatible with the organization. In the scientific and technical professional world, this phenomenon is currently clear because of the SDI, or Star Wars, debate. The mission tends to divide people on a moral or ethical basis as well as on the attraction of the technical challenge of exploring the unknown. So a mission is a communicable and understandable shorthand for talking about and dealing with the essence of an organization. A mission helps to define who will join and who will not. It also becomes a statement to which the public reacts and judges whether the organization is a good one or a bad one.

For those who choose to join the organization, the mission provides a broad statement of purpose against which they can judge the appropriateness of strategies, goals, projects, and activities. It provides a focus for planning activities and aids in management decisions. If it is narrow in scope, the focus is sharp, and if it is broad, it allows the inclusion of many activities. Thus, it shapes the development of the organization. For example, there have been many retrospective discussions of the effect of the mission definition on the development of the railroads. The apparent definition of the mission was the transport of people and materials over fixed route facilities, called rails, which were defined by rights-of-way. Conjecture has it that this narrowness kept the railroad managers from seeing the impact of the truck and the airplane since these appeared to be pursuing different missions. Had the mission been more broadly defined as transportation, without specification of means, railroads could have grown to large transportation industries. In this retrospective look, it is important to note that the government and antitrust laws also had an effect on the outcome. Here are also examples closer to the discussion of R & D:

• Part of the definition of mission for Eastman Kodak must have been to make photography simple and available to the public, as opposed to the professional photographer. This appears to have influenced Kodak's abandonment of sophisticated camera manufacture in favor of more effort on inexpensive cameras. It has shaped the development efforts for years, as we have seen one generation after another of new, simple, low-cost cameras with new formats and new film characteristics. Recent announcements of joint ventures with Japanese manufacturers, however, portend reentry by Kodak into the professional or advanced amateur camera market.

• IBM's entry into the personal computer market required a redefinition of mission, at least as it had been implemented over the years. IBM's mission appeared to be provision of data-processing equipment and services to organizations and companies. Except for a few typewriters, IBM had never sold directly to the public before. The statement of and understanding of a change in mission had to come before managers could develop new kinds of products and lead the company into a new kind of business. Once the change was made, the public began to see a whole series of new activities on the part of IBM that would not previously have been possible.

Thus, missions have a profound effect on what an organization does.

The Need for Excitement

We are excited when stimulated by ideas, events, individuals, and activities. Excitement may come either from the anticipation of the satisfactions that will be generated by the relationship or achievement or from the actual execution, the doing.

It is best—most stimulating, motivating, and fulfilling—when it comes from both. Excitement is a state of being that we identify with stimulation, psychic income, satisfaction, and fun, and it relates both to our perception of the potential for achievement and to the actual achievement. In Western cultural history, excitement and work were not initially paired because work was considered negative, or punishing, and excitement and fun were positive. One message of this chapter is the need to create through mission and excitement a setting or condition that makes work fun. Excitement can do this. Excitement can capture the individual's energy and motivation for the good of the organization. The individual's investment results in what the organization calls productivity, a return for the organization. The organization needs also to capture the individual's energy and motivation for the good of the individual. When this unique pairing is achieved, the individual benefits with psychic income, the return for the individual.

Creating Excitement

Management can create a sense of excitement through five basic actions:

1. By choosing exciting things to do. This technique is not always available, for frankly some R & D work is unexciting, yet it has to be done. When this is the case, the manager must see that the unexciting activity is not continually piled on the same people.
2. By attracting people who can be excited by the mission and giving them the freedom to pursue it in a way in which they feel they are free to be self-managing.
3. By choosing leaders who focus on doing things in an exciting way and who radiate excitement, stimulate it in others, and expand or release excitement when they find an excited, interested person. A quote from *The Soul of a New Machine* (Kidder, 1981, p. 56) embodies this sort of behavior on the part of the leader, West: "West still had a way of making ordinary things seem special; in this case a 32-bit

Eclipse was being transformed into the occasion for an adventure. West's ardor for it seemed to spread the way his neologies did. Others beside Alsing felt infected."

4. By having those managers match their people with assignments that stretch their capability and encourage learning.

5. By making individuals secure enough that they will take the risks associated with the creative-innovative process.

Excitement is contagious when we can join someone who is obviously excited. Unfortunately, a lack of excitement is also contagious. A climate with a depressing lack of excitement is a climate of fear. You will remember that in the Preface I spoke of my impression in many laboratories that we have powerful people who feel powerless. When people are full of fear, they feel powerless. On the other hand, a vital, alive R & D organization is an exciting place to be. When one is excited, one is free to take risks and is not worried about security. Creating an environment of excitement is one of the antidotes to the sense of powerlessness that many technically trained people feel in organizations. By being in it, one catches the excitement. This is one of the qualities important in a quality work environment for the professional (QPL). It is a quality that supports organizations in attracting and hiring the best-trained and most highly motivated scientists, engineers, programmers, and other professionals. It is fun to be with and work with others who are "turned on" to what they are doing.

A quick review of twenty or so management books shows that few if any authors talk about excitement, the need for it, the manager's role in creating it, or how to create it. I suspect that this is due in part to our cultural history, which suggests that work should be painful, not fun. Excitement is somehow associated with a lack of control and is thus viewed as the antithesis of the work-environment image of planning, control, and orderly activity. The need for management to create excitement is (although perhaps it should not be) one of the ways in which managing R & D is different from other management.

Challenge, a key characteristic of good work for professionals, is closely associated with excitement. Challenge means risk and thus fits one of the suggested actions, yet the risk must fit the individual's tolerance range if it is to be motivating. Too much is scary and too little is boring.

Collegial support is another aspect of creating excitement. If the people around are diverse in background but excited about their fields, this provides a climate that spawns excitement. It is a necessary part of a quality research environment.

The style and nature of the leader are each an important input to excitement, as I indicated in the suggested actions. I suggested that the leader should radiate personal excitement and amplify it when found in others. Steele and Jenks (1977, p. 97) say this about generating excitement: "First of all, whether you are a leader in the system or not, generating a climate of excitement can require considerable energy. This may be energy to overcome inertia in the system, energy to challenge and stimulate others, or energy to formulate and articulate a set of shared goals." They make an important additional point, which is that creating an exciting environment is work and thus takes energy and attention from the leader.

The Need to Belong

Many years ago I heard an inspiring management speaker talk about the need to belong and the need to be needed as two very strong motivating conditions. I had known that it was important for me, but I had not understood that it was also very important for other people.

The ability to achieve the sense of belonging is closely related to compatibility with and understanding of mission. Today we break this need for belonging into several segments or aspects. All of these needs are part of what I call the psychological work contract (described in Chapter Three); in its simplest description, the psychological work contract is defined by what we choose to bring to work, what we expect to find at work, and what we expect to take away from work (psychic plus monetary income). In the discussion of mission, I indicated that the need to be part of something bigger than ourselves is an important part of our bond with the organization. Not only is it part of the bond with the organization, but for those who find membership in the profession important, there is a need to belong to the profession. The opportunity to belong is normally one of the expectations about the climate that the individual wants to find at work. The feeling of belonging is normally a specification of one of the things the individual wants to take away; I suspect that individuals relate this feeling of being part of the organization to the ability to achieve an impact. Belonging and being needed are important parts of the bond through which work becomes meaningful.

In the case of the professional, the key person in the high-technology R & D organization, it is very important to be part of a team of trained and talented people from whom one can learn and with whom one can accomplish tasks and have an impact. The potential for collegial support in learning and accomplishment is one of the attractions causing the professional to join an organization and to stay. The organization is the enabling vehicle: It provides the mission and goals as well as the facilities, time, and money to support the activity; it supplies the colleagues, the work environment, and given the right, open environmental conditions, the colleagues supply support. This is an aspect of a quality work environment for professionals. Thus, under the best of circumstances, the organization can become the larger entity and purpose of which the individual needs to be part. For the professional, however, this entity-purpose role is shared by the organization and the profession. For the professional closely related to the field and the profession, the balance of purpose and belonging favors the profession. Gouldner (1957, 1958) classifies these people as cosmopolitan professionals; this is normally the case for the research person in an open, nonclassified, nonsecret activity. For the development professional, the balance usually shifts to the organization, and Gouldner calls these locals, because the person who applies technology is normally more closely related to the product or service and thus to the organization. This positive relationship is something, however, that the organization can achieve only with right mission, right size, right management, and right culture.

But there is no one "right" culture for all individuals. Different personal requirements can make one person feel comfortable in an organization and another feel uncomfortable in the same organization; what is comfortable for one is not necessarily comfortable for another. Compatibility with the organization is one of those aspects of the mission-culture impact that can make small start-up high-technology organizations the place to be for some people. Belonging is somewhat easier under these conditions; it makes the larger and more mature organizations uncomfortable for some, for belonging requires that something large and difficult to describe (often diffuse and unknown) be translated into something desirable and friendly. Yet the intensity of the mission-climate package in the small organization can make it uncomfortable for other individuals. Our needs are individualized and change with personal goals, personality, phase of career, and life stages. Providing this opportunity for belonging, for bonding, in an individualized manner is a key managerial challenge in research and/or development. The ability of the manager to meet the challenge is closely related to the character and clarity of mission, the manager's personality and management style, and the manager's ability to create excitement.

The Need for Meaning and Importance

Meaning and importance are additional elements of this bond between the individual and the organization that relate to mission and excitement. For the professional, doing something with one's educational preparation is an important personal goal. The central purpose of life is one's calling, one's work, for most achievement-oriented people, and that is the type of individual found in R & D. Meaning thus flows first from the choice of profession, but to make this choice have meaning requires that the individual achieve something that builds on this investment. The contribution must go beyond just individual achievement; it must contribute to understanding in the profession, to society, and/or to an enterprise. Because meaning seems to occur on several levels, it is probable that the individual must feel a sense of meaningfulness on each of these several levels in order to achieve satisfaction in the need for meaningfulness.

On a trip to the Orient, I had a discussion with an artist that can help to make the point about levels of achievement of meaning. He said that solely from his sitting on top of a mountain and painting would flow all the meaning and satisfaction he needed. He was talking of the satisfaction that comes from the work itself, the intrinsic satisfaction. Intrinsic satisfaction is what he felt when the paint went on the canvas in a way that pleased him, a way representing what he felt. The meaning created by the work itself, the meaning intrinsic in the activity, is usually important to the professional. The artist maintained that this first level was all that he felt he needed. He felt no need to interface with other people for that extrinsic satisfaction which comes when someone looks at the painting and is moved in some way to comment. I suggested that since he had never truly experienced the mountaintop conditions, he might be undervaluing the need for that meaning which flows from another individual interacting with his painting. I suggested that he would at some point come running down off his mountain and call out, "See, look at what I have accomplished." Most, though probably not all of us, at some point need the sense of meaning that comes from feedback from another person. This is the second level. For the artist, the third level of meaningfulness would occur when his work became publicly acclaimed and he found a broad market for his paintings. Since the artist has not tried the mountain and there is a market for his work, neither of us really knows the relative importance of the several levels of meaning for him. Let us now translate this story into the work world.

For the research professional, the first level of meaningfulness comes from the satisfaction that flows from the successful experiment. Through the experiment, the individual ties down some new fact; for our example, let us assume that this is the discovery of a principle or technology on which the organization can base some new product. The second level of meaning comes from convincing others (usually management) that the concept or discovery should be used as the basis for a new product or service. The third level of meaning comes from the presentation of a paper at a professional conference, where the individual can speak to fellow professionals and get one-on-one feedback, or comes from others taking over and developing a product based on the discovery. Now the idea has taken form in a way that adds meaning. If the organization now markets this product and people buy it, another level of meaningfulness can be identified. Additional meaningfulness flows from the fact that the idea has now affected the lives of other people in a way that can be related to the scientist's discovery.

For the development professional, on the other hand, meaningfulness comes more from the physical embodiment, the product, than from the idea or concept. Meeting production cost and time targets, successful marketing, and positive customer feedback probably take on more importance than positive feedback from fellow professionals.

In all these examples, the organization becomes the vehicle through which the individual achieves meaning. Linkage with an organization becomes part of the equation of fulfillment in life for the highly educated, achievement-motivated, salaried professional.

The Dream: Communicating the Mission

A dream, the vision of a better condition or of an achievement, is important in communicating a mission and is central to getting acceptance of goals. "To be successful, a CEO [chief executive officer] must create a 'compelling vision of a desired state of affairs,' says Professor Warren Bennis, noted author, teacher, and former university president. . . . They are concerned with their organization's basic purpose, why it exists, its general direction' " (Naisbitt and Aburdene, 1985, p. 40). Just as the organization is necessary for the individual to achieve meaning from achievement, the dream is the linkage that helps members of the organization make progress, as a team, from today to a desired tomorrow. It is the translation of the mission into a communicable goal or goals. People have gone to war for the dream of making the world safe for democracy. Alexander Graham Bell was driven by a dream of communicating over wires. George Westinghouse, driven by a dream, spurred his company to light the 1893 Chicago World's Fair with alternating-current electric lights. All other proposals were for direct-current lighting. When he made the proposal and sold it, neither he nor his engineers knew how it would be done. Henry Ford had a dream of making a car the average person could afford. George Eastman's dream was embodied in "You push the button, we'll do the rest." "Better Things for Better Living, through Chemistry" epitomized the Du Pont dream. Edwin Land was driven by a dream and drove his company to achieve instant photography. Wozniak and Jobs were driven by a dream, and their result was the Apple computer.

The dream applicable to the quest of this book is succinctly stated by Roland W. Schmitt (1985, p. 13), senior vice president of corporate R & D for General Electric: "We must build upon, rather than abandon, one of our greatest strengths: our fundamental research capability. But we must also make sure that we put our scientific knowledge to use more quickly than others do. We've got to increase our efforts in engineering research—the link between fundamental scientific research and application." Many leader-managers do not understand the need for, or are incapable of enunciating, the dream that will attract others to invest their knowledge and their energies—but good leaders catch on to the need, probably through experiment, and create dreams. Although Bennis suggests that creating dreams is a top-management function, I believe that it is necessary for all managers to have this capability and to exercise it. The difference may be in degree. The CEO enunciates the grand dream, and the first-line manager enunciates the dream associated with the mission and goals of the small group.

This need to create and translate the dream is key to managing R & D because the creative professional—programmer, physicist, or electrical engineer—pursues a personal dream and therefore understands and responds to dreams. As a professional turned leader, however, the same individual often fails to understand the need for a dream for others or fails in communicating the dream. It is as if in moving from professional to manager, someone waved a magic wand and said, "From now on you shall be incapable of dreaming." Dreaming is not part of the conventional role model of a manager. This lack is probably related to three aspects. First, as I have said, the education that technical people receive biases them against feelings as legitimate data. Incidentally, they seem more willing to accept personal feelings related to their science than feelings related to people, even themselves. Sarason (1977) notes the difficulties, seemingly common to all professionals, that professionals have in speaking with candor about their feelings relative to work, career, and life. The feelings with which leaders must deal are different from those which the professional addresses, for in the managerial role they relate to individuals, and to science. Second, in entering the managerial role, they become part of the business environment—in which feelings and emotion are again downplayed—and this further depresses their legitimacy. For example, teachers of business and technical communication have stressed for years that it should be devoid of feeling (Gaum, Graves, and Hoffman, 1950). Third, the process requires a new kind of creativity—managerial, not scientific. Most professionals see the creativity process as something associated with their field, technology, or knowledge. There are therefore several conditions other than the inherent difficulty in enunciating a dream that may tend to handicap the professional turned manager.

Accepting this explanation for the moment, what is the leader-manager to do? Two things are necessary. First, accept that the dream is necessary and useful and that the manager's responsibility is to articulate it. Second, work in new kinds of creative ways to come up with it, translate it, and communicate it in such a manner that others can buy it and own it. This is but one aspect of managerial creativity, which also includes experimentation, development of one's image of the role, management of change, and interesting uses of organizational structure.

A real example will put this in perspective. One of the leader's first responsibilities is to assess the strengths and areas for improvement in the organization. Once this has been done, the next step is to develop and implement change for improvement in effectiveness. Suppose that after the assessment you determine that one of the areas for improvement is improved coaching for development of capabilities and improvement in performance. What do you do? Here is a possible script:

1. *Develop the dream.* Create a word picture of a new organizational state, where everyone gets the opportunity to participate in creating an effective match with work and where leaders provide feedback for learning and improvement. Include in the dream some evidence that there will be plusses for the participants, such as more fun at work and an increased sense of personal worth.
2. *Share the dream.* Work with the managers who report to you directly to improve their match with their work, with specific emphasis on your coaching role in helping them to be better. Get them to buy the concept of coaching through experiencing personal gain.
3. *Talk about the dream.* Make coaching, individual development, and increased satisfaction from work something the people in the organization talk about. Work it into your speeches. Find examples of good coaching, and use these to highlight your speeches.
4. *Establish ad hoc teams.* After you have some converts in your immediate team, spread the dream by creating participative teams to discuss the need and to establish action plans that will help achieve the goals inherent in the dream.
5. *Implement the dream.* Implement coaching training for managers, new policies that support coaching, and measurements of coaching activities. Train all employees so that the individual sees that coaching is not just something the manager does, but something to which all individuals can contribute. Provide for feedback about progress by setting up a system to comment on and communicate about the improvements that occur.

Motivation Through Owning the Goals

When my goals and the organization's goals are congruent, I am motivated to work to achieve the organization's goals. For this to occur, I must identify and understand my goals and must know and understand the goals of the organization. Knowing, understanding, and believing the goals of the organization is often difficult in R & D because the message seems inconsistent and sometimes actually contradicts the published statement of goals.

In a recent assignment, for example, I had the opportunity to interview scientists in a research organization. There was considerable confusion in their minds as to what the company really wanted. Some felt that the message they had heard was simply "Do your own thing" (pursue your own research interests), yet they could not believe that a profit-making organization really meant that. The message they thought that they heard lacked credibility. Some felt that if they came up with an invention, the company would not pursue it. This group did not feel that they were relating to the organization's goals in a meaningful way. Some felt that there was an inconsistency in what management was saying to them in terms of dollar support from different channels; that is, the dollars for capital equipment were inconsistent with the space available for locating that capital equipment so that it would be useful, or the dollars for the program and the head-count allocation were inconsistent. There seemed in one case to be excellent financial support for the program, but the head-count restrictions were such that the leader could not add the people needed even though the funds were available. As a result of the fact that the dollars for staff seemed out of line with the support dollars for activity, some felt that R & D was maintained just as a show piece, that no real developments were desired. Because the message about goals had not come in one clear, consistent way but had been transmitted in many, sometimes unrelated, actions, this group had no clear picture of the goals in that R & D organization. Consequently, it was difficult for any individual to judge whether the personal and organizational goals were congruent.

As in our story, the professional receives messages about organizational goals in many ways. Strategy documents and published program plans are but one of the ways to discern what is desired. The message is transmitted through many separate managers' actions and often emanates from different parts of the management team, which may well be responding to quite different goals. For example, it is quite possible in most organizations to have a financial group motivated and measured against goals that actually stand in opposition to the goals of a research or development function. Most often the professional views messages from different sources as being different messages. The message's lack of clarity thus makes it difficult to buy and own the goals of the organization.

Individuals are not necessarily clear about their own goals. Individuals' goals change with personal experience and accomplishments and with the conditions and opportunities in the organization. The individual pursuing a project that the individual really believes is a breakthrough may well feel that influencing the organization to implement the project is the most important goal. An individual's goals change with phase of career, family needs, and stage of life. Thus, the goals of the professional who has just joined the organization and one with fifteen years of experience in the organization are bound to be different. The professional nearing retirement, for example, is often driven by a goal to leave a mark, to leave something behind that will demonstrate that the individual was there. This is definitely not a typical goal of the new entrant, who feels that it is more important to be accepted, to belong. It takes self-assessment and career/life management activity to know one's goals, to keep in touch with them, and to understand the costs and risks that one is willing to face to achieve them. Most professionals do not invest sufficient time in this personal assessment and planning. Asking oneself these questions is tough and, for some, too scary. Some individuals are conscious of these shifts in personal goals and can understand and articulate them, but others cannot; either way, they have different needs from those of the organization. They face different challenges in owning the organization's goals. The result of this review of the environment and people in R & D is that the individual may well be trying to match unclear personal goals with unclear organizational goals. That is not only difficult, it is impossible!

Owning, accepting, and buying-in are actions *internal* to the individual, yet there is so much at stake that the manager must work to enable these to happen, both for the good of the individual and for the good of the organization. Here are some things that leaders can do:

- Provide those whom one leads the opportunities to talk about individual goals and organizational goals. Trying to tell someone else about one's goals has the affect of clarifying one's own thinking about them. Thus, by talking with the individual about personal goals, the leader is a catalyst for clarification, and by trying to explain the organizational goals, the leader increases the probability of a match.
- Examine and share one's own process of understanding and matching individual and organizational goals. By sharing this, the manager not only demonstrates by example how someone else pursues this process but also makes it more comfortable for the nonmanager to talk on a personal level.
- Communicate upward about needs for improved definition and communication of the organization's goals. Give the boss evidence of how the goals are unclear and misunderstood so that other levels of management can join you in trying to gain a congruence between individual and organizational goals.
- Both at the process level and through style, do everything allowable within the organization's current management practice to help others see the ways whereby they can participate in shaping and having an impact on the nature of organizational goals. The goals we help to shape can the more easily become our own goals.
- If individuals cannot achieve goal understanding and congruence in this environment, help them find another part of the organization that has the environment (culture-mission-goal balance) that they can match. If both the individual and the manager have worked the problem and there seems to be no match within the organization, admit it—and help the individual look outside the organization for a better match.
- Talk about the fact that goal congruence is only one aspect of those things which the individual and the organization must match. Explore improvements in other aspects of the work/person match (as described in Chapter Twelve).

Participation, the Vehicle for Achieving Ownership

That which I create or shape, I own. This is the essence of the creative process. Thus, it must be a key management concept in an organization whose goals are creativity and innovation. These should be the goals of R & D. In the normal pursuit of R & D work, this emotional bond of ownership is with the idea, product, or service that the individual creates. As such, it can be useful in that it probably causes the individual to be more committed, but sometimes it is not useful. It can become a source of conflict when the researcher wants to take the time to understand what is happening in a scientific sense even though feasibility for application has been proved. It can also become a source of conflict when the organization must move the product on to manufacturing and the customer but the development engineer or software designer wishes to continue to polish it. It is sometimes useful in that "killed" projects in R & D seem never to die; the originator may find a way to continue it even though management has decided in favor of another approach. This can be positive, for occasionally management is wrong. In the current discussion, however, you and I are aiming at building this emotional bond with the mission and goals rather than with the specific task activity of the individual.

In my work with R & D organizations, I have found that the way to achieve this ownership of goals is to have the professional participate in setting them. As Katz and Kahn (1978, p. 394) say: "internalization of organizational goals means that individuals work for these goals since they express their own values. Often the goals of the subsystem are, or become congruent with, the objective of the members. People achieve self-identity with their occupational identification or their system involvement." We are searching for system involvement as a way of achieving this self-identity. This can be done through task groups, through planning committees, and/or through a process that involves all levels in shaping the organization's future. The dangers are that the process will seem to require time and energy out of proportion to the impact the discussions are allowed to have on shaping the goals, that there will be no perceptible impact on goals by the group, and/or that the goals will seem to have little to do with what the organization actually does. I have seen all of these things happen. The most usual is that the program-planning process grinds on, establishing goals, but that in reality the organizational goals seem to be imposed from the top. The expectation on the part of top management in this case is often that the participative group will discover the goals that top management has already decided to choose. This is manipulative, and the professional (manager or nonmanager) is intelligent enough to understand and resent it. It backfires. Thus, the process must be *real* in order to achieve the goal discussed in this section—the emotional bonding that comes from ownership of the goals.

This need can be restated in another way. In working with professionals (both through processes of self-discovery and through assessment and redesign of their jobs), I have discovered a job element that seems to be most important to the majority of professionals in defining *good work*. The single most important element repeatedly turns out to be autonomy—discretion and control over their work. Control over one's work starts with determining what one is to do. This is decided with respect to broad goals and becomes reality when these broad goals are related to the specific job goals of the individual. Thus, participation in broad goal setting is the front end (a sort of precursor action) in establishing control over one's work. But remember that I stated in Chapter Three that autonomy has a strategic dimension and an operational dimension. I believe that in talking about one's participation in setting the overall research or development goals, I am talking about the professional's ability to affect the strategic dimension. In talking about one's pursuit of the work, I am talking about the operational dimension of autonomy. The discussion demonstrates both the necessity for and the power of a process which really involves the professional in broad goal setting for the organization and which satisfies the need for strategic autonomy. But we must understand that all professionals do not exhibit equal needs for control in these two dimensions. In satisfying this need, the leader must really get to know the needs of the individual.

Thus, in talking about the power of participation in contributing to goal congruence, for some we are talking about strategic autonomy, and for others we are talking about operational autonomy as the key that creates the conditions of buying-in and ownership. (These and other job redesign factors are discussed in Chapter Twelve.)

Goal Congruence Between Individual and Organizational Goals

In this chapter on missions and goals, all the subtopics have been aiming at one thing—*goal congruence*—which means that one's goals overlap, are similar to, and are included with the goals of the larger entity, the organization. The purpose is to gain commitment and to have individual energies invested in directions that satisfy the needs both of the individual and of the organization. When the individual can go home at the end of most days with the feeling that progress has been made toward achieving personal goals in the process of achieving what the organization needs, that individual has achieved congruence. This is good for the individual because it moves in the direction of satisfying the need for psychic income through work, and it is good for the organization because it moves in the direction of achieving effectiveness (productivity) in the pursuit of the organization's goals. The individual and the organization come together synergistically when this occurs. Both management and a manager can either contribute positively to this synergism or get in the way of achieving it.

Summary

• Missions provide the raison d'être, the purpose, around which people in an organization can come together and apply their energy and knowledge. Missions are important because they provide the vehicle for the initial sorting of those individuals who should be part of an organization from those who should not. Missions support recruiting efforts. Missions are particularly important in focusing action and motivating people in

R & D because detailed statements of what is to be done are often not possible.

- Missions in the broad sense—and goals in a more specific sense, through representing the direction the organization has chosen to go—become statements of the meaning of success in the organizational context.

- Excitement is critical in establishing a positive work climate, especially in R & D. It is the manager's role to create the excitement. Excitement can be created by choosing an exciting mission, by attracting people who can be excited by that mission, by choosing leaders who radiate and elicit excitement, by giving people jobs that stretch them, and by matching people with work in a way that supports risk taking.

- Professionals, like others, need to belong, but in the case of the professional, belonging means bonding both with the organization and with the profession. The strength of the need for each of these bonds varies with the individual.

- Meaning and importance are additional elements in the bonding of the individual to the mission and the organization. Meaningfulness occurs on a level intrinsic to the work itself as well as at other levels of peer, management, and customer recognition.

- It is necessary for the manager to create a dream, a compelling and attractive vision of a desired state of affairs, in order to communicate the mission and goals, to gain an understanding of them, and to encourage others to buy in.

- When the individual's goals and the organization's goals are congruent, the individual is motivated to pursue the organization's goals. Owning goals and making them congruent occurs most often when individuals feel that they have participated in shaping the goals. The organization's large goals and the specific goals of an assignment become congruent when the individual and the manager have open discussions about matching the work with the individual.

Chapter 6

Building Vitality
and Effectiveness

The Keys to Success

In the growth years of scientifically based industry, there were usually three goals for the organization as an entity: more, better, and bigger. Being the first to bring a new discovery into the marketplace led to growth in size and in numbers of people and to beating the competitor. These were the signs of success. Today, with questions about whether we have lost our scientific and technical forward thrust, with intense international competition, and with dramatic technical, geopolitical, and economic shifts, these former goals are being questioned. Some individuals and groups are questioning the worth of scientific progress in light of the costs, which sometimes show up as the deterioration of certain aspects of the quality of life. Some are questioning whether we have lost the commitment to success. And some are questioning our scientific abilities vis-à-vis those of other nations, who periodically seem to beat us. The world of technologically driven organizations is at least temporarily in turmoil, and industries in Silicon Valley that many thought were recession-proof because of the strength of their growth are facing tough times.

The power of a goal is that it provides a reference against which we can measure progress. It helps us make decisions that result in consistency of direction. Gellerman (1963) cites Chris Argyris as defining a healthy organization as one able to achieve its basic purposes, which are defined by its goals and by its understanding of the obstacles that must be overcome to achieve them. Healthy organizations are equivalent to vital ones. Goals assist the management of vital organizations in focusing their energies. If we take being first in the marketplace as the goal and then find that we do not have the power—the organizational strength—to pursue our direction beyond the first victory, we have a Pyrrhic victory, or at least one confined to the moment. Such was the case with Osborne and the portable computer. I can remember, too, one computer project in which the leader met the technical and business goals, but with a team that was burned out; some members were obsolete technically, and many were suffering stress-related illnesses and needed extensive time for refurbishment. Was this a worthwhile development victory? Does R & D organizational life have to be deleterious to health? Is technical obsolescence a necessary result of technical progress? Results goals, the prime management focus, are not alone enough. They must be joined with other goals of equal importance.

These worrisome questions led me to a search for joint goals—ones that could guide leaders toward meaningful successes, include positive human resource concepts, and emphasize strengthening the organization. This search led me to choose vitality and effectiveness as running mates with results. As I wrote in *Personal Vitality* (Miller, 1977a, p. 1), I feel that "vitality has become critical to both personal and organizational survival. At the same time, however, enhancement of human effectiveness, growth, and a sense of accomplishment, all part of vitality, are becoming more difficult for the individual and the organization." In this chapter, I would like to encourage you to join me in choosing vitality and effectiveness.

Vitality is the power an organization gains today that assures tomorrow's success. It comes from choosing the right activities and pursuing them with effectiveness. As Katz and Kahn (1978, p. 255) write: "Organizational effectiveness is the maximization of return to the organization by all means. Such maximization by technical means has to do with efficiency; maximization by noneconomic or political means increases effectiveness without adding to efficiency. Increases in effectiveness by both means are typically observable as storage of energy, organizational growth, organizational endurance and survival, and as organizational control of the surrounding environment." Vitality and effectiveness goals stress organizational learning, which is especially necessary in today's R & D world. But there is a danger that specialized technical knowledge, which can be the basis for success, may also tend to block the change and adaptation necessary for continued success and survival. Throwing out old goals, a necessary step, is often so hard that organizations fail to survive. In R & D organizations, we see the effects of this when some new, usually small, organization tips the balance against the large established organization. Breakthroughs result from the freedom to take a fresh look and not be encumbered by past successes.

Vitality is aliveness and adaptability energy. It is thus both a means toward an end and a result of pursuing goals in ways that include capability enhancement. In R & D, vitality is measured both in the ability to pursue goals to success and in the ability to question goals and change direction. This balance is particularly hard to achieve in R & D, where the emotional attachment to one's own idea or research direction can be very strong. The attachment leads to commitment and often to success, which are positive results of this emotional bond, but it can also lead to a negative result of the emotional bond—a blindness to alternatives.

A vital organization is vital because of the energies and knowledge of the people that make it up, and the chance of being vital as a person is enhanced if you work with others who are vital. In some sense, vitality begets vitality. Human interactions in a vital and effective organization make a strong environmental or cultural impact on the individual. Stimulation comes from an environment in which vitality is valued. In measuring vitality, one finds that the hard measures are available normally after it is too late to affect organizational vitality through management action. When you find that the new product development is a dud in the marketplace, you have already invested extensive dollars, energy, and years in pursuit of the wrong goal. The vitality drain can be enormous. Managers therefore need to develop quick measures, which are usually soft, to assist in day-to-day decision making and course correction. These subjective measures, like asking yourself whether you feel as vital as you did six months ago, can alert managers to take corrective action in the right time frame.

Effectiveness results from choosing the right goals, the right tools, and the right people and from guidance by a good leader. It requires making good people/job matches where the individual's needs and capabilities are congruent with those of the organization. It comes from excitement, collegial support, and team development. It is built upon open communication. It occurs when people are not afraid to face the bad news, do not spend excessive effort protecting their jobs, and share both feelings and facts. Blending vitality and effectiveness goals and using them as a management tool is a manager's role that can lead to meaningful successes. Those management actions which do this generally include caring, coaching, and the kind of attention to the individuals and teams that provides stimulation and support. Management actions that blend vitality and effectiveness require feedback techniques so that the manager is cognizant of what is happening and is able to choose both direction and style—the managerial approach that fits the culture, the conditions, and the goals.

The Power of a Goal as a Reference for Direction

Goals provide individuals and teams with a sense of focused energy and therefore contribute to their ability to build motivation and commitment for work and change. Goals are a necessary part of providing direction for an enterprise as well as for the individual's career and life. The choice of goals can often make the difference between useful or wasted investment, the difference between success and failure. Goals provide us with a mechanism for assuring effective application of effort. They help leaders and teams do this by providing a reference against which decisions can be made about where to invest attention, energy, and time. Properly used, they can assure that decisions are compatible with missions and overall purpose.

Examples of the power of a goal abound. President John F. Kennedy articulated the goal of putting an American on the moon and thereby focused energy and shortened the time for achievement. This goal also provided an overriding purpose for the nation. The Japanese car industry was failing until, with the help of W. Edward Deming (father of quality circles), it chose quality as a goal and thereby became a real competitor. Success flowed from improved quality. Sometimes goals can repeatedly provide a central focus, forcing the company to get back to its central purpose. Such has been the case of George Eastman's "You push the button and we'll do the rest," which has endured for almost a century. But goals seldom have the long life of Eastman's, for they must be discarded and new ones chosen if in light of changed times they no longer provide the useful focus.

My thesis in this chapter is that R & D organizations need to add vitality and effectiveness goals as equal partners with results goals—for results goals can have destructive effects if they lack attention to the human equation.

Since goals are powerful in the effects they create, leaders should choose future goals with great care. The quality of the goal is important. For example, some years ago Abbott Laboratories' top management went away for a retreat to reassess their goals. They had thought that making the pharmaceutical breakthrough, growing, and being profitable were the appropriate organizational goals, but they came back feeling that the first-order goal of importance was creating the environment in which tomorrow's leaders of the pharmaceutical industry could and would grow. They had discovered that product results goals were not enough. Their answer supports the opening comment in this chapter—that overall goals should include positive human resource climates where individuals can grow.

Vitality and effectiveness goals have as much value as results goals for R & D organizations because they help to balance the thrust for results with the choice of right goals, with an emphasis on process (the how of achievement), with management of organizational learning, and with special emphasis on individual development and increased organizational capability.

Throwing Out Old, Nonworking Goals

In my educational preparation, no one ever suggested or discussed throwing out old, nonworking goals. The underlying assumption seemed to be that a good goal remained good forever. In some sense, this was probably more true in a society of slow change than it is now. It is an assumption to be questioned in a society in which social, technological, and economic change is a way of life. Yet displacing an old goal is difficult because managers and individuals become emotionally attached to goals and people resist change. To get people to support change, they must see the value in the change and feel that it is worth the cost, risk, and energy investment to make the change. Throwing out old goals, modifying them, and/or substituting new goals requires both process support and leadership.

There must be some techniques to learn that can help in goal revision and transition. By first looking at the abandonment of a goal—of something that has most probably worked for us and our team or organization and to which individuals may be personally and emotionally attached—perhaps we can begin to understand the process of revision and transition. In the case of a personal loss, there must be grieving before there can be acceptance of the new status and the forging of new goals. This is true in the death of a loved one and in career endings and job loss. For a group of people, it is probable that a similar effect is necessary. This means that there must be a crisis (such as a lost contract, a lost competition, or the failure of an experiment) to set up the need for grieving and to create the openness to consider a new goal. Managers respond to crises. In fact, much of the managerial behavior that can be observed by watching managers is crisis-response action. The use of a crisis could therefore work where the change is in the present. How about conditions that may lead to future crises if not changed? How about even more subtle changes, as in the case of replacing an old goal with a new one because of a sense of changed conditions? The probable answer is the need for the leader to create a crisis, since events have not yet brought the situation to a crisis level.

The establishment of vitality principles and goals in IBM was an example of the need for leadership to create a picture of a future crisis in order to gain acceptance of vitality goals. For some time, I was privileged to work with Arthur G. Anderson, a vice president of IBM, a physicist, and a person who understood the need for goals that include not only results but also the pursuit of individual and organizational capability gains. We started with the issue of technical obsolescence. If it were rampant and pervasive, it would already have been a crisis and management would have responded, but it was not. Instead, there was evidence that, without a change in goals and management emphasis, obsolescence or a lack of vitality would become a future problem. Acceptance of vitality as a goal for R & D activities required that people believe in the potential for a future crisis. They had to believe that a deterioration in capability would occur unless managers changed their management style today. As a leader, Anderson persuaded others to buy new principles (such as the individual's need for variety in order to avoid obsolescence), thereby getting them to make changes today, even though there was not a present crisis. It was he who came up with the idea of the human resource review (which I described in Chapter Four). He implemented it and made it part of his management style.

In keeping with this need for the leader to picture a crisis in order to get others to commit energy to changes today, I shall help you see the present and future crises that I see if R & D managers fail to put increased emphasis on human resource management. If the thesis is correct, then you will be more open after this discussion to the power and need for goals of vitality and effectiveness. Here are the dimensions of the crisis that I believe R & D organizations are facing and will face.

The Crisis

• "Society should seek to anticipate potential disjunctions between education and work. . . . The most disturbing of these potential disjunctions is *underemployment,* the underutilization of education, training, skills, intelligence, and other human resources. . . . This condition, which has both objective and subjective dimensions, is probably at the root of many of the most severe problems of industrial society, and is certainly a major cause of job dissatisfaction and increasing demands for improvements in the quality of working life" (O'Toole, 1977, p. 36). R & D organizations employ some of the most highly educated people in industry and are guilty of underemployment and underutilization. Sometimes this occurs because the manager is encouraged to hoard human resources so that, when asked, the leader can be responsive and be a hero for having achieved results. This reserve power will turn sour, go away, change careers, and disappear if not utilized. To utilize it, we need managers who focus not just on technical results but on matching people and work, stretching them so that they grow in capability.

• Science and technology face a shortage of new professionals. The shortage will occur because cyclical demand, anti-technology movements, and layoffs of professionals who previously thought they were not so vulnerable to economic downturns have made the field of study less inviting for some. This is hard to prove from statistics and predictions of requirements, for this data is elusive at best, but three pieces of statistical data are hard data. (1) The numbers of eighteen-year-olds available to enter college will decline overall from about 4.2 million in 1980 to about 3.2 million in 1990, with but one reverse trend occurring in the mid 1980s (Wiggins and Johnson, 1975). (2) Undergraduate enrollment in engineering dropped 2.8 percent in 1984. (There are distortions in the percent entering electrical engineering, with the percent going up, and many universities are limiting enrollments [American Society for Engineering Education, 1985].) (3) In many universities, the graduate science and engineering departments have been populated for several years by students from foreign lands, not from our country. In addition a major demand is being created by the phasing out and or retirement of large numbers of professionals graduated in the 1940s and 1950s; thus, it will simply not be possible for industry to maintain the professional levels they now have. Only if R & D leaders can focus on the quality of the work environment is there some chance to turn this trend around by making engineering attractive to top students.

• Professionals are increasingly choosing where they work, and whether they stay, based on the quality of organizational goals, the nature of the leadership, and the quality of the work environment, QPL. They are bringing higher expectations and more specifically defined expectations and goals to the workplace. They expect someone to care about them. They expect the organization to provide career management support. The current generation of managers in R & D has, by and large, neither been trained nor supported in developing an interest in and an understanding of human resource management. One of my reviewers was moved to provide anecdotal support for this aspect of the crisis. He told of a successful scientific endeavor that had attracted and created loyalty because of the charisma, style, and scientific stature of the leader, who made it an exciting place to work. The leader was replaced by a more typical manager. When a talented engineer considered leaving, she was told, "We know we have nothing exciting to keep you here. This is sad, but a fact, so goodbye!" And thus began the demise of the organization. The reviewer also told of people leaving a leading technical organization because they felt that no one cared about them! That organization's managers, having decided that they really cannot keep people, have thus accepted a training role. I remember another incident: I was interviewing a scientist leaving a top laboratory. I asked him if any managers had ever expressed how much they appreciated and admired his work, for I knew they valued him highly. He said, "Yes, after I told them I was leaving."

• The turnover among young professionals, those in their first five years out of the university, is increasing. This is another result of the conditions just described. One cause of this, it is true, is the fact that the current generation has a shorter time scale for achievement than did its predecessors, who are now the leaders. The situation has changed dramatically since the late 1960s. I remember addressing the turnover problem then; my colleagues and I designed solutions that would support the professional who would have been out of the university for five to eight years. Those solutions would now be at least five years too late! Many managers are oblivious to this change in expectations so they sit and tell the young professional how long it took them to achieve recognition or status in the organization. Their personal reminiscing fails to affect the young professional's hunger for quick recognition.

• Potentially even more serious is the professional who becomes dissatisfied, detaches emotionally from the job, and starts exhibiting dysfunctional behavior. It is especially serious if the leader is unaware, which I suspect is often the case. The employee stops trying to communicate with the manager because of a past lack of success and tries to maintain personal balance with negative behavior. A study of professionals who had contacted a job search firm indicated that all the professionals said they had practiced deviant behavior at least once (Raelin, Sholl, and Leonard, 1985, p. 33); while not seeing this as a cause for general alarm, the authors point out that the fact that dysfunctional behavior is used to compensate for conflict "is an indication that management should pay more attention to some of the serious manifestations of dissatisfaction among talented professional employees. . . . dysfunctional behavior in their organizations is a human resources concern that needs to be addressed."

• Professionals seem to be increasingly at war with management, partly because of goal conflicts and partly because they feel that there has been an unnecessary proliferation of management, a bureaucratization of science and technology. Some refer to the change as the "sanctification" of management. I believe that this is because we have administrators and we have technical leaders; we have not developed technical managers with a balanced technical–human resource perspective and the capability to carry it out effectively. There is a crisis in the education and training of the technical leader-manager.

• The productivity of professionals is becoming increasingly important in meeting the organization's goals. Professional activities are making up an increasing part of the total cost of product or service, yet R & D managers are not paying attention to process—not paying attention to the issue of creating effectiveness and of ensuring that work is done in such a way that the people and the organization become regenerated and enhanced. Without this focus, tomorrow can only become more costly.

These elements of a current and growing crisis should convince you that a fresh look at goals, at management emphasis, at managerial styles, and at improving the quality of the work environment is necessary for success in R & D tomorrow.

Vitality in Organizations: A Definition

Organizational vitality is the power that an organization generates today in pursuing its goals. This power increases its capability for and probability of success in goal achievement tomorrow. *Vitality equals adaptability energy.*

It is possible to operate an organization in such a fashion that its vitality is depleted and its growth defeated. It is also possible to operate it in such a fashion that its vitality is preserved and enhanced. Vitality is a quality of aliveness; it occurs when learning takes place and is later applied as increased capability. The chief scientist of the IBM Corporation, Lewis S. Branscomb, once said of organizational vitality, "You can smell it." It *is* possible to sense it. For example, in a vital organization people are "turned on" to their work. When approached, they are pleased with the opportunity to tell you about it. Here are some concepts that differentiate the vital from the nonvital organization:

• *Organizational vitality is a process phenomenon.* There is no such thing as static vitality. If the work process results in psychic incomes for individuals, then he or she will have more capability and energy to apply. As a result of achieving something important for themselves, they will be more motivated to pursue the goals and work of the organization. Thus, the organization gains more capability, and it is management's responsibility to channel the power. If you see this process of learning and increase in capability going on, then the probability is that the organization is vital. If not, then the probability favors a nonvital assessment.

• *Vital organizations provide vitality-enhancing climates*

for people. Since the individual's vitality cycle can be conceived as doing, gaining, and investing, it follows that there are work climates that make this cycle more or less probable. (Personal vitality will be described in the next section.) A work climate which provides support for choosing activities that stretch a person and which thus stimulates learning is an example of a vitality-enhancing climate. One can conceive of, and witness, work climates that are corrosive to people. Such a climate uses up individual energies and vitality in friction. It wastes capabilities.

• *Vitality is enhanced in an organization that chooses a vitality strategy and manages with it.* Management will ensure that it focuses on the important objective of creating a learning organization if it simply challenges each decision or action with the question "Does this action enhance or deplete vitality?" Just as you can see this going on in a vital organization, you can also see that it is not going on in a nonvital organization. For example, one management I know just made a decision to change the payroll cycle without questioning its affect on vitality. That simple administrative change has caused a loss of energy in terms of griping and friction with the professionals who have to rebudget and replan their personal cash flow. The organization lost vitality and technical effectiveness from management's pursuit of administrative efficiency.

• *Vital organizations are flexible, adaptive, and innovative.* They do not resist change; they encompass it and thrive on it. This does not mean that they give up their fundamental beliefs and values; rather, it means that they choose which policies and practices to change based on how each affects the organization's vitality.

• *The managers of vital organizations are conscious of and manage corporate learning and corporate memory.* It is not enough that individuals learn. If the memory of a corporation is totally carried in the heads of individuals, that organization is ripe for disaster. This can be tested by the question "What if a key group were to disappear tomorrow?" A vital organization is conscious of team learning. Teams can and should enhance their problem-solving capability. Teams are powerful when the capabilities of the individuals add synergistically.

• *In vital organizations, individuals are secure enough to take risks and are not wasting energies defending positions and fighting turf battles.* To learn, we must experiment. Experimentation is risk taking. To take a risk, the individual, and thus the organization, must feel that the possible losses are not so great that they cannot be endured and that the possible rewards are worth the risks. If one feels that the punishments for failing are fair and that recovery is possible, then one is more likely to try. The individual must be internally secure to take a risk. It would appear that the slowing of innovation is due in part to organizations setting up environments and policies that discourage experimentation and make the fear of failure a negative motivator.

• *Vital organizations have fewer rigid rules.* If one thinks of hiding behind rules as a hardening of the organizational arteries, then it is easy to see that rule interpretation is a key to vitality. Rules, when properly used, assure consistency and thus should support effectiveness. However, when rules take on a life unto themselves and become tools to block innovation and experimentation, they become antivitality devices. Observing the use of rules is one quick way to judge the vitality of an organization.

The Relationship Between Vital People and Vital Organizations

Frederick R. Kappel (1974, p. 5), then the CEO of AT&T, said in *Vitality in a Business Enterprise,* "What makes a vital business? Vital people make it. The very sense of the word vitality tells us it is wholly an attribute of human beings. It is not to be found in things, in machines, or dollars, or material resources of any kind. Vitality is something people demonstrate through sustained competence; through creative, venturesome drive; and through a strong feeling of ethical responsibility, which means an inner need to do what is right and not just what one is required to do."

I know this sounds self-evident and perhaps even trite, but there is an important concept contained in the statement. If an individual wishes to become and remain vital, the individual should join a group of vital people. This reinforces the professional's feeling of the importance of collegial support (cited in Chapter Three). If a leader wishes to create a vital organization, the quest will be aided by attracting and retaining turned-on, excited, vital people in sufficient quantity. There is a need to reach a critical mass. I was part of an early educational experiment related to this concept. The teachers decided to move one aggressive and quick learner into a slower group of children to cause the others to become better students, but this did not work. The fast one slowed down. Critical mass had not been achieved. Leadership that appreciates and values vitality in people, and demonstrates it through actions, is taking the first step toward making vitality work as a goal.

Vital people are excited by their activities. They are turned-on, learning, accomplishing people. *"Personal vitality* is the desire and the ability, capacity, or power to perform effectively and vigorously in life and at work. The vital person gains personal growth and satisfactions from life and work" (Miller, 1977a, p. 19). Vital people are ones who understand the vitality cycle, in most cases without ever having it described. The individual attains, adds to, and maintains vitality through this cycle. The cycle has several elements. It starts with choosing the right work—work that utilizes capability and stretches or challenges, causing one to learn new knowledge and capabilities. Next, one must apply oneself to this choice through activity, through actually doing the task. When individuals operate on the right activity and apply themselves with vigor, they make a gain. The gain from the right activity is psychic income, including a sense of increased power, energy, knowledge, and capability; as a result, the individuals have the opportunity to invest this increased vitality in another cycle, with an improved chance of gain. Unfortunately, this cycle works in the negative route as well, for choosing and doing the wrong activity results in a loss of interest, of energy, and eventually of capability. This emphasizes the need to choose the right work. Effectiveness means choosing the right work.

This discussion should make the relationship between vital people and vital organizations clearer. A vital organization is one with characteristics of climate and environment that make the individual's vitality cycle possible and support it. The gain and the investment by people are the actions that make the organization more powerful and vital.

Measuring Vitality

If we are to manage an organization with vitality as a goal, it is important to measure our success as a basis for directing our management emphasis. In organizations, that which we measure becomes important. That which we fail to measure is unimportant. Even if the manager's measurement techniques are rough and approximate, the activity of trying is in itself important.

Measuring vitality is difficult. One can measure some concrete things that relate to or constitute a part of vitality, like the documentation of knowledge, the writing and presentation of papers and reports. However, the real measure of vitality is probably a measure of attitudes—of outlooks or a set of values— and measuring these things is considered subjective or soft. This is especially true in a scientific environment, in which most individuals deal with physical or hard measures. How does one put a sense of aliveness on a rational, reportable scale? How does one measure the freedom to think unplanned thoughts or the energy level available to apply to an organizational challenge? And how does one measure the feeling of potential for success versus the feeling of potential for failure? Measures of these subjective aspects are particularly hard to defend. And they are particularly hard to deal with in a fact-oriented environment like R & D. But managers must try in order to ensure that the goal is valued.

Measures do exist. One can ask people whether they feel more or less vital than they did six months or a year ago. Their response probably has a high correlation with reality. One can ask people whether they feel that management and professionals put a high value on learning: If they do, this correlates with a vital climate; if not, the response correlates with a nonvital climate. Managers can ask about attention paid to organizational memory: If professionals feel that organizational memory is not important, this response correlates with a lack of interest in and support of vitality. Vital organizations and vital environments are usually not tranquil and usually include centers of conflict, and it is here that the goal of effectiveness adds to and rounds out the vitality goal: Too much conflict means low effectiveness, and too little conflict probably also means low effectiveness. Yet all these measures or indications are subjective. Hard measures, such as a failure to meet design specifications or a loss in the marketplace, take too long; they come too late for managers to use the input to make decisions and course correction. Subjective or soft measures are the ones that must be developed, refined, and used by R & D leaders.

Defining Effectiveness

I feel effective when my energies result in accomplishments that fit my goals and when the energy expended seems appropriate for the results. Organizations are effective when there is a gain from applied energy; the energy necessary to achieve the gain is not excessive, the time to achieve it is not too long, and the gain furthers the goals of the organization. The results should represent some gain—some profit, some amplification of input energy, and a gain in capability. Thus, the sense of being effective relates to input-output relationships.

Effectiveness and efficiency are different. One can be efficient in achieving goals of low value, but that accomplishment would not be judged as effective because the concept of effectiveness includes an assessment of the quality of the goals.

In context of the R & D organization, *effectiveness* means choosing goals of high value and pursuing them efficiently, with the minimum input of energy, people, and time necessary to achieve quality output.

Measuring Effectiveness

Measuring effectiveness seems easier than measuring vitality. Results measures are considered hard by comparison with those discussed under vitality. The achievement or nonachievement of a technical or organizational goal is measurable if the goal was defined in measurable terms. Thus, meeting experiment goals or product specifications is measurable.

There is a soft part of this measurement as well; it has to do with the need to choose goals of high value (part of the definition). Because R & D work requires creativity and innovation and these achievements are not predictable, the predictability of quality and the measurement of the quality of achievement is based on an opinion, a feeling. Clarity of the value of goals represents a point of view, a perspective, an insight, and these are seldom unanimously agreed upon. It is also not possible to turn the clock back and determine what would have happened if different goals had been chosen. We sometimes do not even know at the time for measurement about real success or failure. I can remember the case of the STRETCH machine in IBM. It was an ambitious project to build a supercomputer. It required pushing the tube technology to the limit. It failed to meet its technical goals by a large margin, and it cost several times the planned development costs. Few machines were built and sold. It appeared to be a failure. Yet the learning which took place made the next generation of computers, the 360 systems, possible. Five years later the same project, which initially had looked like a wrong goal choice, could be looked upon as a success. Consequently, there is room for differences of opinion about goals and effectiveness.

The Relationship Between Effectiveness and Vitality

Vitality, that power which is the gain from the process of doing the right things, is not alone enough. Without effectiveness, it is like an engine running without load. The power must be applied to goals of high value in an efficient manner—and this is effectiveness. So the two concepts must work together and be paired with the quest for results. This can be illustrated by a story of two different laboratories (Miller, 1977b).

Laboratory *A* was very effective, but not vital. Most of the people in laboratory *A* were working on the development of one product. The product was a good one and was successful in the marketplace. Over time, however, the level of unhappiness among this laboratory's professionals rose, for those who made logical extensions of technical discoveries were predicting the demise of the product on which they were working. The professionals were becoming less creative and innovative, in part because of this feeling of a technological limit and the disappearance of a personal career future. Vitality was declining. Professionals were choosing to leave and go elsewhere. There was insufficient variety and freedom to engage in other kinds of technical activity. If an individual was not interested in working on the product or was burned out by too long a stint on the one product, there was no alternative. A solution was then implemented. It was to add several other development projects to this laboratory so that the professionals had a choice of technical activities and an opportunity for variety. With these project additions, they did not feel that their career options were increasingly narrowed. Over time, as a result of these changes, vitality, effectiveness, and results became running mates.

Laboratory *B* was very vital. It was the locus of many creative and innovative ideas. It was a place where there were many development projects. None of the projects, however, ever came to really successful conclusions. Morale was declining because the professionals knew that they, and the laboratory, were not viewed as effective. They knew that they were not seen as valuable because their products did not get into the product line and to the marketplace to affect the profit of the company. The insecurity of the professionals and the leaders in this laboratory rose. This laboratory was vital, but not effective. Professionals were leaving this laboratory for small new start-up ventures where they felt they could gain the psychic income associated with seeing a product go out the door. The solution in this laboratory was to narrow the product scope, to reduce the numbers of different projects. For a period of time, almost all the energies were directed to one promising product family. Vitality, effectiveness, and results eventually became running mates.

How a Vitality-Effectiveness Strategy Can Affect R & D

The anecdotal stories just told about the two laboratories are good examples of how the pursuit of a vitality-effectiveness strategy can affect a development organization. Pursuit of the two strategies can bring about improved morale and result in useful output without using up or depleting the human resources. Here are some of the effects:

• Improving the balance of characteristics of the climate or culture so that individuals feel that they have achieved improved QPL. In the case of the two laboratories, this happened. In laboratory *A* they already felt useful, but they needed increased variety and an improved sense of career future. In laboratory *B* they needed an improved sense of usefulness, and this was achieved when their product successfully entered the product line. Improved morale and increased psychic income resulted from changes initiated by the leaders, who understood the need for all three goals: vitality, effectiveness, and results.

• Improving the useful output of the organization from a corporate perspective. This was what happened in laboratory *B*.

• Improving the balance of emphasis on long- and short-term goals. As an example, the vitality goal of learning and growth in individual capability is a long-term goal as compared to the effectiveness goal of discovering the new technology of high value or to the results goal of getting the product out on schedule. The effectiveness and results goals tend to be short-term, and the results goal one that can be measured in the hard, or physical, sense.

• Avoiding the trap of pursuit of a narrow objective over too long a period of time. This was part of the worry of the professionals in laboratory *A*. They were fearful that they would be expected to work on a product line long after it was being replaced by other technologies. They were fearful of being sidetracked and becoming obsolete.

• Providing management with a clear set of goals and strategies against which they can make decisions that have a positive impact on the people and their activities. An example would be a decision-making base that would avoid debilitating decisions, such as the one previously mentioned in which the payroll period was changed with no real understanding of the impact on the people. Not only does it provide managers with the decision-making base; it also provides the professionals with a conceptual framework within which they can be part of management and help by questioning management's proposals for decisions when the professionals feel that the decisions are not compatible with the goals.

Specifications for a Vital and Effective Research Organization

Because every organization is different, generalized specifications will have to be tailored by the user to the particular situation and the specific organization. What follows is a generalized set of criteria that should be useful as a checklist in assessing the vitality of a particular research organization. The criteria listed, rather than being exhaustive, are a representative group supporting my communication of the concept to you. I realize that they are prescriptive at a metalevel, but I know of no better way to communicate the feelings that the leader who implements the concept of a vitality and effectiveness strategy needs to experience as personal feelings. I am providing the list not as a document to be used intact but rather as a guide for shaping the actions you choose in a way that fits the concept of vitality and effectiveness goals. The more specific suggestions in the remainder of this book fill out these general prescriptions. A vital and effective organization has the following characteristics:

• It is a creative amalgam of goals, leadership, people, and facilities. It results in pushing back the frontiers of knowledge, contributing to organizational objectives, and increasing the organization's capability.

• It chooses important goals, pursues them with vigor, and is managed with a careful balance between freedom (such as a lack of schedule pressures) and pressure (such as a requirement to produce useful results within a five-year period), thereby ensuring that the members feel that they are part of the larger enterprise that supplies the money and facilities. In the case of a free-standing research organization, the larger enterprise is represented by the clients or customers.

- It develops an image of vitality, of being an exciting and fun place to work. This allows it to attract, develop, and retain vital professionals, vital leaders, and vital support people.
- It sets up an environment that institutionalizes caring and nurturing in such a way as to support individual achievement, growth in capability, career growth, and career transitions.
- It makes individuals secure enough to risk experimentation and failure. Only with sufficient failures can the organization be sure that the frontiers are being pushed aggressively.
- It has QPL, meaning that individuals with different personalities, knowledge, interests, and personal goals can all find psychic income through their work. It provides a system of rewards and recognition that matches individual with team needs and stimulates motivation for research activities.
- It chooses vitality and effectiveness as goals coequal with results goals, which causes vitality and effectiveness to be criteria for decisions, which measures vitality and effectiveness, and which has feedback systems that supply the data for course correction.
- Its leaders, managers, and professionals understand the concept of and the necessity for corporate memory and work to manage and preserve it in a way that makes historic research programs and discoveries accessible but does not limit innovation and change.
- It has policies and systems that ensure a good match of people with work so that their skills are utilized. It does not just reuse its people's old capabilities; rather, while making use of their old capabilities, it also gives encouragement and support to their learning new capabilities.
- It is mindful of its responsibilities to transmit and communicate the results of its work. Unless a research organization develops communication styles and systems that provide data, ideas, and technology to those downstream who must apply this knowledge, it has missed its real purpose. Communication with those downstream should not just be one-way, but two-way.

Specifications for a Vital and Effective
Development Organization

The development organization differs from the research organization in one primary group of attributes: Its goals are shorter-term; more specific to the goals of the organization; definable in product, system, or service terms; and generally require the application of technology that is known, although often beyond the level at which it has been previously applied. It is like research in that it requires people to do things that have not been done before. It differs from research in that its major activity can be described as innovation, which, although requiring creative efforts, is not the creation of new technology. Development is also usually involved with massive data preparation in order to communicate with manufacturing and the field; research has a strong requirement to communicate, but the volume of data handling is small by comparison. The requirements for an environment which enhances vitality and effectiveness and which mates these goals with results are similar to those for the research organization, but they are different in some specific ways. Again, I ask you to recognize that my purpose is not to provide a specific prescription that cures; rather, it is to help you understand concepts within which your own specific prescriptions can be created. A vital and effective development organization has the following characteristics:

• It chooses, pursues, and achieves product, system, or service goals which use new concepts or technologies and which contribute to the success of the larger organization. The pursuit of these goals should utilize the skills, knowledge, and capabilities of the professionals, be achievable in a time frame reasonable to that type of business, and provide the corporation with a competitive edge.

• Its management chooses those technologies that are appropriate to pursue and provides its professionals with the facilities and support necessary to pursue these technologies to manufacturable, shippable, and marketable ends of product, system, or service.

• It develops an image (reputation) of excitement, purpose, and achievement of results that helps it attract, develop, and retain vital professionals, vital development leaders, and vital support people.

- It is one that sets up an environment that institutionalizes caring and nurturing in such a way as to support individual growth in capability, career growth, and especially career transitions. The concept of multiple careers as a normal progression should be supported with policies and practices of coaching, counseling, and career management so that the individual can share the responsibility for career development.

- It is one that makes individuals secure enough to risk experimentation, to try approaches different from the past, and to push back the frontiers of the application of new concepts and technologies to client needs and uses in an aggressive fashion.

- It is one with QPL, which can be interpreted to mean that individuals with different personalities, knowledge, interests, and personal goals can all find psychic income through their work. It needs to reward both individuals and teams effectively for their accomplishments.

- It chooses vitality and effectiveness as goals and gives them an importance equal to that of product, system, and service results goals. Its management should establish processes that encourage and allow the nonmanagement professionals to be participants in goal setting and decision making. The result should ensure that the strategy and goals of vitality and effectiveness are used to guide the direction of the organization.

- It creates innovative systems and processes for documentation of that data which is necessary in order for those downstream from development to do their work effectively. It needs to transmit this information across organizational boundaries with clarity and with an understanding of the needs of the manufacturing and marketing people and of the customer population. Communication channels need also to provide for feedback from these downstream people.

- It has policies and systems that ensure a good match of people with work so that their skills are utilized, but not in such a repetitive manner that it stifles the growth of new capabilities or eliminates the variety necessary to avoid obsolescence and to maintain and enhance individual vitality.

- It has policies and programs that support continuing education in the technologies and in personal and professional skills. Learning needs to be considered in terms not only of formal classes but also of informal exchange and of assignment rotation.

Blocks to Creating Vital and Effective Organizations

Why is it that these relatively straightforward concepts are not put into practice in organizations? One of the overriding reasons is that many managements have not and do not consider the concepts necessary. They have been taught by management courses and books that results are what count and that management by objectives is the answer. Many new technology-based companies have been in the start-up phase, in which the managers' main challenge is to add new employees, not to nurture the development of those on board. Also, the emphasis in the start-up phase on just getting the job done at all outweighs any thought of doing it effectively. Thus, in these early phases, little emphasis is put on performance management and on ways of improving performance. Because of their technical education and personal interests, R & D leaders have been biased in their outlook to feel that technical issues rather than people issues are what make the difference between success and failure. Some managers have responded to an employment market in which losing employees was not viewed as serious because there always seemed to be more out there to recruit. Because of the economic cycle, many managements have considered reductions in the employee population to be the key management issue. Managers in government-contract–based industries have been led to believe that the government will not pay for the "niceties" of employee development. Professionals in the industries dominated by government contract have learned that they must take care of their own marketability and their own personal vitality. During periods of layoffs and cutbacks, managers feel compelled to do things that run directly counter to the concepts. For example, responsibilities that were formerly delegated get redelegated back up the ladder. Rather than jobs being redesigned to make them more fulfilling, they are redesigned to redistribute the necessary but unexciting and repetitive work; consequently, individuals do not learn new capabilities.

Even if managers are convinced of the need and are supported by upper management, there are aspects of organizational environment and human behavior that make it difficult to implement vitality and effectiveness concepts. Some examples are as follows:

• Measures and controls often support one goal and impede another. Examples include financial controls over expenditures. Everyone will agree that management must ensure that only necessary things are bought and that payments are made only to legitimate debtors. However, the first example of this need for control, in the absence of innovative managers, is to demonstrate a lack of trust in the professional, and even in the manager, by requiring sign-offs by higher management. Sometimes the signatures required and the time to secure them is such that the message is interpreted by the professional as one of management not wanting them to be productive. Similar controls over communication are a second example. They can also transmit a feeling of lack of trust and thus impede effective action. In one laboratory, there was a time when professionals and managers would take trips carrying correspondence labeled "draft" in order to get the message to the person who could act, because getting through the clearance procedure would have caused them to miss the window for decision. A third example is a control over head count that rewards the manager who moves a person out of the group (for the good of the organization and/or the individual) with a loss of head count; consequently the manager has fewer people to do the work required! Only by concerted effort can these conflicts of goals be avoided. Upper management most often asks for some new goal without ever looking at those controls in place which may negate it.

• Vitality concepts build on the idea that the professional is and wants to be self-managing and to operate as a responsible professional. In reality, leaders are faced with many individuals who want to play a dependent role and who will do everything possible to ensure that the manager takes the responsibility. Sometimes this is seen in career management: The professional wants the manager to decide what the individual should do, so that if the change fails, it can be management's fault. Sometimes this is seen when a manager tries to make a professional a participant in decision making and the professional takes the attitude that the manager, not the nonmanagement professional, is being paid to take those risks.

• I have already mentioned the conflict between short- and long-term goals. Generally, vitality and effectiveness concepts are longer-term goals than are those associated with results. Leaders learn that changes in management and in assignments are so frequent that individuals are seldom around to be measured on accomplishing long-term goals or to get any reward if there is any. What people feel faced to respond to is a system that is strongly biased in favor of the short-term goal.

• Vitality concepts build on the individual matching of people with tasks. The concept is that the organization should utilize capabilities and respond to the needs of the individual while trying iteratively to match these to the needs and capabilities of the organization. Doing this requires that the manager become personally familiar with the individual's goals, strengths, and weaknesses. In many organizational cultures, the manager is discouraged from getting that close to an employee. Recent privacy legislation and court rulings have scared managers and managements, causing them to retreat and deal with individuals as classes or groups. Both these situations make implementing vitality concepts more difficult. Even more specifically, where a union is involved, the manager is required to deal with the union rather than with the individual on many matters affecting vitality and effectiveness. General Motors and some others have begun to make breakthroughs on this with their union leadership understanding the problem. They have jointly agreed that quality-of-work-life issues are outside the union-management bargaining process.

How Management Creates Vitality

Translating concepts like vitality and effectiveness into designs, action, and style is the work of leaders. It is in the translation, adaptation, and innovation of management concepts that many leaders and management teams fail. I cannot provide a specific guide to innovation, translation, and implementation, but I can provide some examples of approaches that other leaders have used. Let me warn again that this section should be read not as a prescription, "Go thou and do likewise," but as a stimulant for thinking about the concepts' application.

Creative Organizational Design. One of my findings is that an organization's structure, or design, can support or inhibit vitality and effectiveness. It is therefore important to experiment with new forms of organization and to measure the effects.

One new form, which has evolved naturally as technical projects have become more complex, is the temporary task group. It is formed to address a problem and is made up of people representing varied capabilities and backgrounds. The task group gains its authority from composition, expertise, and selected problem focus, not from position on the organizational chart. The task group exists for months, normally less than two years. Typically, the task-group members later take assignments that make them responsible, in the classical organizational structure, for implementing some of the concepts or ideas created in the task group.

Another approach is to change the structure of the organization rather frequently, thus preventing people from defending comfortable turf and digging in (as discussed in Chapter Four). The following is an example of how I once used this approach. Model shops support development professionals by making parts for their projects. Because a skilled model maker is often a major contributor to innovation, and certainly to manufacturability, good synergism between model makers and professionals is important. Thus, one organizational design is to assign model makers to professionals for management-leadership, which often means setting up a series of small, independent shops. This assignment arrangement is good because the model makers feel that they belong to the project; it often proves bad, however, because it does not necessarily provide for good management for effective use of the model-making capability. Therefore, another organizational design is to centralize the model shops under skilled model-making management. This maximizes the effective utilization of the skills, ensures development of the individual's model-making capabilities, and usually means support by more sophisticated equipment. But it tends to weaken the bond between model makers and professionals. Neither organization is perfect. Both have their problems. My technique was to go back and forth between the two organizations on about a three-year cycle, thus hoping to reap the benefits of both. One warning is necessary: Overly frequent changes make individuals feel insecure. It is up to the leader to sense the appropriate use of this technique in order to maximize the positives.

Some managements have experimented with small, new organizations deliberately set up away from the controls, rules, and procedures of the parent organization. There is some evidence that breakthroughs in product, system, or service come about more easily when the group is new, small, and unencumbered by the past. Since all such experiments do not end in success, this technique may therefore not be enough in itself, but examples like the creation of the IBM Personal Computer do tend to prove its usefulness.

A last example of creative organizational design can be called the internal corporation. It is not really a corporation, but it becomes a budget center and is managed as a separate enterprise. Entities of this type are usually formed around products that can stand alone and/or are process-sensitive. This has been done periodically in IBM. The technique is to take the development group for a new product and marry it organizationally with the manufacturing group for the same product before the time of transfer of the product from development to manufacture. The new, temporary organization breaks traditional organizational boundaries, ensures focused management, and enhances communication between development professionals and manufacturing professionals. Some of the problems it avoids are described by Riggs (1983, p. 130): "Where departmental barriers are high and engineers are encouraged or permitted to be myopic, design engineers will attempt to maximize product performance and manufacturing engineers will try to redesign the product to reduce its cost. The high-technology company that manages this transition well stands to gain timing, cost, and quality advantages that can have substantial payoffs in the marketplace." This unique organizational approach facilitates the joint pursuit of improved design and contributes to a more effective process, reduced costs, and improved quality.

Vitality and Effectiveness (V/E) Groups. Task groups have been established in some organizations to gain understanding and acceptance of the V/E goals and to create action plans. Breaking the vitality topic into subtopics such as "the use of sabbaticals to enhance vitality" makes it possible for individuals to get their arms around the concepts. Because they have participated and cooperated to design action plans, managers and professionals take on ownership of the plans. Most people are of two minds about change. On the one hand, individuals interpret not changing as safety; on the other, they know that their growth and development are a result of change. One way to make change more comfortable is through participative activities. Thus, establishing task groups to discover what can be done to enhance vitality and effectiveness can be an effective management tactic. Task groups should be composed of both managers and nonmanagement professionals. While these groups may seem to rehash much of what is known, the process creates ownership of these new goals.

An Open Process for Mission and Goal Setting. Interviews of professionals in R & D organizations reveal significant problems in their clear understanding of and commitment to organizational goals. This confusion contributes to a lack of vitality, of effectiveness, and of result-oriented activity. In fact, I have repeatedly found that one of my major contributions in helping groups to become more effective has been to assist them in understanding and becoming clear about their mission and goals. Managers can avoid the need for external help by making the mission- and goal-setting process one in which all can participate, an open process. Leaders who can use participation and open processes—or who can find other techniques for achieving the same end—for goal and mission setting will gain committed followers and unleash new power.

Decontrolling Front-End Controls on Projects. Because of the influence of business school training, and in some cases because of significant overruns and growth in the cost of R & D, most managements installed new planning, budget, and financial controls in the 1960s and early 1970s. Although these controls make sense at some stage in the research and/or development cycle, they have and often are now being applied too strictly and too early in the process. Thus, in an effort to avoid waste in R & D, organizations often force the professionals and/ or their managers to predict the schedules, costs, and profitability of an idea when it is nothing more than an idea. Systems of selective control, which allow less tight control during the early pursuit of an idea or project, stimulate the innovation process. Systems can be designed that progressively tighten the control by means of predetermined checkpoints based on dollar, staffing, and time levels.

Limiting the Energies Applied to Budgeting and Finance. Many R & D organizations misuse professional and managerial time in the budgeting and rebudgeting of finances. Certainly these processes are necessary, but something seems to have driven the proportions out of balance. I have seen more than one organization spend time keeping track of time down to the minute, and I have seen many that extend the budgeting and rebudgeting process (known as the "silly season") to several months, sorely distracting the attention of their professionals and leaders from their primary goals. Several cures come to mind. The first is to use higher levels of management and staff to make estimates, which are often all that is really required, and to stop involving lower levels in iteration after iteration. This is accomplished by requiring a decision about importance and not fighting all budget requests with the same-size hose! In one organization, this technique increased the professionals' respect for the upper layers of staff and reduced the unnecessary involvement. Another cure is to design a budget system that supports R & D leaders by providing the necessary "what if" answers without involving the whole line of management and professionals each time a question is asked. Another cure is to start at a higher level of trust at the first iteration and not put the lower management levels and the professionals through games to try to get them to come up with the predetermined answer, which is often characteristic of a budgeting process.

Bridge Building Between Ideas. Much of the creativity in organizations comes from associating two previously unassociated ideas, concepts, or technologies. Organizations must necessarily subdivide themselves in order to make themselves manageable, but this process establishes organizational boundaries, some of which are barely penetrable. The impedance of communications at border crossings limits the opportunity for a creative intermingling of ideas. Organizations have tried various ways to increase the cross talk. One is to create short television movies, composed by recording short visits to the laboratories of different individuals, and to show them openly. This idea was used in IBM many years ago; the movies became noontime diversions when circulated to the several laboratories. A half-hour program can show many people what five professionals are doing. Just increasing the knowledge of what is going on increases the probability of building bridges. Another idea is to hold an annual or semiannual state-of-the-organization meeting at which some professionals tell all the other professionals about their work and their ideas. Another concept, where the majority of professionals have computer terminals, is to set up a "half-baked idea" or "technical gossip" system. By taking advantage of the interoffice mail capabilities of computer networks, professionals can query others or put an idea on the waves to see where it goes. Still another approach is to set up special groups who have the responsibility of visiting and trying to bring people together when they suspect that there may be compatible interests.

Paying Attention to Under-the-Table Projects. Early in my career I had the opportunity to work for a director of development who, by his interest and style, stimulated innovation. After reviewing the planned program, he would ask to see the *interesting* work. By paying attention to the unplanned and unauthorized activities, he legitimized them. His attention made individuals less fearful and motivated them to seek his attention by doing unplanned things—by being innovative. His active interest in what they were doing made the message clear that innovation was desired and that he knew that not all innovation was limited to the planned and funded activities. While I am convinced of the power of this idea, it is hard to get R & D executives to find the time on their busy calendars.

Improved Performance Management. Most organizations have a performance planning and appraisal system, but in most organizations people feel that they are going through the process for someone else. Vital and effective organizations find a way to make professionals and managers feel that the system is a necessary activity for ensuring joint goal setting and measurement of progress. Instead of doing it for the personnel department, they start doing it for themselves. (This is more fully discussed in Chapter Ten.)

These examples reflect but a small portion of the actions that creative leaders can take to improve vitality and effectiveness. Transplanting them without proper preparation of the organizational soil will not work. To work, solutions must be culture-specific. They must fit the culture of the organization, much as the plant that grows best in the sun will not thrive in the shade. Workable solutions fit the problems, crises, and opportunities of that organization at that time. Indeed, they seem to erupt spontaneously from within the organization when the proper climate, or culture, has been established.

Summary

• Goals provide a powerful reference base for decision making and thus help managers ensure an organizational focus. Goals should change with changing times, but throwing out and/or modifying old goals is a difficult process.

• To move people and organizations to change goals, managers must identify a crisis or picture a potential future crisis. Today, serious problems are emerging in R & D. One, for example, is that many technological organizations are giving up trying to retain and challenge their highly educated professionals. Another is that managers are neither trained in handling nor in some cases sensitive to the professional's discomforts and dissatisfactions.

• Organizational and individual vitality are created by choosing the activities that contribute to increasing capability rather than using it up. Effectiveness is mated with vitality when the right goals are pursued efficiently using the minimum energy necessary to achieve quality output. A V/E research organization is one where management establishes a quality work environment for professionals and nurtures their development. Similarly, while encompassing the concepts of vitality and effectiveness in research, a development organization provides the opportunity for development professionals to achieve psychic income through pursuit of well-chosen product goals utilizing new technologies.

• Vitality and effectiveness are useful goals because they tend to offset the narrowness of results goals for products, systems, and services. Vitality and effectiveness goals should join results goals as coequals in order to ensure that results are achieved without paying the price of burnout, obsolescence, and disengagement.

• Vital people populate vital organizations and provide the organization with its vitality. Vital organizations attract and nurture vital people, who in turn stimulate vitality in others.

• Those things which are important in organizations gain their importance, in part, by managers' attempts to measure and report them. Vitality and effectiveness goals join results goals in importance when management begins to measure these aspects.

• When paired with results goals, the effects of vitality and effectiveness goals contribute to an improved work climate and to management's ability to improve the productivity of the organization.

• One of the foremost reasons why managers find it difficult to implement vitality and effectiveness concepts is that they have not been convinced that these concepts are necessary. Measures and controls often support other goals and block vitality and effectiveness goals. The implementation of vitality and effectiveness concepts is sometimes blocked by the personalities and attitudes of the professionals. Such is the case when some professionals avoid taking responsibility and acting like professionals.

Chapter 7

Establishing Environments
That Enhance Creativity

Recent writings in management have emphasized the differences
that corporate culture can make on organizational success.
Books such as *Corporate Cultures: The Rites and Rituals of
Corporate Life* (Deal and Kennedy, 1982), *In Search of Excellence* (Peters and Waterman, 1982), *Organizational Culture and
Leadership* (Schein, 1985), and *Gaining Control of the Corporate Culture* (Kilmann and others, 1985) are representative of
the increased interest in the topic. Yet the idea of affecting performance and satisfactions through environmental design is not
new. The broad recognition of and acceptance of its importance
and the emphasis in the literature are what is new!

Both Kappel (1960) and Watson (1963) demonstrated in
their speeches at Columbia University that chief executives recognize the importance of principles, beliefs, and transcendent
values, the components of culture, on the success of an organization. In order to increase recognition of the need for vitality
and for accepting and supporting individual learning and growth,
I wrote some years ago (Miller, 1977b) of my own experiences
in redesigning the environment of a development laboratory. I
showed how the inclusion of specific performance evaluation
and appraisal of the manager on the subject of stimulating employee development changed the manager's priorities. In this
chapter, I will update and broaden my previous writings with

specific emphasis on what to do to make R & D organizations effective through the design of cultures and/or environments. One opening caveat is important. Environmental or cultural design, including management of the culture, is not alone enough to improve effectiveness. It is but one part of the orchestration of organizational success.

Climate, culture, and environment act as a backdrop for all that goes on in an organization (the three terms are defined in the following section). A well-defined culture can support and encourage certain actions as well as highlight and provide conceptual blocking for actions that are out of keeping with goals. As Harris (1985, pp. 31-32) says: "Culture influences us to form basic assumptions about human nature, reality, truth, relationships, and the myriad of activities or events that occur in our lives. Our culture affects how we view the nature of work and the worker, what we consider satisfactory performance and productivity, what we see as adequate education and training of employees, and the like." Culture can be used as a management device for reinforcing the right behavior in the absence of specific instructions or rules. For the organization, therefore, cultural and environmental cues can assist in improving goal-oriented performance. Culture can enhance the image of quality in the work environment so that competent people are attracted; it can improve work experiences so that people stay and aid leaders in gaining commitment to the organization's goals. It is important to note that I have emphasized the positive aspects of a well-designed culture. But, cultures grow in the absence of design and management and can persist after they are out of keeping with the organization's needs and goals. It is possible, therefore, to have a culture that is counterproductive.

For the individual, compatibility of climate with the individual's needs and beliefs is important if satisfaction is to accrue from work. In a recent study of managers, Posner, Kouzes, and Schmidt (1985, p. 293) say, "The results from a recent nationwide survey of American managers shows, we are convinced, that clearly articulated organizational values do make a significant difference in the lives of employees, as well as in their organization's performance." It is an important contributing factor in the achievement of psychic income and the support of individual development. The climate is especially important in R & D. Since the nature of the work is the exploration of the unknown and the new idea or thrust is easily killed, the right R & D climate can act as a protector and supporter of the untried and the new. R & D culture should provide support for the needs of professionals who are working on creative events. It should provide a set of expectations about the energy, time, and facilities necessary for research, contain support for the value of research and its usefulness to the organization, and should provide development professionals with understandings about expectations for and value of innovations. It should also provide some basis for others in the organization, outside of R & D, to understand the need for and characteristics of R & D. By so doing, it can help protect R & D from the conflicting pressures of other organizational forces and goals that might destroy the opportunity to bring creativity and innovation to fruition in the market and in their contribution to the profit.

Company cultures and R & D cultures within the company are not necessarily the same, nor are they always compatible. It would seem that successful high-technology ventures more often have compatible company and R & D cultures than do other organizations. Yet this is not necessarily true, for whereas the goals of the organization are to sell to a market and make a profit, the goals of research often have a much more tenuous connection with market and profit. Conflict between cultures within the organization means that the individual receives mixed signals about what is expected. Mixed signals use up human energy needlessly. They are like friction in moving parts.

Even in the absence of intent or design, a climate or culture is created by the accumulation of experiences and their transmission to other members. That is, it grows out of the need to interpret the meaning of events that occur in the organization. In this case, a culture is like a series of synaptic junctions that have fired previously and, as a result, have a tendency to fire more easily the next time. The culture is the organizational learning about what works and what does not, and thus tends to make certain actions more probable. One can differentiate organizations in terms of whether the culture has been designed or has simply happened. The careful observer can spot the absence or presence of deliberate design.

My approach in this chapter is to encourage deliberate design and management of environment. I will do this by first setting forth specifications for the ideal research or development environment and then looking at the elements of the environment in more detail. As a result, you will be able to distinguish between those leadership actions required to establish an intellectual climate and those required to establish the expectations about work behavior. The several elements of climate can either reinforce or conflict with each other, so it will be important to learn how they can be made to have a uniform effect and thus reinforce each other. For example, IBM's basic belief in the importance of the individual reinforces specific policies intended to support the continuing study for the professional, programmer, accountant, scientist, or engineer.

This chapter ends with a conceptual script, or cultural design–implementation scenario. The scenario is not intended to be a cookbook, but a checklist that managers can use to be sure that they have attended to the important elements of environmental design.

The Importance of Environment and Culture on an Organization's Success

It is important to start any discussion of climate, culture, and environment with some definitions. Because so much has been written about culture, it is the buzzword of our times. But all three words are used here. My purpose is to ensure that the reader understands the concept, not to debate definitions. Although there are slightly different meanings, I do not care which word you use in your mind's eye as you read this chapter. The definitions:

- *Organizational climate* is what the individual feels when working in an organization. It includes the expected effects of organizational values, beliefs, policies, and procedures on the behavior of individuals. It is a collection of behavioral norms (unwritten rules), whatever their origins. It reflects unique characteristics of the type of business, the organization's chosen mission, the technological base if any, the goals, and the management style. In sum, it is the essence of the organization as it effects the attitudes, beliefs, actions, and style of those who work in the organization.

• *Culture* is defined in the dictionary as "the integrated pattern of human behavior that includes thought, speech, action, and artifacts and depends on man's capacity for learning and transmitting knowledge to succeeding generations." Culture seems to emphasize more what happens than what causes the happenings. Climate, by comparison, seems to suggest more emphasis on causes (partly because we spend our lives reacting to weather). But in both cases, in this book, I am referring to causes and effects, the whole of which results in Marvin Bower's definition (Deal and Kennedy, 1982, p. 4) as "the way we do things around here."

• *Environment* is the term I have used for years to describe the total effect of values, beliefs, policies, and practices on the behavior of individuals in an organization. Like climate, it includes the effects of the style of the leader, the nature of the business, the maturity or youth of the organization, the technological base, and the goals of the organization. It, too, is used to describe causative factors. Thus, it is possible by using this term to talk of environmental design and environmental statements as ways of influencing behavior. In the conventional uses of the three words, individuals seem more willing to feel that they can control environment than climate or culture.

If we react to the subtleties of the differences between the words, it is possible to talk of the importance of building an environment to create a climate that ultimately results in a culture. It is important to design, implement, and manage an environment because it:

- Affects individual's beliefs and values and thus affects motivation.
- Can assist leaders in making an organization more or less effective.
- Attracts or turns away people who are potential employees.
- Affects the potential for quality person/job matches.
- Affects the potential for the individual to achieve psychic income.
- Affects the amount of negative stress inherent in organizational activities.
- Can influence leader-managers so that they are more consistent in decision making and style.
- Increases the probability of consistent and harmonious behavior on the part of individuals because it contains clues to desirable behavior.

By designing environment, management provides the individual members of the organization with guidance, which, in the absence of specific managerial direction, influences behavior. This influence is communicated through the culture, for it is spread by individuals sharing experiences and anecdotal stories, and it is communicated by deeds, what individuals and leaders do, because members observe and copy. Thus, both words and deeds contribute to the individual's understanding of what is expected. It is communicated by the choice of capital equipment, for these decisions reflect the appropriate use of human energy in the organization. It is communicated through the decisions about whom to promote, for in each decision management reveals its standards. It is also communicated through bricks and mortar, because the physical facilities represent the level of commitment and the image of the organization. It is as if the walls exude behavior cues.

People put on special behavior (the behavior that all these different cues suggest is desired) as they pass through the gates or doors of the enterprise. One would hope that this behavior would be a subset of the individual's normal behavior. If the organization requires an unnatural shift in behavior, this causes stress and contributes negatively to person/job match and performance. So, while it is desirable for an organization to build an environment, climate, and culture that support its goals, it is important also to attract, select, and indoctrinate people who are compatible with this climate. It is also important that this climate not be too deviant from the larger culture and societal climate in which the organization is set. Excessive deviance begets conflict and negatively affects the ability of the organization to achieve its goals. Each organization owes its right to exist and pursue its mission to the society that has granted it the right.

Historically, it was possible for managements to build climates or cultures that were significantly different from the cultural surround, and to extend, support, and maintain them. This ability had both its good and bad aspects. Today, because of improved communication and because of the existence of unions and increased governmental influence over the relationship of the organization to its employees, it is much more difficult to establish and maintain a climate that is different. As an example of the change, I will cite some of my early experiences. When one searches for a job, the pay and benefits are among the most important aspects compared between the prospective organizations. When I left Columbia University employment, I discovered that employees in the organizations where I interviewed were often unaware how their pay and benefits compared with those offered by others. Internal communication in that era was more effective than external communication. Companies were able to gain belief that their plans were good, even if not, because the employee had poor sources of information about other organizations. Today such isolation, and difference maintenance, is not possible. Professionals receive annual reviews of pay and benefits in their professional society publications. Computer-based services bring professionals information about offers from other companies in their fields. Our newspapers report union settlements on the front pages. With open communication about pay and benefit plans, no company can set up a condition in which unsupportable beliefs about its benefit plan can endure. In addition, yesterday's employee felt more dependent on the corporation than today's employee does. One has but to look at the court calendars to see the significantly increased numbers of times that employees or exemployees take employers to court to demand and get redress for perceived wrongs. Our culture has changed its feelings about the right of the organization to take advantage of employees. Closed cultures were once possible, but they are much less possible today.

The Importance of Environment and Culture on the Individual

In the opening section of this chapter, I discussed the importance of culture for the organization. Now it is important to look at the relationship of culture to the individual. It is equally as important for the individual to match needs for environmental and cultural support as it is for the individual to match needs for specific job elements that contribute to fulfillment (discussed in Chapter Twelve). In both cases, a mismatch can create negative stress, thus affecting the opportunity to achieve success and often affecting the individual's health. A good match reduces negative stress and can contribute to positive stress (eustress as defined by Hans Selye (1978)) which leads to achievement. A good match improves the potential for achieving one's needs from the work in the organization. A mismatch can be corrosive to the individual, actually eroding capability and self-respect. An appropriate match can be enhancing for the individual by contributing to increased individual capability and self-respect. We can see a parallel in plants. One does not plant a shade-growing plant in strong sunlight. One does not plant a sun-loving plant in the shade. The environment appropriate for the individual is one in which that individual can thrive.

A compatible environment, one good for the individual, provides the individual with:

- Proper conditions and support for achievement, development, and growth.
- Collegial and social support from other people who, by se-

lecting and belonging to the organization, have or develop
compatibility of values, outlook, and goals.
- Reinforcement, recognition, and reward for positive behavior, as defined by the beliefs, values, and norms of the climate.
- A longer, more healthy, less negatively stressful career and work life because there is no need to fight the environment.
- Improved potential for psychic income through a good cultural fit, which in turn should lead to a good person/job fit.

The feel of the workplace has a profound impact on the psychological health of the individual. Unfortunately, when making one's choice of employment, it is not always possible to assess all the aspects of the environment. However, properly aimed questions can assist in discovering some aspects that are important in making the choice. For example, I remember one young woman, with a master's degree, who taught me how an applicant can assess environment. As she said of herself, she was a scarce commodity. There were few female graduates with her background, so almost every major corporation she interviewed wanted to hire her. They offered her more money than she thought she was worth, and usually a uniquely tailored job to fit her interests. She searched for other ways to differentiate between organizations that would be good or poor places to work. She developed the concept that some organizations could be corrosive to people and others good for people. When she went for an interview, she asked to talk to some people who had worked in the organization five, ten, fifteen, and more years. If she discovered that these people were alive and vital, interested in their work, she reasoned that something in the climate was good for people. If these people were turned off and seemingly nonvital, she reasoned that something in the climate was not good for people—that the environment was corrosive. I believe she was ahead of her time in making this type of assessment, but I also feel that more and more professionals will make similar assessments of climate, culture, and environment in the future.

Our personal needs for climate differ with our personalities, our fields of interest, and our work goals. For example, the research scientist needs an environment that provides support for the autonomy and freedom necessary to pursue the unknown and to be creative. Ginzberg and Vojta (1985, p. 19) write: *"Tight controls on managers' [professionals'] time in the office are more and more inappropriate.* I am talking about individual contributors, R & D scientists or analysts—not people who are having to manage people all day long. I don't want everyone to disappear from the office! . . . Some people can only work at night, and so on. As it is now in most companies, it's much too rigid—a time-conditioned system for a world in which ideas and output are the important things." This means not only freedom from excessive management direction but also the intellectual freedom to think unpopular thoughts and the work freedom to do unusual things. Support for research must also include policies and actions that demonstrate that managers put a high value on research work and on its potential for outcomes of value to the organization. Support can come from policies that give the research project the necessary time, sometimes long, before having to face a review and a possible cutoff because of lack of progress or results. It means holding off the natural organizational forces for control and accountability long enough for something to happen in the time frame of research, which may not be compatible with the time frame for results in the organization outside research. It can mean supporting the researcher with an amount of computer facility, accessibility, and time that seem excessive to other members of management. The research professional who senses that management has held back on the necessary support is quick to assess the climate as nonsupportive. It does not meet the professional's needs. It does not feel right. QPL is in the eyes of the beholder. So the individual's productivity, psychological health, and even physical health depend on finding a compatible environment, climate, and culture.

The Unique Impact of Culture on R & D

R & D organizations are populated by sensitive, often insecure, people with high expectations because of their long educational preparation. R & D organizations are unique because of the percentage of uncharted work. They have many more people working in a self-directed mode than do other parts of the business or industry. Universities, hospitals, and professional service organizations in social work, accounting, or management consulting also have high percentages of people who are self-directing; consequently, many of the statements that I am applying to R & D also fit these organizations. These characteristics cause professionals and others in these organizations to search for signals as to what is right and what management expects. This makes the people more sensitive to environment, climate, and culture—since it is from observation of behavior, listening to experiential reports, and observing norms that they will find out what the expectations are. Culture, therefore, has a greater impact on what happens in R & D than it does in some other parts of an industrial or business organization where there are more clues to expectations in the specific plans and management directives.

Much has been written about IBM's culture. IBM is known as an organization with a strong culture. Its culture, along with the beliefs and policies enunciated by Tom Watson, is dominated by a marketing outlook. How have the marketing outlook's sensitivity to customers, service orientation, and drive for success in the marketplace affected IBM's R & D? Has IBM been able to create the unique R & D culture that supports this particular kind of work, and if so, how have they done it?

The market influence is strong in the IBM development environment because it is here that the product planners try to anticipate and interpret the customer and potential customer needs. Interpretation of the market has caused some good product developments, from a technical perspective, to be scrapped because it appeared that they would not be successful in the marketplace. It has sharpened the responsiveness of development professionals' efforts in satisfying customer needs and in handling customer feedback about problems. Both these effects of a strong marketing culture are good. However, this culture has supported the imposition on development of financial and planning controls that I believe have stifled the creation and incubation of new ideas. For a new approach, an idea, to get into the planned program and to be supported financially, it has been necessary to predict its profitability five years out in the marketplace. This puts a tremendous pressure on the programmer, scientist, or engineer who has a new idea but who has not yet developed it to the point where it can stand careful examination. Decontrol of the front end of the development activities (as discussed in Chapter Six) and encouraging under-the-table activities were seriously considered several times but were never successfully implemented in my days in the company.

   Out of a deep management understanding of the need for a unique and productive research organization, IBM has tried to insulate the research environment from some of these pressures of the culture. It has separated its research facilities physically from sites where other activities take place. The only research facility on the site of other activities has been in San Jose, and IBM is now moving research in California to its own site, south of San Jose. One story will show how subtle cultural pressures can be damaging to an R & D environment. In the early days of the pursuit of technical vitality, development management decided to have a series of seminars on science in areas unrelated to the product programs of the site. Our thinking at IBM San Jose was that the vital person is one with wide interests but that most professionals are too busy to read outside their field and explore them. Management, in development, wanted to expose people to what was going on in other areas of science for the professional's personal benefit—but with the outside thought that what was happening in another field might elicit a creative connection to their own work. R & D ran these sessions on company time and invited outstanding speakers. Because both research and development shared the site with a manufacturing organization in San Jose, laboratory management wanted to open these sessions to manufacturing people as well. Manufacturing management felt it necessary to assign tickets for attendance and for managers to decide who could go or not. They were worried about lost productive effort in the short term, and within their goals this was a legitimate worry. Manufacturing management wanted R & D management to implement the same approach. Unlike R & D, where management truly expected some long-term gain and trusted the professionals and others to make the choice about going or not, manufacturing management was afraid that employees would goof off by going to these sessions. The two managements had a different tolerance for risk of short-term loss to support this long-term goal of increased vitality. This difference in climate almost caused cancellation of the sessions!

The Relationship of Company Culture to R & D Culture

We have already examined a part of this issue in the previous section. Not all aspects of a company culture are supportive of the kinds of activities that management wants to see take place in R & D. There need to be differences in the environments, climates, and cultures in subunits of an organization while maintaining some overall, shared beliefs. Sometimes the company culture and the research culture are actually incompatible. For example, several organizations have tried unsuccessfully to support a research organization. Some have failed to provide the insulation from the short-term tight financial control necessary for the research environment. I suspect that these failures may have come about in organizations in which tight and strong financial controls were considered a virtue in the company culture.

One more illustration from my past experiences in IBM can further demonstrate this clash of cultures internal to an organization. In the late 1950s, in an attempt to reduce obsolescence and to enhance technical vitality, IBM established a program to send scientists and engineers away to graduate school as a full-time work assignment. It was an expensive program because, in addition to salary, IBM paid moving expenses, temporary living expenses, and educational expenses. It meant that IBM invested a large amount of company money in a relatively small number of people. This action ran up against company culture in two ways. First, it was the antithesis of the egalitarian approach of IBM, where treating all employees equally was important. Second, it ran against the goals of the tight financial controllers, who were at that very time worried about underestimated development expense and project cost overruns. Arguments were raised in favor of spreading this money over larger numbers of people. These arguments missed the point, for IBM was already supporting part-time graduate study and supporting larger numbers through that program. One important point was that this, and only this, program made an environmental statement—it shaped the culture by declaring, in an environment in which technological obsolescence was a severe problem, that *study is work*. It announced that the enhancement of the capabilities of unique employees was a legitimate business investment for the future. Unfortunately, these other forces, supported by the overall company culture, were allowed to erode the program over the years. First, management reduced the salary support to 75 percent, arguing that the employee should share in the investment. Some managers did not understand the risk taken by the individual and that going back to school was in itself a large personal investment. Over time, the budgets, and thus the numbers of employees selected and supported, were reduced. Still later, other minor reductions in support were implemented. Supporting a unique culture within another culture, that of the organization as a whole, is a constant struggle and takes strong leadership on the part of the managers of the subunit. Even with strong leadership, it is possible that the people of the organization will see the differences and that their commitment and attempts to create congruence of goals with the company will be negatively affected by mixed signals. Mixed signals leave the individual guessing about what is important, using up energy needlessly. This is one of those types of loss which argue for a pervasive strategy to make vitality and effectiveness important goals.

Company cultures can be compatible with and supportive of various components of the necessary subcultures for units like research and development or they can be nonsupportive. Edwin Land's influence on the culture of Polaroid is an example of the first. His heavy emphasis on innovation as a way of life for the corporation supported the necessary research climate in Polaroid. Previous examples discussed cases where company culture and research culture were in conflict. The important point is that the leaders of R & D must decide what elements of culture are necessary and work to establish and support them. Design of environments should be a conscious managerial strategy.

Creating an Environment, Climate, or Culture

Dominant personalities create climates. They do it sometimes without thinking about it and other times with deliberate intent. Environments are created in the absence of deliberate design or management attention. Cultures grow out of the folklore of the organization. Passed along informally by word of mouth, often in the form of anecdotal stories, behavioral expectations represent the accumulation of experiences about what works and what does not, about what is important and what is not, and about who gets ahead and who does not. But environmental design can be initiated by managers who understand the value of a climate in making more probable the right kinds of activities and in encouraging effective interaction among members of the organization. However, it is important to note that insecure managers will not be able to implement positive cultures. Any program of design of environments must first address the role of the leader-manager and ensure that these people are secure. They must be secure enough to take the risks of using culture and environment rather than a specific directive style to influence the behavior of employees. Here are some of the steps in the design of an organizational environment:

• Determine and document the organization's goals. Goal writing is extremely important; many people do not do it at all, some try but do not do it well, and a few do it well. Goal writing requires identifying what is important and, to the extent possible, what is necessary to achieve it. Goals provide a way of measuring progress. Good goals are specific enough to be communicated, are built on cost-benefit analysis, and are committed to by those who must pursue them. Some years ago the management of one laboratory decided that one of its goals was to change the culture so that it would be considered acceptable for the individual to ask for a change of assignments for individual development—for stimulation from variety and change. They had a process, but an assessment of it showed that managers and professionals felt that the act of implementing it would, in effect, label the individual as a discontented person and thus as a problem. The more that people believed this, the more it became true, for only those who were desperate (had real conflict with their managers) initiated it. Stating the goal was the first step in a process that eventually led to open posting of openings and a culturally accepted process of bidding for the jobs.

• Examine all elements of environment, climate, and culture through an audit. In the example just reviewed, the first step was to study the current condition so that management knew what it was changing from. Various people have devised much more sophisticated environmental audits. The *Kilmann-Saxton Culture-Gap Survey* (Kilmann and Saxton, 1983) is one of these which attempts to document the differences between desired norms and actual norms. A very short human resource climate audit was included in *Working with People* (Miller, 1979). I suspect that the market will soon be flooded with instruments because of the heightened interest in culture and climate.

• Determine which climate elements support the goals and which do not.

• Participatively discuss ways of eliminating those elements which do not reinforce the goals and of replacing them with supportive environmental elements.

• Institute the plan, and follow it up with assessment so that changes can be improved and strengthened.

When trying to come up with actions to support vitality and avoid obsolescence in IBM, we experimented with environmental design. In one case we determined that there was a need for expansion and change in the nature of continuing education. We surveyed professionals, and they told us that the message of support was coming through weakly because it was not properly supported by management. Since we knew that management supported it, we looked for hidden messages that detracted from the goal. The professionals told us that often when they enrolled in a continuing education class, their managers would interfere in a way that caused them to drop the course. They would schedule the professionals for overtime, thus interfering with the course, or would send them on a business trip, causing them to miss class. The professionals therefore felt that continuing education was something management talked about but really did not support. We fixed this with an environmental statement—a management requirement to get permission to interfere with attendance at a class. An environmental statement costs little but transmits a big message. Its importance is in the message rather than in the specific act. We required that any manager who felt need to cause a professional to miss a class, in a program which the manager had approved, secure the laboratory director's approval for this action. We called this process administrative friction. It was surprising how few managers needed to cause professionals to miss continuing education classes after they found it necessary to go to the laboratory director and ask.

A second example of environmental design has to do with the same time period and the same desire to support education —in this case, reeducation. We determined that many of the more senior engineers had either forgotten or had never really learned differential equations. We considered inviting the senior engineers to a program. However, this action would have sent the message that we thought they were obsolete. Management considered it undesirable to so label them and/or embarrass them. So we set up a program with an inspiring instructor and enrolled all the young engineers. The senior engineers demanded to be let in and wondered why they had been discriminated against! Admittedly, we had done the whole thing with a bit of drama, many kinds of publicity, and scheduling the auditorium for the class. Here again was an environmental statement, an action that tended to shape the culture, but was rather simple in itself.

A third example occurred in a different part of the company but was again related to the issue of vitality. The message we wanted to get across was that spending company time on improving personal capabilities and career management was OK.

We took a corner of a technical library and converted it to a Personal Enhancement Corner. The library, like most libraries, was essentially brown in tone, so we painted the corner and the shelves white. We populated the corner with books, audiocassettes, slide programs, and videocassettes on topics of improvement of personal capabilities. Everything from how to make a better speech and how to write better to career management, stress management, and health care was included. We spent about $3,000. The message was clear, however, and people who had never been in the library before opened the library door. We had again used an environmental statement to change the environment, to change the apparent value of a type of activity in the organization. Eventually, this type of action should contribute to a changed culture.

I would like to tell one additional story. While interviewing in one of my client companies to determine how to support a better climate for career growth, I ran across a case where one policy was interfering with our goal. I was talking to some managers about the need to free up professionals from one's group to allow rotation and transfer—as a method of stimulating capability enhancement. Several managers commented, typically saying: "Do you know what would happen if I let an employee leave my group? If I did, I would lose the head count, my group size would be reduced, and I would have less people to meet the requirements laid on me." Obviously, a manager faced with this will not let people go. Management's attempt to control staffing levels was interfering with their goal for enhancement of capabilities. They had to decide which was most important and make the environment consistent in its support.

These stories should encourage you to think in terms of environmental design. Do not limit your thinking to the physical environment, although this is also an area for action. I remember one time when we were trying to control entrance and exit to a building for security purposes. People were propping open back doors with stones because the controlled entrance was out of the normal path and required them to walk a considerable extra distance. We put in a controlled access entrance, with a closed-circuit television arrangement that displayed badge and person to a remote guard, in the normal path, and the infractions stopped. Climate design can include work on the intellectual climate, work on the social climate, and design of the goals, policies, and programs that support the goals. Climate design is more an outlook, a perspective, than it is any particular action.

Environments for Vitality and Effectiveness

In Chapter Six I set forth specifications for vitality and effectiveness goals, and one specification was to identify those important elements in the environment which are necessary to support these goals. An environment that supports these goals must demonstrate in every way that these goals are important. The specifications that follow for quality research and quality development environments are examples of this type of environment. You will notice similarities and overlap of specifications, but the perspective is different. In Chapter Six, the list was in support of goals. In this chapter, the specifications list is written from the perspective of environmental design.

Specifications for Quality Research Environments. In the broad sense, a quality research environment is one that supports quality research activities, makes it easier for professionals to pursue research goals, and improves their effectiveness and vitality in the process. The following is a checklist for the leader who would design an environment supporting these aims. A quality research environment should provide:

• A climate in which the expectation and the practice are that goals are participatively set, so that the professionals feel that the goals are theirs and that they own them. A culture in which creativity is a goal, is asked for and not blocked, and in which the outputs of research are seen as meaningful and contributory to the overall organizational mission. An environment in which the experimental philosophy pervades management style.

• A climate in which goals are clearly stated, effectively communicated, understood, and nonconflicting (where they can be) and in which, when goals do conflict, and established hierarchy of relative importance assists everyone in knowing which comes first.

• A culture in which leaders are carefully selected, effective, well-trained, and perform their roles with an understanding of the need for balance between goals for results and goals for effectiveness, excellence, and vitality. An environment in which decisions are made in a consistent fashion so that the organization feels like one organization, not several competing organizations.

• A culture in which there is respect for the professional's role, high trust, open communication both of feelings and facts, and mutual support so that people are personally secure enough to take the risks associated with their work.

• An organization populated with outstanding talent in an environment that exudes a feeling of excitement, establishes importance for goals, promotes collegial support, and in addition provides support and respect for the need the professional has to relate both inside to the organization and outside to the profession and the world. It is important to note that companies with strong cultures typically expect professionals to identify with the company first. This tends to support ingrown professionalism and weak connections to the profession at large. In companies with weak cultures, professionals know that, for their own protection, their relationship to the profession comes first. These professionals also leave one employer for another with greater ease.

• Support for the practice of providing individuals with challenging work and sufficient strategic and operational autonomy and freedom for the individual professional to pursue assignments in unique ways. Every professional should feel that the expectation is that the individual will be self-managing but also able and willing to be a team member when program requirements support that mode of pursuing goals.

• An organization that provides the support and facilities necessary to make the pursuit of the work goals as effective as it can be in the world of the unknown.

• Support for practices through which people get managerial support and feedback about their work, interest and attention from management (caring and nurturing), and fair evaluations of performance—evaluations in which the primary aim is performance improvement, future growth and development of capabilities, and appropriate reward and recognition.

• A culture in which there is freedom for the individual to change assignments and/or careers—freedom to grow and not be locked into nonvitality-enhancing activities after they have ceased to provide psychic income.

Specifications for Quality Development Environments. The first significant difference between quality research environments and quality development environments is the need for contact and communication with the customer, thus ensuring that development shapes and is responsive to market needs. The second is the need for a relationship with that manufacturing or implementation organization which takes the fruits of the development professional's work and turns it into reality. The third is a need for a development-cycle time which is compatible with the individual's needs for reinforcement with results and yet which fits the time frame for the technologies involved. For development environments to be exciting, stimulating, and supportive of the individual, they must be tied in to the real world. There must be concrete, measurable results that affect the profitability and success of the enterprise.

The Institute of Electrical and Electronic Engineers (IEEE) has been searching for ways to support the professional in the need for QPL, and several years back it initiated support by creating the Career Maintenance and Development Committee (CMDC). Rather than present a specifications list that represents primarily my personal point of view in the case of development, I shall present theirs (Institute of Electrical and Electronic Engineers, 1983). One important feature is the acknowledgment of responsibilities for both the individual professional and the employer of the professional. There are thus two lists. While I am referencing this work under development activity, it will be obvious that many of the points apply equally well to research.

Employer Practices:

1. Adopt a stable employment practice as a general goal.
2. Consistently provide for the continuing personal growth and technical development of the professional.
3. Recognize alternate career concepts.
4. Commit to and promote internal mobility.
5. Improve rewards for technical performance.
6. Increase the scope of assigned responsibilities with increasing experience.
7. Increase recognition for technical performance.
8. Improve the environment [QPL].

Engineer Practices:

1. Take responsibility for your own career.
2. Participate in the leadership.
3. Improve your value.
4. Communicate upward.
5. Perform like a professional.
6. Avoid routine work.
7. Be a mature realist.
8. Maintain appropriate registration/certification.

As can be expected, the employer practices read more like an environmental specification than do those for the engineer. However, it is important to note that the expectations that the employer will design, implement, and manage improved work climates will only be realized effectively if the professional acts as a professional and lives up to the improved opportunities to become a partner with the organization. The reader should also understand that this IEEE/CMDC list is considered supplementary to an earlier list endorsed in 1978 by twenty-eight professional societies. This, along with the mission of the CMDC, explains its focus, which is primarily on the career support aspects of environment. Under employer practices, the IEEE/CMDC used the category of improving the environment (item 8) to collect many aspects, such as improved communications openness, adequate secretarial support, conference attendance support, and the need for an opportunity to do personal research. Since registration and certification as a topic is sufficiently complex for a book on that topic alone, and since it is far afield from this discussion of environment, it is best that readers interested in that aspect seek other sources.

Elements, or Dimensions, of Environments

In order to sharpen our understanding of environments and how they are created, I will review and discuss several elements, or dimensions, of environment. Perhaps we can enhance our understanding of the whole by looking at the pieces.

Creating Principles, Philosophies, and Values as Environmental Building Blocks. Environments are supported by the beliefs and values of the organization. In the same sense that buildings take on a character that relates to the materials of which they are built, environments take on a character that relates to beliefs and values as they are implemented in philosophies and policies. If it is believed that salary should reflect performance, then it is necessary to have a salary system that relates pay to performance. If it is believed that satisfactory work over a period of time should be recognized by some closer tie to the organization, then one can implement this with a policy that rewards time in the organization with more vacation, more retirement, or other additional benefits. These types of policies are typical of the building blocks of environment used in most organizations.

A more unique policy may make the point clearer. Westinghouse has developed a slogan, "You can be sure," to represent its commitment to reliability of product. This has been reinforced in their environment by quality assurance programs, by quality circles, by meetings at which the theme is explained, and by buttons and other reminders. It has been reinforced by award programs that recognize people for contributing to the theme.

Establishing the Communications Climate. An open communications climate contributes to effectiveness by assuring clarity of goals and contributes to the comfort the individual feels through being accepted as a member of the organization and "in on the know"; this in turn allows the individual to feel safe enough to take risks. Openness is thus desirable. How does one design an open communications climate?

1. By top management setting an example, sharing openly.
2. By complete, timely, and accurate formal communications.
3. By teaching managers how to create trust in one-on-one relationships. If one gives trust, one will receive it; if one does not give trust, one will never receive it. Trust is built slowly over a long period of time. It is built through sharing potentially self-damaging information with another person and learning that this person will not use it in a way to hurt you. Trust can be killed instantly by a misuse of information.
4. By standing by one's word and by making one's actions consistent with one's words. I remember an early mentor or counselor, a vice president in charge of a manufacturing operation, telling me about rumors. He indicated that rumors represented the need for communication—the absence of communication. He said that he took a rumor walk on the shop floor once a month and listened to what people told him were the rumors. He then came back to his office and made a couple of them true! He recognized that an open communications climate had to be responsive to needs.

Creating the "Organizational Feel." In *The Feel of the Workplace: Understanding and Improving Organizational Climate,* Steele and Jenks (1977) describe climates in terms of the metaphor of the weather. They suggest that certain organizations feel gray and overcast, some feel sunny and warm, and others are periodically stormy in certain departments.

One important source of the feel of the workplace is the personality and style of the leader. Leaders who have short tempers tend to build short-tempered, stormy organizations, and leaders who are warm, open, and sharing tend to build organizations that reflect the feel of their personalities. So one way to implement the appropriate feel in an organization is to pick leaders with personalities and styles that reflect the belief about how the organization should feel.

Another is to reward behavior that fits the pattern of the climate you wish to have. I shall repeat a story from Chapter One which is applicable to this point. Sensing a closed, non-trusting environment in an interview once, I said, "I get the feeling you don't share feelings very openly around here." The response was "Right, we don't even share facts." One could encourage people to share feelings by establishing support for open career discussion between manager and employee. This could be reinforced (rewarded) by recognizing and acknowledging the positive outcomes of career counsel and career discussions.

Organizational feel reflects the social climate, the morale and attitudes of the people. If people believe that work is fun, you can sense it when you talk to them.

Emotional-Attachment Anchors. For the professional in R & D, choosing the work that uses the individual's skills is critically important. Because much of the work is chosen by the individual and because individuals work alone much of the time, they become emotionally attached to their accomplishments. This emotional attachment has both good and poor aspects. On the good side, it ensures that the individual is committed and owns the goals. It ensures pride in work and usually fosters quality work.

On the poor side, it can mean that taking a discovery or a product from the creator for use in the business can be a traumatic event. The engineer may want to go on perfecting the product long after it should have been released to manufacturing, or individual professionals may become so covetous of their work that open communication is impeded. Sharp management, conscious of this aspect of an R & D environment, uses the emotional attachment in a positive way. For example, this might mean assuring the creator-innovator that his or her name will stay with the product in some way. In many laboratories, products have been known by the names of the key professionals on the project. As projects have come to involve more people, however, this has become less practical.

Creating the Physical Environment. Most modern research or development laboratories look like college campuses, for organizations are increasingly trying to create pleasant supportive physical spaces for professionals to work in. After the attention to the outside came attention to the inside, such as putting offices on one side of the hall and laboratories on the other, creating for the researcher a sense of a personal laboratory. More recently, attention has been paid to the relationship of one group to another. For example, managers who feel that people doing one kind of work should communicate with others doing another kind of work have discovered that this communication is furthered when the two groups bump into each other in the course of daily activities. Management has begun to understand that informal, unplanned communication is an important part of the creative-innovative process. Making the physical layout support this is important. I became sensitive to this point years ago, when I was responsible for physical facilities and had to rent many outlying locations. Small groups in outlying locations became isolated and took on their own behavior patterns; communication with them became ever more difficult. So I established a pattern of alternately moving groups to and from outlying locations, thus keeping no group separated too long from those others with whom they needed to communicate. The latest frontier in facility designs that support the type of environment you wish to establish has been in the office space itself. The trend has been to create common areas and to make individual spaces smaller so that people have to bump into each other.

The important point is that one should look at physical space as an element of the environment. It should reinforce, not block, the other positive climate elements.

Creating the Intellectual Climate. The intellectual climate is very important in R & D, because it sets a standard for the work. The intellectual climate is established in part by who is hired. If the members of the organization are leaders in their fields and professionally alert and vital, this goes a long way toward ensuring a vigorous intellectual climate. Other things can also be done to ensure that intellectual activity is valued in the environment. For instance, most research organizations establish expectations for professional documentation of work, speeches before professional organizations, and personal activity in these organizations. For professionals whose work can be published, this is a part of the intellectual climate. In one development organization, while trying to establish the environmental support for writing, the management and I discovered that people write for two reasons: because they like to write (only a small portion fall into this category) and/or because they are expected to write. Using this knowledge, we set up a publications strategy that included documented goals for publications and involved managers asking specific people to write.

For those working in secret areas or in areas needing proprietary protection, however, that fact that others can write and that they cannot may be depressing and may create a negative feeling about the environment. So the environmental designer, recognizing this, creates other mechanisms to stimulate the intellectual environment. For instance, the designer could set up secure colloquia, restricted to those who are cleared, where open exchange can take place. With respect to documentation, in one organization, the creative solution was to publish internally and hold the document until it could be released externally. In our rapidly moving world it is often not an issue of not publishing at all but rather of establishing the time when something can be published.

Creating the Human Resource Climate. Human resource climates are primarily created by policies and practices affecting the relationships of individuals to the organization and to each other. Whether or not these policies are implemented and reinforced effectively is as important as the policies themselves. I will use one example to make the point that it is important to design this element of the R & D environment with care. I have said that professionals in R & D are somewhat insecure. Knowing this, it is important to design human resource policies that improve personal security so that individuals will be secure enough to share the information necessary for creativity and innovation. Specifically, the individual professional needs to know that the failure to reach a goal does not mean the loss of job. Thus, it is important through policy to let individuals know which types of failures will be tolerated (because they are positive failures necessary in the pursuit of the unknown) and which failures will not be tolerated (because they are unnecessary failures and represent a failure to learn). Such a policy can be implemented through a well-defined performance appraisal program in which manager and employee jointly set performance goals and jointly determine measures of success. Fairness in evaluation will go a long way toward helping individuals feel safe to make mistakes.

Reward and Recognition as a Climate Element. As a climate element, a fair, responsive salary system that reflects job value, capability, and performance is a basic necessity. Von Glinow (1985, p. 194) puts it this way: "Since an organization's culture involves the basic values, assumptions, and beliefs of its members, culture can be seen as influential in the types of rewards that are available in an organization, the conditions according to which the rewards and their criteria would be selected, and the manner in which the total reward system would be administered. Often the impact of culture is quite direct, and can be seen in ruthlessly performance-oriented cultures. . . . Indirectly, culture can influence the reward system through its human resource philosophy. . . . Human resource philosophies which are sensitive to the differences between professional and nonprofessional employees have corporate policies that include 'job content' rewards, peer appraisals, career development, dual ladders, and autonomous working environments."

On top of this, it is important to ensure that what people see as the reward responses by managers reflect the organization's policy and intended culture. For example, several organizations I know have a fellow program. This program is intended to recognize those professionals or managers who have made significant contributions and to reward them with status, salary, and the freedom to pursue their own work, unhampered by the plans of the organization. The concept is a powerful one and a good one. In its implementation, however, its positive effect is often blunted or destroyed. This is because managers, feeling that they need some way to handle cases of burned-out or obsolete managers, have used the fellow program as a technique for providing these people with a safe berth. To the scientist, this distorts the intent of the program, and reduces the recognition accorded those who are appointed as fellows based on significant accomplishments in a technical field. They believe that the only intent was to reward the scientific accomplishment, not the loyal, or even creative, performance of a manager. I suspect that the scientists are partly right. Once designed, a climate element must be appropriately used to carry out its intent. Managers do need a technique to handle those who have been loyal contributors, managers or not, but they should be careful to see that satisfying this need does not destroy another goal. Some organizations have created different levels of fellow to enhance the opportunity to use this powerful tool; I understand that Texas Instruments is one of these. Others have set up committees of peers to select fellows; this tends to ensure that it is not used as a reward for management more often than technical management should really be rewarded. Still other organizations have made appointments to fellow limited time assignments, thus assuring the freedom to make the reward really responsive to current affairs.

Creating the Work-Style and Team Characteristics. Whether people work together, cooperating in a synergistic way, or whether they are highly competitive in a personal sense is an element of the climate. Cooperation can be encouraged by making people individually secure and safe, as discussed earlier. Cooperation can be supported by rewarding it and paying attention to it and by managerial example.

In one organization I was trying to help, the climate was one of turf battles, of argument and lack of cooperation. I asked the top-management group what they felt that people in the organization saw them doing in their offices and the halls. I tried to get them to understand that their own behavior, which was one of argument and lack of cooperation, was setting the environment for those under them to do the same.

In another organization the work style was one of putting in long hours. It was the habit of the top people to schedule meetings at quitting time, to stay until 7:30 P.M. or so. This expectation was so dominant in the environment that top managers sometimes snuck out the back door so as not to be seen leaving at 6:15 P.M., an hour and a quarter after quitting time! It is probable that this unfortunate work style grew from one person's style, the leader's.

Establishing the work style for the environment is more a problem of paying attention to what the leaders are doing and the message inherent in their actions than it is of setting up policy. People react less to policies than to norms, the unwritten rules.

Establishing the "Normal" Management Style. I have already indicated that the style of the leader can imprint a style on the organization. Is it possible, then, to choose a normal or expected style and support this through environmental design? The answer is yes. Management can establish expectations through policy and the training of managers, and expectations have a way of shaping behavior.

One of the theses of this book is that managers must move toward a more participatory style, especially in R & D. If participation is the desired norm, we can help it to be practiced by: telling the employees so that they will demand it of their managers, hiring managers who represent the raw material for this type of management style, training the managers in how to establish participatory activities, supporting team-building events in which managers and individuals learn in groups to learn together, and making managers secure enough in their roles that they will take the risk of sharing their management responsibilities.

These examples of elements of the climate have been presented to assist in creating the perspective that managers can and should design environments. One of the driving forces behind the need for leaders to take an active role in the design, implementation, and management of climate is the change in the nature of work itself and our attitudes about it. Harris (1985, p. 41) underscores this change: "As we seek to cope with the new work environment and its management by information, we are creating a new culture. We literally are redefining the nature of work, the role of the worker, and the relationships required by the new situation brought on by the microelectronics revolution. Our work customs, traditions, habits, practices, institutions, and legislations are being transformed.''

Summary

• Environmental design leads to a climate that supports a desired culture.

• Through environmental design, management can establish cues for behavior that will make more probable a desired behavior intended to support effectiveness in achieving organizational goals.

• Environment is important to the individual as well as to the organization. A proper fit with the environment increases the probability that the individual will achieve the needed psychic income.

• Clearly articulated, communicated, and understood missions, goals, and beliefs are the building blocks of culture. They do make a difference in individual behavior and organizational performance.

• Culture, climate, and environment have a unique and important impact on R & D because in pursuit of the unknown there is an absence of much of the detailed management direction present in other parts of the organization. As a result, individuals become sensitized to climate in search of clues as to what is expected. R & D professionals are keenly aware of the environment and are thus in or out of tune with it.

• Company culture and R & D culture are by necessity different in some ways since the organization is usually in search of profit and research is in search of knowledge. Knowledge must not be sought in a vacuum; consequently, the work must be tied to the corporation's goals, but in a flexible way. Managements that understand the need for subtle differences protect the R & D environment from some of the business pressures that may be deleterious to creativity and innovation.

• One creates a changed climate by assessing the current climate and determining what aspects are supporting and not supporting organizational goals. The first step is to eliminate the nonreinforcing elements; the next is to design and install new supporting elements.

• The environment, the feel of the workplace, is established, whether managers take a deliberate role or not, but it should be a result of design and management of these many separate elements by the leaders. Only by taking the responsibility for environment design and implementation can managers ensure that the environment (culture) supports the goals of the organization.

Chapter 8

Leadership Style

How to Manage the Self-Managing Professional

Accurate communication between two people is close to a miracle. When two people have shared experiences, shared values, and work together in a supportive environment, the resulting communication can lead to a productive and effective relationship. The organization benefits through productivity and goal achievement when the manager and employee can and do communicate effectively and develop a positive, supportive relationship. It is important that the word *supportive* not be interpreted so strongly that the manager becomes a crutch. The aim is development, not dependency. When I talk of style I am talking about the way in which the leader goes about trying to establish and maintain this type of productive relationship; this means communication on all levels. Style includes all the differences in approach that can be used when one human tries to build a relationship with another. I am talking about how the manager builds trust, and how he coaches without destroying the other's self-management; style affects peer and upward relationships as well as those between leader and employee.

Where do we get our style? Certainly, one source is from

watching others and trying what they do, and another is from training and experience. Individuals tend to utilize an approach that they feel has worked for them, and thus it becomes part of them. Style is made up of many aspects, including basic character, personal security or insecurity, self-image, attitudes about people, expectations of others, word choice, voice tone, message timing, body language, and empathy. Style reflects an individual's values, beliefs, self-knowledge, self-confidence, and ego strength. The environment, climate, or culture of the organization affects the individual and thus affects and shapes the individual's style. Just as people tend to stop doing things that seem to be in conflict with the environment in which they work, they also tend to do more of those things that are accepted within and reinforced by the environment, by personal experiences of success, and/or by management and colleagues.

The leader, peer, or subordinate may affect and/or influence others through inspiration. Perhaps the most obvious source of inspiration between two people who respect each other is the interactive communication that occurs when one of the two is inspired. This inspiration is a breathing in of influence. One can also inspire by example—by translating the dream of a goal into images to which another person can relate, by actions that reflect one's values and goals, and by that almost indefinable aspect of a relationship called chemistry.

Some aspects of interpersonal relationships can be discussed in terms of how one is affected by another's specific impact. For example, studies of personal success suggest that what has made people successful is the impact of another individual who cared about them and their development. We know that different individuals need different levels of attention, caring, and feedback; therefore, the frequency and nature of the manager's contact with the individual makes a difference. Some leaders help their groups establish a feeling of uniqueness (such as in the Marine Corps), and I shall call this the unique-clan approach; belonging to a special group can support the individual member in achieving success, but it also can create difficulties for team members in relating to others who are not part of the clan. And some leaders are so unique and outstanding in their personality, style, and personal accomplishments, that they affect others by causing them to seek to emulate that image.

At the frontier, and this is especially true in R & D, it is lonely. Often the individual is pursuing a direction over objections and without support, in which case the ego strength of the individual is very important. Belief in oneself makes it possible to fight the odds; this same ego strength can make relationships with others difficult, however, because they find the individual closed to assistance from another. Closely related to ego strength is another aspect that affects leadership style. This is the personal need for control on the part of the leader. If the leader's emotional bond with the goal and process is strong, usually the need for control will be strong. This strong need for control can stifle others and interfere with their development. It can also destroy the freedom needed for creative endeavor by those who are being led.

Classical management books are replete with references to management style. Generally, they classify styles and suggest, based on research, which styles work best under what circumstances. Styles are classified on continuums or two-dimensional grids, with the dimensions ranging from employee-centered at one extreme to job-centered at the other (Likert, 1961) or from authoritarian to participative (Miller, 1979). I will spend little attention on this material because I believe that an R & D group must operate on the participative end (Likert, 1961) and because the material can be found elsewhere. Most books on management eventually suggest that the leader should fit the opportunities for participation to the needs of the individual and the group. This book is no exception. R & D is unique, however, in the fact that professionals have an unusually high need for participation. As I said in describing professionals (Chapter Three), they view their participation as a badge of professionalism.

This chapter also seems the appropriate place to make some comments on the international level—on the effects of country culture on style. In closing this chapter, I will suggest that the participative style is required in R & D leadership, despite the conflict with the leader's need for control.

Interpersonal Style: The Basis for Relationships

Style, which is a combination of the effects of our values, appearance, vocabulary, delivery, timing, body language, sense of who we are, empathy, and all other aspects of self, is the basis for contact with another human. Style is the sum of a lot of little things. I remember being with General Eisenhower, then president of Columbia University, on a day when he went to the French embassy to receive an award. Even though he was not announced, when he entered the room every eye turned to him. He had a magnetic personage—a bearing, a style, a presence —that caused this to happen. So our first contact—how we walk into a room, how we greet someone—is part of style and affects reactions to us and how others will attempt to communicate with us. We do not get a second chance to make a first impression. This is why, in the nineteenth century, young women were taught how to walk. This is why actors and their directors spend so much time on designing the entrance of a character in a play.

We also take cues that affect communication from costume. One of my friends, who taught costume design, says that the most important visual cue is the hat or headpiece. She suggests that the remainder of the costume can be approximated if the hat is correct. In the organizational world, costume, how we dress, affects our ability to communicate with others, to lead, to inspire. I have used the effect of costume in teaching graduate students about career/life management. I ask them to come to class in costume. Costume is defined as anything they would not wear to work or to the university. We then spend an hour or so talking about the reasons for costume choice, how a different costume affects how we feel, and how others react to the costume. Students discover the power of costume on shaping their style and the impact that costume, alone, can have on interpersonal relations and their careers.

After we get beyond the first impressions of appearance, of entrance, and of costume, we usually start talking to the other person. At this level of relationship, one reacts to vocabulary: to accent, if any, and to delivery and timing. We react to the other person's openness to our responses; to evidence in

204 Managing Professionals in Research and Development

what they say that they have heard and understood what we said; to their need to dominate, to be right, to be in control. Individuals react to the appropriateness of the choice of the opening topic. If in this exchange one finds a common ground of interests, of experiences, of other relationships, then one is usually open to letting the relationship grow. If one finds no common ground of interest, then, as at a cocktail party, one moves on to spend time relating to someone who shares our interests. Sharing is the basis for good communication between two people. But unlike the cocktail party, in the organization one must continue to relate to the manager, co-worker, or subordinate whether or not one initially finds or achieves comfort in sharing. It is up to both parties, who must relate in the organizational sense, to be open to exploration in building the relationship, to be open to adaptation and personal change, and to allow the relationship to grow. When one is required to continue to relate to another person—by role, by the nature of the work, by the goals of the organization, by the need to be part of the group—one cannot let the struggle to relate stop with the first unsatisfactory exchange.

Style therefore continues after the opening to affect the relationship—the communication success, the opportunities for one person to have an impact, an influence, upon another. Style can affect the potential for building harmony, credibility, and trust. Based on style, on behavior, one makes judgments about the other person's values and goals, and these judgments affect the probability of success in the relationship. In the organizational sense, success in the relationship between manager and professional has to be measured in terms of how it influences effectiveness. Success is also measured in terms of its effects on vitality, trust and openness, commitment to organizational goals, morale, attitudes, and people's willingness to continue relationships.

In recent work with an organizational group, I discovered a low level of trust of the manager, poor morale, high turnover, and other signs that the organization was becoming less effective, although it still showed signs of vitality. I found that one reason was managerial style. The leader was very intelligent and had been a successful professional. His appointment won initial approval from the professionals. In my view, when he became a leader, his personal insecurities, his need for new forms of psychic income, the poor leadership above him, and the lack of available help in his transition to manager affected his style. Negative aspects of his style included his withdrawing to his office, his short temper and sharp verbal exchanges, his apparent preoccupation with image and advancement, his perceived unwillingness to be influenced by input from professionals, and the perception that he was enamored with the power of the position and needed to be in control. All of these behaviors reduced trust and caused a deterioration of communication. As is usually the case, the leader did not see himself as he was seen.

Personal Style: Origins

Individuals start developing styles from birth. One learns that different styles work better or worse in different contexts and thus develops different styles for different goals and different situations. One's initial range of styles is developed without benefit of understanding the work environment. It is developed at home, at school, and at play. Styles are developed both from experience and from watching others. I am reminded that my wife and I could tell with whom our children had been playing by their use of vocabulary and behavior styles. Styles are developed in climates very different from the work climate. It is probable that styles are deeply integrated in personalities before one enters the world of work and are thus difficult to change.

In the work climate, therefore, one starts by trying some of the styles that have worked in other contexts. Individuals learn new styles in the work environment, where certain behaviors are reinforced and others are not. For the professional promoted to manager, the sources of style include pre-work life, work experiences as a nonmanager, observations of other leaders, personal experiment as a manager, organizational policies, and any managerial training.

Style: Components

Style is a word used to describe the overall effect of how another person comes across to us. It is a summary word. No listing of components can be complete, but in order to assist others in developing appropriate managerial or interpersonal styles for R & D, I shall first list the components. Then I shall discuss some of the elements that have a significant impact on the managerial role, on person-to-person functioning in the organization, and on team behavior. Here are some of the components of style:

• Individual values and beliefs affect how one behaves, the relative importance one assigns to various goals, and thus how one relates to others. Values and beliefs are a component of style.

• One's self-image, self-esteem, ego strength, self-interest, caution and reserve, trust, and personal separateness—all these aspects of self affect who one is in others' eyes. Herman and Korenich (1977, p. 65) put it this way: "A good sense of your own boundary and what is going on within that boundary can be tremendously useful in helping you to know who you are and where you are. People who have this good sense of their boundaries and of themselves are often good people to be with: they tend to be comfortable with themselves, easy to communicate with, clear and direct in communication to others, and sure of themselves." And Jourard (1974, p. 150) notes: "Everyone experiences his identity differently, but everyone experiences who he is. A person acts in the world and interacts with other people as the person he believes himself to be."

• One's appearance, the way one talks, one's vocabulary, one's tone of voice, speed of delivery, one's gestures—all these aspects of communication that can be assessed by another are parts of one's style.

• Individual roles, and especially one's interpretation of these roles, are part of style. When one assumes the position of manager, one to some extent begins playing the role as understood, in the same way that an actor studies and develops a character.

• Style is affected by the context in which it is seen—which in our discussion is the organization's environment, with its values, goals, and mission. The organization's climate and culture affect role interpretation and how individuals are viewed. It may be helpful to think of the individual as the figure and the organization as the ground. When we look at something, we see it with respect to its ground, or setting. If an individual plays a part on an organizational stage set in muted colors (soft values), that individual will be seen differently than on an organizational stage with harsh lighting and strong colors (clear rights and wrongs). R & D organizations are unique stages on which professionals and technical managers perform.

The Impact of One's Values on Personal Style

Since values shape behavior, and are the basis of motivations, they affect how others perceive and react to us. Values are not unlike icebergs, in that what one sees above the surface is but part. What one sees is behavior. From behaviors, one infers values.

This inferential approach can be demonstrated by talking about a research group. Several of the professionals in a group described a former leader of the group as someone running for the next higher management position. They interpreted the leader's behavior to mean that promotion was valued highly by the manager. In the absence of actual information, they saw behavior that only made sense to them if the leader was trying to look like a candidate for a higher management position. In a research climate, this type of behavior is looked down upon. The same behavior in a marketing organization would probably be interpreted as normal self-interest in career growth. This demonstrates the figure-ground phenomenon. Once these professionals had come to this conclusion about the manager's values, it affected how they related to the manager. Their interpretation negatively affected the manager's ability to lead that group. It makes little difference whether the inference was correct or not. Once it was believed, it affected the group's interpretation of every other action the manager took.

For a manager to be an effective leader, that manager's behavior must make sense to those being led. One makes sense of behavior in the context of the values represented, whether they are real values or not. Some individuals are much more open in telling others about their values and beliefs than are others. This sharing of values on the part of the leader can help to avoid the kind of incident described. It is important for managers to understand their values and to be open about them if they are to be credible and trusted. Credibility and trust, important effects of style, result from consistency between understood values and actions. Individuals must do more than know their values and be open about them; these personal values must also fit in the organization. It was this conflict which aggravated the situation in the running-for-promotion story. Aggressive behavior aimed at a higher management position was not condoned in the context of a research organization. This does not mean that there was any organizational policy against it or any stated organizational value against it. Rather, such behavior flew in the face of the commonly accepted set of values among professionals in research. It would have been more acceptable in a development environment.

The Impact of the Organization's Values on Personal Style

One tries to fit into and to be comfortable and compatible with any environment, climate, or culture in which one finds oneself, for just as in the case of weather, if one spends a lot of energy fighting the climate, one does not have that energy to spend in pursuit of a goal. Value compatibility exists when there is similarity or overlap between one's own values and those expressed in the organization's culture. An individual chooses to join and to work in an organization whose climate is felt to be compatible. Once in the organization, one tends to conform, and so the organization's climate reshapes one's values. In most cases, conforming is not a conscious act; rather, it results from the feedback one gets. If one does something and it is accepted and reinforced, one tends to repeat that behavior. If one does something that leads to a feeling of rejection or lack of success, one will tend to stop that behavior. Individuals who grow and adapt are constantly adjusting their style, their interactions, with respect to the environment and with respect to each other.

Climate therefore shapes the individual's and the group's values, behavior, and style. This makes culture important in interactions and productivity. As managers use the thoughts in this book to design environments in which effective, vital research and development activities take place, they will also be shaping values and style. These managers then have one piece of the leadership puzzle under control. Organizational values affect style whether the individual is compatible with them or fights them. In both cases, the individual's behavior is affected, but in different ways. In the one case, the behavior is effective in the pursuit of the goals; in the other, it is counterproductive. It is wrong to feel that 100 percent congruence will ever exist or is actually desirable. What the individual needs to do is to become sensitive to a range of compatibility that does contribute to effectiveness. In my own case, as a manager I came to feel that if I could not agree with from 50 to 90 percent of the values and goals of the organization, I would leave. The balance was close several times, but it changed so fast that I never had to take up my resolve and leave.

Leadership Style: Classical Principles

By now, you know that I advocate a primarily participative management style in R & D. Studies have shown that participation is a paradoxical concept; as Nurick (1985, p. 355) points out, it simultaneously implies "tension and stability, freedom and well-managed boundaries, and attention to formal structures and informal processes." I also favor a high-contact, high-attention style, with the manager demonstrating that he or she cares about what the employee is doing. For those not familiar with management literature, it is important to know that I have picked one style out of a range of styles.

Likert (1961), for many years a leading researcher of

management, defined four styles, which he called systems: (1) the *exploitative authoritative* system, representing low trust, motivation with fear, and primarily downward communication; (2) the *benevolent authoritarian* system, in which the leader is a kind master, but paternalistic; (3) the *consultative* system, in which the leader keeps control but communication is more open than in systems 1 or 2; and (4) the *participative group* system, in which the leader is supportive of networking and group decision making. In the early part of this century, many if not most of the leading innovators used the leadership style of system 2. Likert favored system 4 for an R & D organization, and so do I. However, it is important to note that there is a *situational* aspect and that different styles thus can and should be chosen for different situations. If the building is on fire, I will not call a meeting to decide what to do; even with scientists, I will be authoritarian!

Another classification system is to think of leadership as being mechanical, organic, or a process. In the mechanical view, leadership is a closed system and the leader finds leverage points and prods. If leadership is thought of as organic, it is adaptive within limits and the leader sets the limits. If it is thought of as a process, it is a system of high change and the leader is a catalyst for change, a process observer and designer.

Hersey and Blanchard (1976) are proponents of a system of situational leadership similar to that of Blake and Mouton (1969). Both systems use a two-dimensional matrix, with one scale representing low to high (bottom to top) relationship behavior (Hersey and Blanchard) or low to high concern for people (Blake and Mouton). The other scale goes from low to high task orientation (left to right), which can be thought of as directive behavior in both systems. They suggest matching the situational style to the maturity of the followers, with high-maturity followers needing a participative, or low task-oriented, management style. People oriented in the GRID system (that of Blake and Mouton) go around describing leadership behaviors in numbers; for instance, 9/1 is a nice guy with a low task orientation, and 9/9 is a team manager.

The approach I shall follow is more closely related to a

discussion of managerial roles. Thus, either here or in other parts of this book, I will talk about managerial roles as: coach, figurehead, liaison and interpreter, inspirer or lowerer of the threshold of action, risk taker, decision maker, monitor of flow, barrier eliminator, problem identifier, teacher, conflict resolver, and negotiator.

Inspiration Through Example

As a young professional, I remember hours spent with other professionals trying to interpret the signals given by our leader. I watched his behavior, and that of other leaders, to find out how to be successful in the organization. Yet many managers and senior professionals are not conscious of the fact that they are being watched as exemplars. In R & D, leading by example is very important. It is important (as I have indicated in discussing missions, goals, and culture) because the work is less well defined, consequently, people in R & D are in search of cues.

Studies of creativity and what cause it to happen have revealed several ideas about creating effective research climates. One lesson is that you should populate your organization with people who have demonstrated that they can be successful as researchers. Having world-class scientists and Nobel laureates in the organization provides the organization with exemplars. These people, in the process of working with others, can provide mentoring; they can teach; and they can exert influence, because other professionals will be watching what they do. This does not mean that the best scientist must become a manager. It does mean that the person who does should have done some credible work as a researcher. Thus, a lesson is that the behavior both of managers and of others will have an influence on establishing behavioral norms for the group. If exemplars, including managers, are carefully chosen, and if leaders think about the potential effects of their behavior and choose it accordingly, then another element of leadership has been mastered—another piece of the puzzle.

Managers would like nothing better than to supervise people, professionals and nonprofessionals alike, who show commitment to their work. Commitment, which contributes to effective, goal-directed behavior, is important to the organization. It comes from believing in the goals (owning the goals) and from the individual's compatibility with the goals. Thus, some aspect of commitment is internal to the individual. The commitment of the manager can affect the commitment of those being managed. If the behavior of the manager is seen as successful, then there is inspiration by example. If nonmanagement professionals feel that the manager is not only committed but believes in the goals and is having fun on the job, then they will tend to do similar things.

Inspiration Through Communication

We live in a word-oriented culture. In fact, one of the dangers in our society is that words are interpreted as actions. We tend to believe that the way we influence someone else is by telling them: one-way communication. Although its effect on behavior is minimal, one-way communication is what people do much of the time. We react to it much as we react to a well-constructed, well-delivered sermon. As we leave church, we comment on the good ideas and the inspiration and think about what we might do differently, but most of us have experienced the fact that a sermon seldom motivates us to change our behavior.

Two-way communication is important because it gives us the opportunity to get feedback, to have other people tell us what they have heard and how this affects, or may affect, what they do. Two-way communication influences behavior much more than one-way communication. It is the way to inspire action, change, and commitment in others. This two-way managerial communication in R & D is most effective and has the following characteristics:

- It is two-way communication.
- It is open, frank, and represents a sharing of topics in which there is some risk.

- It is consistent with the behavior of the individual delivering the message.
- It elicits self-direction from the other person; it does not impose direction on the other person.
- It is delivered in a way that demonstrates respect for the other person.
- It is frequent.
- It is followed up with observation of and positive comments on those changes which are in the right direction.
- The style of delivery fits the context of the organization's mission, values, and cultural expectations.

Within these precepts, inspiration through communication depends on the creation of a vision, a word picture of the improved situation. The leader needs to be able to create a picture which can be talked about—which is transmittable and understandable in terms the receiver can understand and relate to. This means that the new situation must have characteristics that make it attractive and thus make it something that the other individuals might wish to accept as their own. Two failures are common: First, many leaders do not understand the need for the word picture of the changed situation; second, many leaders are not able to create the picture in a way that can be effectively communicated.

Inspiration Through Action

In general, the message one delivers through actions is clearer and better understood than the message one delivers through words. I remember a particularly rough time; business was poor and we were having to take unpopular actions. Regularly, management meetings were held to decide on necessary measures of cutback and conservation. These were not happy meetings. Somewhere along the line, it dawned on me that these meetings, in themselves, were making things worse. Through observation and thinking about it, I recognized that at the end of each meeting, as the managers were leaving, everyone was watching them. The rumor mill telegraphed the managers' facial expressions and actions right after the meetings as signals of what was up, and the signals were usually worse than the reality of the situation. Once aware of this, I helped the managerial group make their faces and their actions reflect a message more nearly approximating the real message of the day's meeting.

From this story of negative inspiration, we should move directly to the task of influencing the work of the research scientist and development engineer in a positive way. The actions of managers and management and of other professionals are the inspiration sources to consider. Since the scientist is biased against management, and since many actions that managers have to take tend to reduce their credibility, it is probable that the actions of fellow professionals have the stronger impact. Yet this should not mean that managers give up in the battle to influence. Managers can take the following actions by way of influencing the work of the scientist-engineer-professional positively:

• *Continue those activities both inside and outside the work environment which demonstrate that as individuals (even though as managers) they continue to have an interest in and a desire to work in technological areas.* As managers, they must keep in touch with their basic fields of technical knowledge through reading, study, talking with those in the field, and attending professional meetings.

• *Manage through the use of the random walk.* By physically getting out of their offices and into the work areas of the professionals, where they come into *physical* contact with professionals at work, managers reduce the barrier to other communications and demonstrate an interest in technological as well as management work.

• *Provide recognition for good technical work.* Managers must know about the work and make positive, reinforcing comments about it to the professional.

• *Practice their enabling function.* What the manager does should make the task of the professional easier to accomplish. The manager should break down barriers, supply assistance in funds and facilities, and generally try to reduce the energy the professional must spend fighting blocks imposed by the organization.

• *Provide some protection from the irrational world of management requests.* The professional's time should not be used up in needless reworking of estimates, useless meetings, and answering unnecessary questions. Providing protection without setting up an unreal environment that cannot continue to be supported is a tough challenge. Managers seem to err on the two extremes, either letting too much through, and thus becoming transparent, or protecting too much, and thus not preparing the professional to live in the real world.

• *Demonstrate commitment to technological goals.* R & D managers should be seen carrying the technical imperatives upward and fighting for the technological perspective, which often gets overcome by other management, business, and marketing goals.

Inspiration Through Personal Chemistry

One of the best managers I ever worked for had a way of causing me to aspire to, and achieve, a higher quality of performance than I would have sought without his influence. Although the things he did fit the suggestions we have covered, there was some extra factor in the relationship. I believe that this is what I am trying to identify when I talk about the chemistry of a relationship. Personal chemistry seems to work something like the fit between the appropriate two pieces in a jigsaw puzzle. There is something about the personalities, the outlook, the experiences, and the way in which the two people come together that makes communication easier and better. This does not mean that the two personalities are identical, for they are usually not, but that they achieve an unusual level of communication. When this happens between teacher and student, between senior professional and junior professional, it is good for the organization and good for both individuals. What managers should strive for is a way to make this miracle more probable.

Since the relationship is personal, it would seem that one of the ways to make this chemical reaction more probable is to provide the opportunity for individuals to work with different people. Only by exploring, by experiencing relationships of different quality, can the individual learn what good chemistry feels like. Thus, an organizational design that ensures that the new professional has a series of experiences working with different people is desirable (and it should be supported by policies); this can help put that individual in a position to choose the most stimulating relationship. Another technique that can increase the probability of the miracle is to involve professionals in the process of recruiting new professionals; particularly if they are asked to focus on the compatibility of the new person with the environment, the work style, and the people, their input can make a positive difference as to who is hired. Still another technique is to provide training for professionals and managers that helps them to develop and to become comfortable with allowing their feelings to provide input, for it is on this feeling level that reaction between two people takes place.

The Impact of the Caring Factor on Success

A friend of mine, now deceased, Dick Schmeltzer, formerly a member of Rensselaer Polytechnic Institute's administrative team, was asked several years back by RPI to study the 100 to 150 most successful graduates. The institution was interested in finding out whether there was a factor that stood out above all others in contributing to success. I suspect they were hoping that this factor was something that could be included, or had been included, as part of the RPI education. Since RPI is a technical university, many of the graduates were, as they started out in professional life, scientists or engineers. He sent questionnaires to these people and interviewed many of them. The only consistent factor he found in each of the cases was that some other person or persons had cared about the personal development and growth of that individual. He concluded that individuals who give of themselves in nurturing another person—and who show that they really care—do impact that other's life in a positive way. From similar data, people interested in career development have concluded that coaching, nurturing, and mentoring are powerful forces in the development of individuals. The caring process can be taught, but making it real depends on the personality and interests of the individual manager. The mentoring process, however, seems to relate to chemistry and has eluded most attempts to formalize and organize it.

I suspect that caring becomes a personal, private goal, a way of giving to another person. Somehow, caring people develop the empathy necessary to actually reach another human. The only managerial training with which I have ever experimented on this subject went this way: First, I asked each person to recall times when, as individuals, they felt that they had been nurtured at work or in life outside work. To this list, I asked them to add incidents when they felt that they had nurtured another person. Second, I formed the managers into small groups and asked them to share these experiences. This process was intended to cause them to identify the constituents of a nurturing event. Once these constituents were identified, I had the managers proceed to generate ideas about how caring and nurturing could be enhanced in their organization. I feel that the exercise was a success. It therefore seems possible that an organization could make caring a value within the culture and cause more of it to happen through training. Success in this process should increase effectiveness, personal growth in capabilities, and success in achieving the organization's goals.

Some of the thoughts generated by one of these groups of managers may be helpful. The group concluded that the first need was to have an open, frank communication base between employee and manager, for they felt that nurturing and caring cannot happen if there is a lack of trust and respect. One of the ideas for creating this openness was to have joint manager-non-manager educational activities, specifically those including small-group processes. The point was that they felt it necessary for managers and employees to experience the fact that they are not as differently oriented or different in their interests as is usually assumed. The group concluded that the second need was for the manager to understand the power of the communication process and to feel that the organization not only condones communication but encourages it. This requires not only statements of intent to support two-way communication and real participation but also an actual reduction in the manager's tendency to interfere with or stop nonproductive (unplanned, spontaneous, or random) activity because of pressures from upper management supporting control by the manager. They really felt that if they were seen too often talking informally with an employee about anything other than current organizational events or problems, they would be criticized. They talked, too, of the need for informal space if they were to accomplish this goal of open communication. Mindful of the structure and relationship of authority imposed by most offices, they felt that the communication process would be encouraged if managers could have a small, living-room-like setting.

The Impact of the Attention Factor on Creativity

In support of their thrust for achievement, humans need different amounts of attention from other people. The manager who understands this and is providing the appropriate levels of attention and recognition suiting the needs of the individual professional has found a way to encourage creativity.

How does a manager become sensitive to the amount of attention that someone needs? The best way is probably the direct way—to talk about it. The manager can determine the levels of attention that individuals require simply by asking them to report their feelings. If individuals report that they feel ignored, then the manager can increase the frequency of contact. I suspect that professionals in a creative group need a relatively high level of attention, by daily contact or contact at least every few days. This need leads me to suggest that any one manager should be required to supervise only a small number of creative, innovative professionals.

Attention is an expression of interest, not a matter of interfering or of telling someone what to do. It creates the opportunity for interchange, if interchange is needed. Attention shows another person that you feel that what they are doing is *important.*

Attention and recognition are related. Attention is the simplest, or most primary, form of recognition. Many people think of recognition in terms of prizes, certificates, and dollars, but a more powerful type of recognition is that appropriate to the needs and the expectations of the individual. Appropriate recognition reinforces behavior, improving the probability that the individual will try more of that behavior—whereas inappropriate recognition (that which the individual feels is either too much, wrongly timed, or given with a lack of sincerity or understanding of the individual's needs) is nonreinforcing. Understanding the individual's need for the recognition to fit expectations is a necessity for any manager who sets out to design recognition policies, programs, and systems. In R & D laboratories where the environment has been designed to support attention and recognition, policies and programs guide and support the manager in these activities. Often the manager perceives limitations to recognition that are not actually there. Here is a list of creative ideas for managers who wish to increase recognition:

• Giving the other person some one-on-one time, with the attention of the manager exclusively focused on understanding the other individual's needs, interests, and goals. I still remember an early manager who took me on trips with him and thus provided this one-on-one time. I flourished as a result.

• Rewarding successful performance by increasing the individual's input into the choice of assignments. If managers could set up a situation in which the freedom to control one's work were earned through achievement, this would give the professional high-quality recognition. When I look at my total work career, I feel that I earned the right to influence my career through performing for the company. This is a good feeling.

• Rewarding successful performance with the opportunity to talk about it with peers. Providing opportunities for ad hoc or bootstrap seminars within the group can increase its effectiveness. Seminars give individuals a chance to rub ideas together and provide opportunities for peer recognition of their work.

• Rewarding successful performance with the opportunity to write about it and to talk about it at professional meetings, beyond the confines of the organization. An opportunity to present a paper at a conference can feel like a reward for professionalism.

• Recognizing successful performance with the opportunity to do more private or personal research: allowing the individual a greater percentage of total time to devote to special interests, even if these are not directly aligned with the goals of the organization.

• Recognizing the need for personal refurbishment and learning through the exploration of ancillary activities. This could be done by rewarding performance with the opportunity to study and to visit with and explore the work of others, at both universities and other laboratories. (I realize, however, that the openness of laboratories to visitors is often circumscribed by proprietary controls over information and sometimes by governmental controls.)

• Providing short-term special activities that allow individuals to gain perspective by being able to get away from and look back at their work. Sometimes this is travel, especially for the professional who normally does not travel. Sometimes this is a task force assignment that temporarily puts the person in touch with a different group of professionals and new problems.

• Using the recognition and reward systems of the organization to ensure that the professionals in the group are appropriately recognized within the organization's culture.

The Impact of the Unique-Clan Factor

Belonging to a group with special characteristics, believing that one is part of a select group, can have a strong motivating effect on individuals. Various branches of the armed services try to build these special characteristics and to use them as motivating forces. The Marine Corps is a prime example. Organizations use this technique too. I can remember freshman orientation at the University of Rochester, where I was told that I was part of a select group. It was said that each of us could find a university where we could come out on top scholastically, but that at the U of R, some of us would flunk out. Only a small portion did survive the rigors of the U of R's brand of education. This feeling of being exclusive is also part of the culture and the motivation in being part of one of Silicon Valley's high-technology start-up groups. Here the special characteristics relate to being technological frontier people—to packing more function on a chip, to doing something better than the competition. Being special relates to being part of a small, select group.

Within organizations, managers can use this concept to improve the effectiveness of their subunits. For one thing, of course, they can select their people with special care, setting higher-than-normal specifications for entry into the group. They can also make use of special characteristics in terms of the unit's mission, for if the subunit's mission can be a little tougher, more challenging, and pose higher risks than the unit's mission, this will help differentiate the group in an R & D environment. If the mission is closer to a technological frontier, this, too, can help to make being part of the group special.

Groups can also be differentiated in terms of the work climate's quality. For instance, if the leader fights the bureaucracy and gets special relief from some organizational requirements or rules, this makes the group special. If the manager can make it more fun to work in this group, then entry into the group becomes a goal to be attained. This could happen, for example, if the manager's nurturing efforts and the group's success in achieving goals established a reputation that led to graduates of the group being perceived as desirable candidates for promotion to other parts of the organization. The group needs to be successful in achieving its goals, and if in the process of doing this it can differentiate itself in vocabulary, style, attitude, and clout, these characteristics will contribute to creating the unique-clan factor. All these characteristics and efforts can contribute to a positive attitude and thus to the group's effectiveness.

However, attempts to create special conditions can also have negative aspects. First, the group's uniqueness may make dealing with other parts of the organization more difficult. To the extent that the group is seen as getting more than its share, as having it easy, or as being aloof, jealousy can develop. This can create fiefdoms within an organization and thus be the cause of border wars and even diminish overall team synergism. Second, much of the uniqueness is usually associated with the leader. Groups whose uniqueness is attributable primarily to the leader may find themselves unable to function effectively in the larger organization after the leader has gone. Third, uniqueness can become a kind of personality cult. Fourth, it can be a contributor to the "not invented here" phenomenon, which causes duplication and blindness to alternatives. Therefore, the manager's challenge is to create that degree of unique-clan atmosphere which contributes to the group's effectiveness without destroying the effective operation of the larger organization.

The Impact of the Ego-Strength Factor

It is lonely on the frontiers of technology. There are many around who are quick to attack or to express negative feelings about one's efforts and chances for success. Often, professionals must persist over long periods of time when both the organization and their peers seem to be against them. Survival under these conditions requires ego strength, a belief in oneself.

Like the unique-clan factor, however, ego strength has a negative as well as a positive side. Early in my professional career, I had a manager who advised me to be wrong occasionally —he actually wanted me to propose wrong answers and make wrong decisions. I believe that he was reacting to my ego strength. He said that others found it difficult to be around me and to work with me because I was generally right—*right,* even when they could cite the reasons why I should be wrong. At that particular time, I was pushing a frontier; I needed that ego strength.

Over the years, I have had the opportunity to be around outstanding leaders in many fields, and being with them has often been uncomfortable. (This, incidentally, is the negative side of recruiting world-class scientists.) While generalizations are dangerous, frontier people tend to be dominant personalities. Too often, they run roughshod over others, are poor at listening to alternate approaches, and are impatient with fellow professionals who do not understand that they have "the answer." They are combative personalities who ignore or who express distaste for the necessary organizational policies and practices.

How, then, can managers create an environment that allows and even encourages the development of appropriate ego strength without developing unruly prima donnas who detract from rather than add to the effectiveness of the group? Recruiting people with personalities who may develop ego strength is the first step. One of the manager's initial acts with the group is to talk about the need and about how one develops it. It is also appropriate to reinforce ego strength by giving it attention. But here is where the danger comes in, for in reinforcing the ego strength, it may grow very rapidly; if one gets on the swelled-head track, almost everything tends to make it worse. So it is important to emphasize the fact that the organization is not a sandbox and constantly to reestablish the necessity of doing things within the system, of meeting the goals of the organization. As in the training of a child, it is sometimes important to pull in the reins and not allow the strong ego to play games in order to get power.

The Impact of the Personal Accomplishment Factor

In Chapter Six, I discussed the vitality cycle. In this cycle, accomplishment leads to a gain, which is a result of doing the right things. Accomplishment is a psychic income. Receiving it reinforces the individual's motivation and increases the probability of a repetition of success. It is necessary for the manager to make assignments in such a way as to set up an environment that supports this cycle. But the amount of risk, the amount of challenge that each individual can take, is unique. A good match of people and work can improve the opportunity for accomplishment and thus the effectiveness of the individual and of the group.

The Leader's Need for Control

Because of the insecurities and the risks associated with being a leader, there is a tendency for managers to stress control over those things which they manage. Thus, whatever previous need the person had for control is enhanced by the managerial role. If, as a result of experiences as a professional, the individual had built a strong, emotional tie with accomplishments, this would reinforce the need for control as a manager. Ownership of goals makes it hard to delegate them and to risk the fact that others may not carry them out as one wishes. The need is further worsened by the fact that the failure of those who report to the manager is the manager's failure. The manager's reputation rests on their performance. The result of a strong need for control will be a stifling of the freedoms of those being led. This means that the professional who works for such a manager will not have the chance to learn, to be creative, and to take risks needed for growth. A probable result will be a closed rather than an open managerial style. Typically, this manager will continue to pursue duties held as a professional, fail to delegate, fail to address real managerial duties, exhibit a lack of patience, use fear as a motivation technique, and play favorites (which is a way of trying to minimize risks by trusting those felt to be most loyal). Almost certainly, the professionals working for this manager will report a poor quality of work life and low respect for the professional.

With a story, I can show how the characteristics I have been describing support the need for control on the part of the leader. Typical professionals in R & D are self-managing. As professionals, they have control over their jobs, and they are dealing with science, which is generally predictable. As previously described, they also tend to be uncomfortable with interpersonal relations because these are uncontrollable. The person who has excelled at technology is now promoted to the new and strange responsibility of being a manager. Generally, the new manager is not aided in this transition by the organization. Training, which usually comes later, does not address those fears and needs which support managerial overcontrol. One can almost guarantee that a first typical experience as a manager will be to be called to an upper manager's office and asked to explain something that seems to have gone wrong. It may be an overrun of a budget, some professional's decision to leave the group, a technical failure, or a missed schedule. Usually, the new manager is caught off guard—and may not even know of the incident or subject. The lesson learned is that to be safe as a manager, one must be on top of everything. The manager must know all the answers! The natural result is to try to control things in order to know where everything stands. The next natural result is overcontrol. A second typical experience is to be asked to report the status of some technical work. Understanding that the development of those being managed and the needs of a professional argue for letting the professional tell the story, the inexperienced manager brings the professional to the meeting. After the meeting, the manager is called aside and told that the other management at the meeting would rather the manager had made the report. If this had been so, they would have felt free to talk about alternatives that they did not want to discuss in the presence of the professional. The pressure is, again, for control. I have seen this incident occur at the highest levels of technical management!

The indoctrination does not stop with the new manager. The pressures forcing the manager in the direction of control are numerous, and there is almost no counterpressure. Counterpressure, for balance, must come from the manager's own self-assurance and trust in the professionals that the manager leads. From these experiences the leader learns that one of the risks of being a manager is to be treated one way from above (expected to know details and be in control) and to be simultaneously expected to treat those whom one manages differently (give them freedom and the opportunity to learn). The challenge is for the manager to find the ways to make the job of managing fun despite these pressures and strains. One of the fun aspects is helping someone else develop and grow. Providing professionals with opportunities for development will be reinforced in management development programs but not often rewarded by upper management. Most of the measures, pressures, and rewards will tend to reinforce overcontrol.

Everyone's Need for a Participative Style

From the discussion of style, we have seen that the organization's and the individual's needs are for participation, in order to achieve healthy and effective operation, but that the forces of the organization are against it. As Cummings (1980,

226 **Managing Professionals in Research and Development**

Preface) says, only open management "encourages participative management and democratic leadership styles by concentrating on the worth, value, and dignity of the individual employee" and offsets the normal negatives inherent in any human being's (leader's) style, because participation makes the professional an owner of the results, someone who shares in the management. The organization needs participation in order to achieve its goals, which are to harness the power and creativity of professionals, who resent being managed. The individuals need participation in order to achieve a good match between their needs and capabilities and those of the organization. *Participation is one of the most necessary and effective concepts in the management of R & D and professionals.* Yet this does not mean that the manager and management must give up their responsibilities of managing. Too many managers have interpreted this need to mean that the absence of leadership and managing is the desired style, the desired goal, of the manager.

Participation means sharing, not giving up! Participation means delegating, but continuing to be interested and attentive, to follow up, and to measure results. Participation means risking not knowing every detail, risking not being in total control (no one ever is), and trusting that when others know that the group's reputation and success, as well as the manager's reputation, ride on their performance, they will rise to the challenge. Individual professionals will rise to higher achievements when allowed to participate in goal setting and decision making. Participation means establishing a style that radiates trust. *Trust* is a key word. When I study R & D groups that are not functioning properly, the characteristics that reflect the reasons for the problems are: a lack of mutual trust between professionals themselves and between the professionals and management, a lack of openness of communication, a lack of understanding of goals, a lack of commitment to goals, and a lack of mutual support. These characteristics will be negative in an ineffective group. These same characteristics will be positive in an effective, result-producing, vital group. Not only is trust related to participation, but the other factors are also. Openness of communication—between professionals and with management—is a characteristic of an organization in which participation is the style. In an organization in which they participate, professionals know and understand the goals. In an organization in which they do not, goal understanding and commitment are poor. Mutual support grows through sharing and participating.

International Aspects of Leadership Style

National cultures affect the appropriate style by setting up transcendent societal values and accepted behavioral patterns. Hofstede (1980, p. 42) notes that "Many of the differences in employee motivation, management styles, and organizational structures of companies throughout the world can be traced to differences in the collective mental programming of people in different national cultures." My basis in this book has been the U.S. culture. A few comments to demonstrate contrasts and dangers are appropriate. First, I want you to know my biases. I strongly favor having multinational organizations use nationals for all key management-leadership positions, because they understand the culture of the country. People on assignment from the United States and other countries should be temporary and in an advisory, not a management, role. There are exceptions, of course; these are often individuals who by experience have become international in their own right. This does not mean that foreigners are relegated to unimportant roles. One case from my experience was a U.S. technical manager assigned to IBM's LaGaude laboratory in France. I talked with this person before, during, and after his assignment. He had no managerial role except as adviser. As a result of involvement in meetings, he discovered that one issue affecting effectiveness and hampering local leadership was a constant reference to "they" as causes for problems, rules, and limits to freedom. The "they" was of course U.S. based management. His primary, and important, role turned out to be interpreting the intent, meaning, and goals of the technical leadership in the United States. This was a good role, but I am worried that often we come across as experts trying to tell others how to do things. We must increase our sensitivity to their cultures and needs and study their ways to find the creative adaptation of multinational managerial concepts. This does not mean that I am a proponent of importing the Japanese or the German way. These ways work in their home territory because of the support they get from the national culture. Our country's culture may not supply the necessary supporting outlooks and beliefs. With this a background, here are some comments:

• In discussing management styles and training of managers in different countries, we need more than the generalizations that are currently popular. Hunt (1981, p. 62) suggests, "Such generalities as 'The French hate MBO,' 'Family is vital to Norwegians,' 'Success in Asia is family first,' 'Organizational loyalty is the clue to Japan,' and 'the British are individualistic with low commitment to work organizations' are all supportable—but we need more." Experience and studies have brought us these generalizations, but they only provide a surface clue to differences. In another article, Harris (1982) talks of the need for consensus, the deliberate solicitation of other points of view as essential in managing where more than one country's culture is involved. Experimentation can and should lead to new forms of participatory management that meld the good points of several cultures.

• For a U.S. multinational organization, our country's management style tends to be dominant. This is not in itself bad if the Americans understand that it is American, listen to the feelings it elicits, and adapt to special needs. I remember one Englishman, a technical leader, who, after his experience in the United States, felt that our style was a powerful tool for improving effectiveness; he went back to England with a personal mission to infuse our style into English industry. So our reaction should not be that all we do abroad is wrong. When in the Philippines, leading a management-development program for a multinational U.S. company, I had a cross-cultural experience that underscores the need to be open and observant. We had a role-play exercise in the program where the manager was to practice coaching and where the employee had a legitimate complaint that the manager had failed to keep his end of the "contract." For those steeped in our culture, "getting the manager" in this case was fun. For those from India, the exercise did not come out at all well. In our discussion, we learned that in India the employee does not let the manager fail. This was not a realistic example when seen through their cultural eyes, and when playing the employee, they were unable to confront the manager. (The Spring 1986 issue of *Human Resource Management,* which reports on a conference on international human resource management, is one of the first sources of information on this subject; see Tichy, 1986.)

• U.S. decisions, which reflect our practice and style, can sometimes put organizations outside our country in uncomfortable positions. Usually, the U.S. manager is not even aware of the results. During my IBM experience, I spent an afternoon receiving a lecture from a vice president of IBM France. He went to great lengths to explain to me that because of our technical leadership, he had been left with three ex-directors of the French laboratory. Each had been moved out after a time in the position that was appropriate in the United States. The French company's management, however, had no viable positions for these three leaders at appropriate levels and status commensurate with their pay and experience. I had not made the decisions, but I felt responsible for the lack of understanding on the part of U.S. management of the impact in France.

• Another potential for differences, even conflict, in cultures comes again from an IBM experience. French engineers in the laboratory in LaGaude discussed their feelings openly with me one afternoon. What was bothering them was that several of them had recently gone to an alumni gathering at the École de Polytechnique. They had discovered they had less in common with their former classmates than they had with their U.S. peers or with engineers in IBM Germany or IBM UK. They were worried and sensitive to the fact that their work in IBM was alienating them from their own culture. This is but one level of a problem that can become even more severe. Members of the management team in a specific country, on the rise in responsibility in a multinational organization, come at some point to feel that they must make a decision between country and company. They reason that if they choose to go up in the company with the requirement to work in other countries, they will eventually be citizens of no country. One friend of mine in Holland chose to leave IBM at that point; he joined a Dutch company, KLM Royal Dutch Airlines. He was motivated to grow and had the talent to take on increased responsibilities, but for him the break with his country would have been too great a price to pay for increased pay and responsibility.

I have just begun to scratch the surface of an important topic that could easily become a chapter or a book. Researchers and practitioners have only begun to gather the data we need, especially in the management of R & D where technical direction often spans country borders and the applications of technology definitely cross country borders.

Summary

- For an organization to function effectively, there must be open communication between all members. The leader-manager's style can foster communication or block it. The styles of professionals can shape both interpersonal and upward communication.
- One's style comes from education, experiences, watching others, and it is seen—and is effective or not—in context of the organization's culture. The components of style include values and beliefs, self-image, appearance and communications approach, and our interpretation of our roles. Style would not be evident in a vacuum, since it is seen with respect to a background. The background is the environment, climate, or culture of the organization—as overlaid and influenced by the country's culture.
- Relationships, the ability to work together or not toward shared goals, are affected by the values of the individuals in the organization as well as by the values of and the climate of the organization. Manager's actions, which are based on self-image and style, interpret and shape the work environment. Not only is style seen in context of the organization, it is also shaped by the organization's mission, goals, and expectations—all of which become the norms, the unwritten rules for behavior.

- Classical books on management classify styles in several different ways. Two-dimensional grids were discussed briefly; variations in the amount of attention to people as opposed to jobs (or in our case, technology) and variation in the amount of direction, relative autonomy, provide a picture of the range of possible styles for managers. Generally, for R & D, appropriate styles are on the participative end of classifications as opposed to the authoritarian end and tend to provide high contact between leader and professional.

- Managers can inspire through example, communication, actions, and personal chemistry. Some of these ways are under the more or less direct control of the manager, while some can only be influenced through organizational design and culture.

- There are things the manager can do that tend to influence the effectiveness of the individual positively. These include: nurturing and caring; attention and recognition; careful establishment of a group difference, a unique-clan approach; supporting ego-strength development; and setting up the work environment to support personal achievement, accomplishment, and individual development.

- Professionals who become managers develop leadership styles that are influenced by their prior experiences, their personalities, their needs for psychic income, and organizational pressures. For those professionals or managers who are pushing back frontiers, the lack of support is creatively offset by ego strength. However, experiences as a professional and emotional attachment to goals often mean that the professional turned leader tries to maintain control. These forces are so strong that there is a tendency to overcontrol—with few forces supporting the other side, the need for professional autonomy and freedom.

- Establishing participation as the management style is most important in R & D management because of the needs of the individuals and the nature of the work. Participation means sharing, not giving up the manager's role of leadership. Participation in R & D is especially important because it assists the professional in gaining control of work both strategically and operationally. The professional's ability to control work is one of the individual's measures of personal professionalism.

• National cultures provide a kind of programming of individual behavior and values that can be compatible with or in conflict with organizational cultures. It is particularly important for leaders in multinational organizations to be sensitive to the origin of styles and to their impact on other countries' cultures. Openness, listening, and experimentation are important in creating new innovative blends of the best management concepts from several cultures.

PART III

▼▼▼▼▼▼▼

Strategies and Systems
for Long-Term Success

The impact of leadership on the direction and success of an organization depends on the manager's choice of strategies and systems. In this part, the reader is introduced to several systems and is assisted in gaining an understanding of how to design organizations and implement different structures. For example, performance management, the topic of Part Two, is explored here in terms of building a culture that supports the manager through effective measurement and reward of achievement.

The leader's challenge starts with building a team and is quickly followed by the need to maintain it and enhance its capability. Pursuing these tasks requires understanding how to recruit, why people join an organization and choose to stay with it, and how individuals develop. Managers match people and work. The goal is to gain congruence between the needs and capabilities of the individual and the needs and capabilities of the organization. Accomplishing this goal requires an ability to implement and manage change and is one of the most difficult aspects of the manager's role.

Chapter 9

Recruiting, Developing,
and Retaining Professionals

For an organization to build a research or a development team, it must make itself attractive to potential employees who have and can bring the right educational preparation and personal characteristics. It must therefore begin its recruitment drive with meaningful communications about its nature and mission, including information about its unique characteristics, culture, and work opportunities, about who thrives in the organization, and about how it satisfies its people's needs. Since universities are the primary source of recruitment, the organization must build relationships with faculties and with university placement offices. Organizational information is sometimes best communicated through former students and informal professional networks, and sometimes through brochures and printed matter; which communication medium works the best depends upon the organization's prominence, its technology, and its relative abilities to attract a Ph.D. for research or an M.S. engineer for the development team. Recruiting begins by getting the organization's image out where the potential employee can see it, assess it, and be attracted by it.

Individuals are attracted by different aspects of an organization. The relative importance they attach to the several aspects depends on their personal goals, expectations from work, and stage of life and/or career. Scientists are usually attracted

235

first by the nature of the work itself, the freedom to pursue their own research interests, and the people with whom they will associate. Engineers are often attracted by the opportunity to join an emerging area of technology and an organization key to that breakthrough. Sometimes a professional is attracted by geography, especially if it allows the pursuit of a hobby, is near family or potential family, and/or provides relief from the pressures of work. The most important aspect of successful recruiting is honesty; it is wrong to give the feeling that one will be free to pursue one's own interests, for example, when in reality the organization must impose restraints. Unfortunately, what the recruit hears is often what the recruit wants to hear. The organization's representatives must therefore bend over backwards to be sure that the negatives are heard at a time when they are trying to emphasize the positives. A failure to do this leads to unfulfilled expectations, poor morale, and unnecessary turnover.

When the contact has been made and interest generated, the screening, selection, and indoctrination start simultaneously. It is necessary to ensure that the psychological work contract (the expectations on both sides) is clearly understood and that the best-qualified person is selected in the fairest manner. One of the challenges is to assess the person's present competence, ability to achieve in the organization's environment, and ability to learn and grow. For example, the organization needing immediate expertise will often opt for the current expert, but this may not be the person who can grow and find a good match in the organization over the long run. Once the person has been chosen, the offer is made in a way designed to gain an acceptance. Competition for good professionals is so keen that this part of the process is very important. Whether the offer is accepted depends not only on the nature of the offer but also on the contacts made during the person's visit to the facility and on the indoctrination that began at the time of the recruiting interviews.

An organization's ability to attract, develop, and retain professionals depends on its environmental support of the individual. Increasingly, individuals are making career choices based on their assessment of and experience with the presence or lack of QPL in the organizational environment. An organization that supports the growth and development of its people has a better chance of attracting and retaining outstanding employees than one that does not. But even more important, policy and environmental support for individual development have an effect on the effectiveness of the organization in the long run. Typical professionals will be with the organization through several assignments and probably several careers. Continued effective matching of individual and work depends on environmental elements like dual ladders and the support for capability development and career evolution. Support is needed for personal, professional, and technical growth. It is better to avoid obsolesence and burnout by building vitality than to try to correct these problems after they occur, yet revitalization, refurbishment, and retraining steps are possible and necessary.

The organization is led by managers, and many R & D organizations have failed to put proper emphasis on their selection and training. Training is especially crucial for professionals because that performance which causes the professional to be noticed, and thus considered for management, is often not the type needed from a leader. Support in making this transition is crucial to organizational effectiveness. Many organizations fail to state what they expect of managers, leaving the managers to guess about the expectations. Since these guesses are often wrong, this leads to frustrated managers and makes them ineffective as leaders. Training can help establish expectations. Above all, it should provide a conceptual framework for managing. Thus, the manager's early training should focus on concepts, roles, and processes; later, it must cover the development of specific skills, such as interviewing, and must provide training for senior leaders on the organization's philosophy and on their responsibilities both inside and outside the organization.

Attracting Professionals

Professionals join an organization because they are attracted to it (its mission, culture, and people), to the work itself, and often to the geographical location.

Von Glinow (1985, pp. 196–201) defines four cultures,

each having different attractions for the professional: "The Apathetic Culture . . . with its lack of concern for people and its weak expectations regarding their performance . . . typically offer[s] high job security. The Caring Culture has weak performance expectations of its professionals . . . is highly concerned about its employees. [It] will attempt to attract professionals by playing up the human side of the company through its management practices." In the "Exacting Culture managerial leverage is used to help professionals increase team output. . . . Strategies used to attract professionals are aimed at those who are success-oriented or performance-driven." In the "Integrative Culture . . . high concern for people is matched with strong performance expectations. . . . The Integrative Culture generally offers well-above-average compensation and benefits to professionals . . . offers significant job content and career-oriented rewards" to attract professionals. Obviously, in this book I am talking about the integrative culture, the fourth management system.

Professionals, unlike most support people in an R & D organization, come from the national labor market. Technicians and administrative people usually come from the local labor market. This means that the organization's reputation (its image) must be big enough, bold enough, and unique enough to be seen at a distance; the exception to this might be a small laboratory which is located in a university town and which gets the majority of its professionals from that university. Thus, large organizations that have gained name recognition as the result of selling a product to the public or being in the news regularly have an initial recruiting advantage. But these initial advantages of recognition are not enough; they must be supplemented and enhanced. Sometimes they must even be overcome because they have established a negative picture, as, for example, in the case of news coverage resulting from suspected wrongdoing or technical failures.

Here are some of the ways that an R & D organization can get name recognition and become sufficiently known that potential professional employees will respond to recruiting efforts:

• Advertise nationally, both for general and for specific

image building. The first should be done in widely circulated magazines; the second, in magazines read by professionals in fields that the organization needs.

• Operate on the basis that recruiting is a year-round business, not something that is turned off and on at will. Understand that it is serious, for there is no better way to affect the quality of employees than by recruiting quality employees.

• Support their professionals in professional activities, speeches, presentations of scientific papers, publications in professional journals, and occasional public lectures. Appropriate activities range from support of high school science fairs and career days to presence at national professional meetings and to dramatic events and presentations at EPCOT and at world's fairs.

• Distribute news releases to the press and alumni publications concerning the achievements of individual professionals, technological breakthroughs, and unique product, system, or service announcements.

• Establish an ongoing relationship with those universities which are potential sites for recruiting. This can range from grants, equipment gifts, scholarships and faculty research support, guest lectureships, and faculty loans to participation in university events and to deliberate cultivation of placement-office people and members of the faculty and administration. Appointing an employed graduate as the representative to the university and hiring professors as consultants are techniques often used for promoting these relationships.

• Publish and distribute recruiting brochures and literature to universities (and especially placement offices) that describe the work in the organization and the types of careers that professionals can find. Recruiting brochures have a greater effect in the recruitment of engineers and scientists below the Ph.D. level than they probably do at the Ph.D. level. O'Toole (1977, p. 64) observes that "Paradoxically, as the investment value of education slumps, the importance of its credentialing function soars"; thus, part of the message in these brochures and in direct contacts must cover the organization's openness to growth for noncredentialed people and the relative class differences, if any, accorded degree categories.

One aspect of attraction over which R & D organizations

have little control is the current interest in their particular mission or field. For example, it is hard to recruit for automobile designers when the nation is intent on putting a person on the moon, and it is hard to recruit for large chemical organizations when the new-fibers era has given way to the computer era—but organizations can work to make their particular missions sound exciting and challenging. Organizations also have little control over the current public sentiment about bigness versus smallness; for some time it was considered right to join big corporations because of their facilities, monetary support for work, strength of benefits programs, and things like that, but currently the public seems to be favoring small organizations. Big organizations are counterattacking by emphasizing their opportunities for internal entrepreneurs and their extensive support for career growth. Management must be cognizant of these shifts in popularity of work and must then use them or offset them, as necessary, in order to build the image that will currently attract potential employees.

The Impact of the Nature of Work on Recruiting

For the individual professional to have a good person/job fit, the work itself must be attractive. It may be attractive because it matches the extensive educational preparation, knowledge, skills, and interests of the individual or because of its mystery, its challenge, or its being on the currently hot frontier. Or it may be attractive because of goal congruence; that is, the work's and the individual's goals coincide. This would occur, for instance, if a research scientist's goal were to discover a new circuit element and an organization's goal were to find a faster electronic switching device.

It is also necessary to fit the characteristics of the recruits to the role needs of the work. This type of matching requires that there be an understanding of the role needs. For example, Roberts and Fusfeld (1981, p. 22) have identified five behavioral functions critical in the innovative process—"*idea generation, entrepreneuring or championing, project leading, gatekeeping,* and *sponsoring or coaching*"—and have paired them with significantly different personal characteristics.

Therefore, one part of the recruiting effort must be to project an image about the work that will attract the individual, and another part must be to develop an understanding of the different behavioral skills needed and the characteristics of people who generally have these skills. On the college campus, the latter can be done only by someone who is or was personally engaged in the kind of work that will cause the fit. In the work environment, it can be done by showing the recruit what actually happens and by discussing what these people like to do in behavioral terms. Building an attraction with the work itself is one of the strengths of cooperative programs, summer employment, and postdoctoral appointments, for all of these devices give the individual an opportunity to experience the work and determine whether, in fact, it fits. Often, however, managers are not careful about the type of work given temporary employees, and sometimes the work that can be given is not exciting because of that employee's inexperience. It is possible to turn off the potential employee with the work experience if it is not carefully designed.

The Impact of the Presence of a World-Class Professional

Individuals attract individuals. There is an accepted principle among scientists that working in the presence of someone who has made a technical breakthrough increases the probability that you will make a breakthrough. Building on this concept, it is important to work with someone who, because of his or her successes, is important in the field in which you wish to work. It therefore follows that an organization that has attracted professionals who lead in their fields will find it easier to recruit others who wish to become leaders.

This sounds simpler than it is. First, to attract the world-class scientist, one must identify the individual. If the person has been recognized with a Nobel prize or has made a significant invention, it is easy. For the great majority of world-class professionals, however, there are differences of opinion about who is and who is not one. Second, world-class professionals are often people with strong egos (which are necessary to work on a frontier), personally overcommitted, individualists, and perhaps wild ducks. Fitting them into the organization may be difficult or prove impossible. One of my clients attracted such a person, and in order to pay him enough and to give him enough prestige, made the mistake of giving him a key managerial post. The person never fit into the organizational culture, hated managerial duties and did not perform them, and was most often away meeting other commitments. A mutually agreed upon separation was the only answer for both parties.

The Necessity for Continued Relations with Universities

The source for the majority of professional employees is the university. The recruiting efforts of the R & D organization therefore depend on building bridges with universities. Probably the most important bridges are built between individuals, although these must be supplemented with financial and other relationships. People in universities seem to prefer continuing (and to some extent, unchanging) relationships. Perhaps they are confused or thrown off guard by the rapidity of change of people in industrial organizations. I remember talking with a representative of Cornell University years ago, when I was with IBM. This person was complaining because IBM's system at the time was to assign university relations to the local branch sales manager. In that era, people in these jobs turned over in less than two years. The complaint was that IBM kept changing its representative and that the university was always having to get acquainted with someone new.

The organization that can find the right combination of informal and formal ongoing relationships that make the university representatives feel that the organization is not just interested in the product, the graduate, opens important doors. From the perspective of the university, the balance between relationships of quality and harassment is tenuous. Naturally, the university prefers financial support without strings; university representatives are very reluctant to enter into relationships that have any real or implied commitments on their part to do something for the organization in the future. Another successful, but potentially risky, area of relationships is the use of former graduates; if these people flock to the campus in an uncontrolled fashion, this is seen as harassment, but if these people build personal relations in an orchestrated and coordinated fashion over time, the results can be very good. One of the results of such contact is the identification of potential recruits several years before they finish studies. Faculty loan programs, in which the organization loans the university one of its scientists to teach a subject area for which the university is having difficulty finding the right person, build a substantive and positive relationship. But this loan program can have its danger if the individual seems to be teaching a parochial point of view; such would be the case when the company's products are the only examples used in the class. Hiring faculty as consultants can also build bridges; but again, it must be done with care. Despite the dangers, the payoff of good relations is important to both the university and the organization.

The Impact of Geographical Location

Professionals are recruited from a nationwide market thus one of their opportunities upon entering the world of work is to choose where to locate. It is a time when they can choose not to move because of roots in a particular area or perhaps to move in order to be near a potential partner. It is a time in their lives when they are free to move, usually unencumbered with houses and possessions, and when their dreams of living where they can sail or ski or be in the great outdoors or pursue some hobby have a possibility of being accommodated.

Geographical location thus becomes an important issue in recruiting. In fact, some laboratory organizations, uniquely situated in an attractive place, have been able because of their geographical location to attract people at lower than the going salary level. While paying a price for geography is not the point here, being able to recruit someone whom you could otherwise not recruit is the point. In recruiting, therefore, if you have an attractive location, flaunt it!

What can an organization not located in a desirable spot do? Try to find alternate attractions. For example, being in the New York City suburbs does not do much for one's suntanning interests, but it can sure attract someone interested in art, music, and drama. Being in Athens, Georgia, does not do much for the ski enthusiast, but being in a university town does have cultural advantages, and a small town attracts those who wish to avoid big cities. The type of climate can also affect where you recruit. If your operation is in Tucson, Arizona, it may not look attractive to someone in Boulder, Colorado, but it will sure look good to the person who has suffered through the gloom of southern New York State, at Cornell.

A Creed for Honest Recruiting

Because recruiting the best talent for R & D is a highly competitive process, some organizations and some recruiters become overzealous in selling the benefits of working for their organization. Typically, large laboratories need to hire hundreds of people with specialized educations each year, and so they must interview thousands. Organizations often end up with fewer than they wanted to hire and carry a continuing set of unfilled openings. I do not believe that recruiters and managers who interview either distort recruiting intentionally or have a real understanding of the impact on a career of a slight distortion in information. Nor are they aware that the applicant wants to believe the best and filters out the negatives. Both parties are biased in favor of the positives. Selling each other sometimes outweighs the desire to establish the basis for a good person/organization and person/ job match, the beginning of indoctrination. Selling each other can get in the way of really defining the psychological work contract. The psychological contract was described in Chapter Three, and its establishment will be described in this chapter, but for our use here suffice it to say that it is the internalized agreement the individual has about what it is necessary to invest in work and what will be taken home from that investment.

Some of the mistakes in recruiting and interviewing include:

- Failing to really listen for the applicant's needs and desires
- Doing too much of the talking
- Overemphasizing the positives

- Selling too hard
- Not discussing the negatives
- Responding to questions from the insider's perspective without understanding the applicant's perspective
- Talking down the competitive organization
- Failing to take sufficient time to explore the potential for acquaintance between the individual and the organization and to start indoctrination that can contribute to compatibility and effectiveness

Failures in the recruiting and indoctrination processes contribute to low morale and increased turnover. This does not mean that making 100 percent perfect choices is possible, but it does mean that proper attention will minimize the negatives. Some distortions are so subtle that even an experienced interviewer will fail to recognize them. I remember a case where an applicant asked a lot of questions about the policy and benefits having to do with illness. The interviewer responded with the facts from the company's perspective, never catching on to the true question. The true question was, "Does the company dismiss for illness?" The answer was, "Of course not!" Later, when this employee was sick, she felt that normal attention from her manager —phone calls and visits to inquire about how she was doing—was directed at building a case for firing her. She complained to higher management. Apparently, she had the idea that they would dismiss her for illness, which must have been based on experience prior to this company or on the experience of friends. Dismissal for illness was the opposite of the company's policy and/or intent.

The most typical failure in research organization recruiting is to distort the freedom that the applicant will have in continuing the pursuit of personal research interests. Typically, the fresh Ph.D. is closely attached to the research base for the dissertation and desires to continue in that vein, especially if the area has not been explored because of lack of funds, time, or facilities at the university. The recruiter, trying to sell, emphasizes the freedom that will exist in the new organization to continue this research. In the worst case, the impression made is simply that the locus of the individual's work will change. There is a real failure to talk about or transmit an understanding of the constraints imposed by the mission and goals of the organization, such as limitations regarding the time and energy that can be devoted to personal projects. All good research organizations do provide some time for the pursuit of personal research projects, but all good organizations also have organizational missions and goals to pursue. The distortion comes both from applicants hearing what they want to hear and from the interviewer trying to sell too hard.

To minimize the negatives in the recruiting process and to maximize the probability of establishing a positive psychological contract, here is a sample recruiting creed:

- In a fair and balanced fashion, we will discuss (1) both negatives and positives about our work climate and human resource policies and (2) the nature of the constraints surrounding the work.
- We will ensure that every interviewer representing the organization is trained in the process both of representing the organization and of listening to and responding to the needs and interests of the applicant. "The prospective employee's first encounter with the organization is a major opportunity to confront him or her with the business beliefs of the firm" (Posner, Kouzes, and Schmidt, 1985, p. 306). We will ensure that interviewers sample the applicant's understanding of the organization's values and beliefs and begin the process of building a compatibility of values and beliefs by talking knowledgeably about organizational culture.
- We will ensure that subsequent interviewers do not just cover the same ground with the applicant but really supplement each other so that all aspects of work and interests are covered.
- We will struggle to make the psychological contract about work as explicit and well-defined as is possible and will ensure that both the new employee and the manager are agreeing to the same implied contract.
- We will take the time necessary for the applicant and, in the case of geographical relocation, the spouse to become really

acquainted with the organization and its community before getting the signature on the offer.

The Selection Process

The selection process begins with the manager determining the nature of the need and specifying the qualifications the applicant should have. It is followed by some type of external search. This may include local or national advertising, interview days in remote or local cities, the use of an external recruiting organization, and university campus contacts. Usually, for campus recruiting and for interviewing an experienced applicant in a remote location, the gathering process occurs at the same time as the initial screening. It is simply good economics to do it this way, and it conforms to expected practices.

The next step is the preliminary, or paper, screening of applications and résumés. At this stage, there is an attempt to separate those who are obviously not qualified from those with good potential as applicants. Preliminary screening eliminates wasting effort, time, and money on applicants who are out of the normal range for consideration.

The next step consists of on-site interviewing, intensive screening, early indoctrination, and the establishing of relationships. At this stage, there should be an effort to get to know the applicant and for the applicant to get to know the organization, to make what is said about the organization believable, to understand its work, its climate, and some individuals. The primary effort should be to establish whether or not there can be a good match between that person and the organization, the work climate, and the specific work. This means (1) exploring the applicant's needs and capabilities and (2) describing to the fullest the needs and capabilities of the organization. Sufficient time should be taken in this process to ensure that all questions on both sides are answered. It is important, too, to develop a strategy for interviewing that ensures that sequential interviews explore different aspects and do not repeat the same questions, for technically trained people normally explore technical knowledge; thus, if interviewers are not trained and this tendency is not managed, repetition will result. While it may seem supplemental to screening, it is important to make sure that personal contacts are made at this time, since in the case of a later offer these personal contacts will often contribute to a positive response to the offer.

For those who would like the process pictured, see Miller (1979, p. 79). For those who desire more information on the conduct of interviews, the types of questions to use and not use, see Fear (1978), Drake (1972), and McCulloch (1981). McCulloch provides special warnings about the legality of questions and practices in today's business world, where pressure groups, the courts, and legislators audit the interviewer's actions.

Choosing the Interviewers and Contacts

In the previous section, I alluded to the need to build a personal relationship with the applicant. While this is most useful in continuing the offer and hiring process, it is also a necessary part of the rejection process. My first graduation came during World War II. Engineers were scarce and in high demand. I could have had as many offers as I took interviews. Our placement director was interested in making the interviewing day worthwhile for each of the company representatives, so she asked us to fill interview schedules, to add our names to create larger numbers. This resulted in my signing up for a Gulf Oil interview, with little real interest in the company. That interviewer listened, and in a short interview I felt that we really got to know each other. He understood that I was not interested in Gulf at that time, but he assured me that if I ever was interested in Gulf, they were interested in me. The quality interview and the quality organization leave friends, not enemies, behind.

Choosing the interviewers—the representatives of the organization—is very important. For the applicant, these people are the organization. The interviewers, whether professionals or managers, should be chosen with the following criteria in mind:

- The type of initial impression they make and whether it is representative of the organization. The interviewers should be genuine in representing the quality of their relationship to the organization and their excitement about what they do.

- Their communications abilities—both in representing the organization and in listening to the applicant.
- Their compatibility with the type of applicant. For example, it is desirable to use professionals and managers whose own work is similar to the work the applicant might do in the organization.
- The need to select interviewers who represent a range of personalities—so that each applicant can find someone in the interview process with whom it is easy to build a relationship.
- The need to cover human resource issues and concerns. This usually requires using a representative of the human resource function.
- The need to live in the legally restrictive world of equal opportunity—and thus to avoid certain questions and any actual or appearance of bias in the interview process. This reinforces the need for training interviewers.

Not only is the selection of interviewers important, but the style and locus of contacts is also important. I can remember screening processes after which my colleagues and I realized that we had succeeded in hiring the right person as the result of some unnoticed or unplanned event: for example, choosing the right combination of people to go to lunch with the interviewee at a place where the interviewee felt secure in bringing up a sensitive question or concern that the individual was not secure enough to ask on company property; or having a qualified person take the spouse around the community to look at housing and schools or to pursue some specific family need; or deciding on the spur of the moment to hold the interviewee for another day to meet specific people. On one occasion, the most important event was an apparently chance meeting with the large organization's top executive, who welcomed the applicant and indicated that he knew she was there that day. Imagine the impression the fact that the top person knew of her presence made on the applicant! In another case, a manager in the process of the interview aborted

the planned interview schedule and responded immediately to
things the interviewee had said, which represented interests not
previously known, and this made the difference. When conducted by the right team, interviewing is a dynamic adaptive
process in its best form.

Selection Interviews

Good selection interviews are based on planning by both
the applicant and the organization's interviewer. Good interviewers demonstrate early in the interview that they have done
their homework; they have read the résumé and the application
and do not intend to spend time asking those same questions
over again. Good interviews start with making the applicant comfortable. Often this means that the manager or professional
should choose the informal setting rather than sitting behind the
fortress desk, which creates a physical barrier that must be overcome. I have a strong bias in favor of one-on-one interviews,
although some organizations have successfully used group interviews. The danger of group interviews is vivid to me: An unini-
tiated, scared, fresh graduate, I was once confronted in a campus
interview by three people alternately asking questions! I felt like
I was being accused of some wrongdoing.

It is important for the interviewer to have a plan, but not a
detailed script to follow, and for the interviewer to give undi-
vided attention to the applicant. In another personal experience,
I had traveled two hours by plane to get to an on-site interview.
The interview took place in an office, and a minimum of three
other people were present the whole time, all the while carrying
on nonrelated conversations. Despite a large salary offer, I did
not join that organization. The interviewer should be a catalyst
for good open communication. Often this means sharing some
personal experience, letting the pause of silence be filled by the
applicant, or allowing some diversion from plan that increases the
applicant's comfort. In following a plan, the interviewer should
guide but not dominate the conversation. This is a difficult balance. On the one hand, the interviewer must get the data necessary to make the hiring choice, and on the other, the interviewer

must answer the applicant's questions. The psychological work contract must be discussed and a meeting of the minds assured. This means learning what psychic incomes the applicant needs from work, learning what the applicant feels that he or she can contribute, and discussing whether there is a probability of a match between the individual, the culture, and the work. The interview should be closed with the applicant understanding where he or she is in the process and when the information will come about rejection or offer. The interview must be documented with sufficient information, gleaned in the interview, on which to base a choice, but with care to ensure that no defamatory or illegal statements are made.

Making the Choice, the Offer, and Gaining an Acceptance

The manager has the prime responsibility for making the choice, determining which of the candidates should be offered employment. Usually the human resource function assists, but it is best if their role is one of counsel. This ensures that the manager wants the new professional and has a stake in having the applicant be successful. This positive motivation can help in ensuring that there is real attention paid to indoctrination and the match of the person and work.

The choice should be based on as factual a foundation as possible. Thus, education, research interests, previous experience, and the individual's input about goals and work desires are all important parts of the decision. However, there are intuitive aspects of the hiring decision that cannot and should not be denied. One of these has to do with the manager's and other professionals' assessments of the compatibility of the proposed new personality with those of the group. This judgment gets into the chemistry of interpersonal relationships and is an art, not a science. Yet compatibility is an important aspect in achieving effectiveness. Another part of the intuitive process is understanding the motivations of the applicant. The question is, are these motivations compatible with the goals and climate of our organization? Another important assessment is understanding how strongly the individual wants to work for this organization. Compatibility with the community and the geography are also important assessments. However, despite all this complexity, today's manager can expect to have someone look at the decision and judge whether it was fair. The decision must be defensible. Unfortunately, this can pressure the weak manager into making a decision favoring the applicant who is most defensible on paper but may not have the best potential. It is in this area that the manager needs assistance from the human resource people.

The offer must be specific, and it is usually made with a form letter prepared with legal advice. Ideally, it should be signed by the manager, by the prime contact with the applicant, and by the person for whom the new professional will work; hopefully, these are one and the same person. The offer letter covers the financial and legal aspects of the bond with the organization. These are important. As discussed in Chapter Three, the psychological contract is also important, and it is in the interviewing, in discussions about assignments, and in early indoctrination that it is formed. (It will be addressed again in Chapter Twelve, where matching people and work is the chief topic.)

Communications Integrity and Promptness

Many a good relationship between person and organization has been lost as the result of not communicating well and promptly. The individual entering the world of work has a schedule within which to make a decision. Ideally, the individual would like to have all the possible choices at one time to make the decision about which offer to accept. The organization has a schedule and, ideally, the manager would like to have all the qualified possible applicants on the desk at the same time. Neither of these ideals can be totally met. Things have a tendency to happen in sequence, and often the offer one has been waiting for comes in after the choice has been made, or the applicant you have been waiting for comes to your attention after the choice has been made. All this puts a premium on good, prompt, and complete communications. Both the applicant and the organization should communicate clearly about their time frame for decision. This should be part of the offer letter, in the case of the organization. The time for the applicant to establish the time frame is at the close out of the screening interview.

Communications integrity requires that what is said be real and be specific to that individual applicant. Many organizations process so many applicants that they use form letters for communicating with applicants. This is not in itself wrong, but it puts a burden on the signator to make sure that the form letter fits the conditions. One hears stories of applicants receiving two conflicting pieces of correspondence from an organization in the same mail; at worst, these are a rejection and an offer, and it has happened! The key seems to be to establish one person—hopefully the potential manager, and preferably someone the applicant has met—as the contact with the offeree. All correspondence, however trivial it may seem (such as a request for an additional fact or scheduling a medical exam), should be routed through this key contact. Management should ensure that all communications have been read in context and have integrity.

As a part of communications integrity, one should be sensitive to the applicant's necessity to make commitments between the time the offer is accepted and the time the applicant reports for work and the resultant need for frequent contact during what may be an extended period. My own processing as an applicant for IBM, way back in 1952, can still be remembered as an almost serious misfire. I was given an offer in April. I accepted it, resigned my position with Columbia University, and searched for a home in the new community. I committed to the purchase of a home and a mortgage. The time for leaving Columbia, early June, was approaching and I had heard nothing from IBM since April. I finally called and "forced" commitment on a start date. There was a serious communications gap. Only after joining the company did I discover that IBM had actually considered withdrawing my offer, and many others, during the period between offer acceptance and reporting. They had instituted one of their periodic "hiring freezes." Managers with a longer view and a strong ethical sense had triumphed, convincing others that the commitment to the employee should be honored, short of real disaster. Many years later I had the opportunity to interview people being laid off by Rockwell, and among them were newly hired people who had just relocated and reported for work, only to find out that they had been laid off. Here again was a case of failure to communicate during a critical period for the newly hired and for the companies involved.

Indoctrination: Learning the Ropes and Becoming a Member

One's first work experience as a professional can shape one's work attitudes and determine one's relative success for a lifetime. In years of investigating open doors, grievances taken to a very high level of management, I discovered that the roots of performance difficulties were often in the early relationships with work. Indoctrination, the process of introducing the individual to the work culture, work expectations, fellow employees, and the work itself are very important in establishing a high-quality fit between the person and the job. If the first fit is a good one, the individual experiences the gain (the psychic income) and establishes a positive outlook toward work. If the first fit is a poor one, it reinforces fears and suspicions that work is bad and unfulfilling.

One of the worst practices in indoctrination can be used as an example. I have seen it many places. The new manager says hello and hands the new professional a stack of papers and manuals to read, saying something like, "Until you have read these, you don't know enough to do anything around here." Consequently, the first experience in the world of work is boredom and loneliness; it is a put-down for this person, who has invested what seems a lifetime, learning knowledge and skills to apply to work. The first experience is thus nonfulfilling and has no psychic income. Contrast this with a manager who spends personal time, most of the first several days, with the individual. And contrast it with the manager who says something like, "You bring a fresh point of view, and that is valuable to us. For your first few weeks I want you to make notes of everything you see us doing which you do not understand, which you question because of something you know, or which looks stupid,

odd, or old-fashioned," and then adds, "I want you to talk
these over with me each morning."

In addition to getting acquainted with the work and gaining some positive reinforcement early in the work experience, it
is necessary for the professional to get in touch with the environment, climate, and culture. This is learning the ropes, getting
to know what the beliefs, values, and goals are. Getting to know
what the expectations are and how things get done in this organization is also part of this important experience—and this,
too, happens by encouraging the new entrant to have a questioning attitude. Much of the learning about environment comes
from informal talks. So it is important to have co-workers take
time out to get acquainted and chat about their experiences.
For those who would like to learn more about this topic, I recommend *The Ropes to Skip and the Ropes to Know: Studies in
Organizational Behavior* (Ritti and Funkhouser, 1977).

One of the more successful ways of helping the young
professional get started is to pair the professional off with a
senior professional. This can provide someone who is constantly
present to answer the myriad questions, and it can lower the
threshold for asking them, since asking the manager may be
tough and the manager may not be readily available. Secret
work poses an additional challenge to the indoctrination process, for often the new professional must spend nine months
outside the fence because of lack of government security clearance. Unless there is special attention paid to arranging interesting nonclassified work and unless the insiders go out of their
way to get acquainted and talk, this first nine months is almost
certainly demotivating. Assigning a senior professional the responsibility of utilizing and working with the new professional
can help turn this potentially negative period into a positive
experience.

Continual Learning and Development: Technical

My assignment in the late 1950s was to find out how to
overcome technical obsolescence, which managers were noticing
at that time because we were at the end of the vacuum-tube era
and the beginning of the transistor era. We were trying to get

engineers to design with transistors who never had studied solid-
state physics, the technological base for the transistor, because
it was not taught when they were in the university. Others
studying the problem at the same time came up with the concept of a technical education's *half-life,* defined as the period of
time within which the content of a university technical education changed by 50 percent. The half-life for electrical engineering at that time was about five years. From this work, it became apparent that educational preparation, however long, does
not end with the completion of the degree. Technical change is
so pervasive that continuing technical education for the life of
the professional is necessary. I am more and more convinced
that this is true for us all, but the case is easier to support for
the technical professional. Therefore, a quality work environment for the technical professional must include facilities for
continued technical learning, both informal and formal. There
needs to be a recognition within the organizational culture that
learning from the work itself is equally as important as class
study. Both managers and management must by policy support
continuing education as work. This topic is included here because more graduating professionals, understanding this need,
are judging whether or not to join an organization in terms of
its continuing education policies and practices.

Continual Learning and Development: Personal

Technical management was slower to discover the need
for continuing education and development on the personal
level. Personal development includes acquisition of interpersonal skills, communication skills, negotiating skills, and career
management skills as well as others that support more effectiveness and a greater satisfaction from work and life.

The need for personal development cannot be argued on
the basis of obsolescence, for these skills and knowledge fields
change at a slower rate than technology does. Rather, the argument for this need rests on the facts that these areas of development are not covered in the education of the professional,
or are only minimally covered, and that the individual only
learns of their value after work experience. It is difficult to mo-

tivate the accountant, lawyer, engineer, or scientist to study outside the special interest area at the college level; after some work experience, however, the individual becomes aware of the personal need for development and thus is self-motivated. The quality work environment for the professional is one in which management understands this need and supports the development of personal skills. As is the case with technical education, many graduates are in part judging whether or not to join an organization in terms of its support for this training.

In recognition of this need and of the fact that it was not being met even though personal development courses were available, in the late 1960s we developed the Professional Development School in IBM. This was a one-week residence program designed to develop the individuals' personal skills in managing their relationship with the organization. It included project management information, presentation skills training, exercises that put the nonmanagerial professional in the role of the manager, information about human resource policies, career management information, and an insider's visit with an executive. It was offered to outstanding professionals, as measured by their performance appraisal, and was aimed at those professionals about five years out of formal education. This time frame was chosen because it was the time when most professionals started questioning their relationship to the organization. A similar program today would need to be aimed at those one and one-half years out of the university, for the time of questioning comes sooner now. This was one of IBM's most successful training programs. It raised the professional's level of understanding about the environment and how to manage oneself within it. This breakthrough concept has yet to be picked up as a necessary one by most technical organizations.

Dual Ladders: An Environmental Element
Affecting Personal Development

Unfortunately, we live in a world in which the person with the managerial assignment is valued more highly than the nonmanager. This is a public evaluation, as well as a management feeling, about the value of managers. The manager's role is seen as being higher than that of a worker, or professional (in the case of R & D). In many ways this is proper, but in the R & D environment, if management is the only route to higher status and pay, it is damaging to individuals and to the organization. It tends to push nonmanagement professionals to aspire to management, even though they are not psychologically prepared for the role and may find it difficult to get the psychic incomes they need from the role. This career route is socially reinforced as well; across the back fence, our culture supports the idea that the person who is a manager has higher status.

The solution is to present the individual with a choice of career growth opportunities so that one does not have to aspire to management. A dual ladder can do this. It provides the individual with an opportunity for growth as a technical professional. For those who try management (as their choice or as management's choice), it provides the freedom to move out of management without losing pay or status. It also gives management the opportunity to promote and to pay more for higher levels of technical work. In concept, the dual ladder provides two tracks for upward movement: one track for an increase in managerial responsibility, and one track for an increase in technical responsibility and/or competence. On the managerial side of the ladder, the promotion is responsive to organizational needs for leadership and a definable increase in responsibility. On the technical side of the ladder, the promotion is responsive to acknowledgment of increased competence and a hard-to-define—and sometimes missing—increase in technical responsibility. Increased technical responsibility comes gradually (it is not a step function like promotion to management), and organizations acknowledge increased competence with promotion and without a change in job duties. Thus, two technical professionals, one at a higher rung on the ladder than the other, may actually sit alongside each other and do the same work.

The dual-ladder solution is not perfect. An additional problem is that if management does a good job of creating equivalency, then the managers may complain that they are not being paid for additional responsibilities (responsibilities over and above those the nonmanagement professional has at the same rung on the ladder), for what they have given up (such as the opportunity to do technical work and gain technical recognition), or for the increased risk of technical obsolescence that may push them into a sort of technical exile status. The best-functioning dual ladders receive about equal complaints from nonmanager technical professionals and from managers. In addition, promotions on either side, or from one side to the other, will elicit complaints if others do not consider the promotions fair or feel that the wrong person was promoted. Moving a manager who is seen as having failed as a manager by professionals up the ladder on the technical side, even though it may be the right assignment for the individual and the right one for the organization, may be wrong because it may generate the feeling among professionals that management thinks the technical ladder is primarily for managers who have failed. It is hard to make the two sides really equivalent; sometimes even a thing as small as the ex-manager not receiving the communications she used to receive can give the appearance of unjustified differences.

Nevertheless, I firmly believe that R & D management needs to use and refine multiple career opportunity paths—three or more developmental opportunity ladders. The organizational problems that occur in its absence are worse than those which occur in its presence. It is but one piece, one element, of a quality work environment for professionals, QPL.

Career-Development Support

Whether or not an environment is considered a good one in which to work is often measured by the support that one feels one is getting for growth and development, especially career development. I interviewed professionals in one organization to find out whether it was a good place to grow, and their comment was that "Management believes the cream will rise to the top, and so no one has to do anything about it." There was no formal support for career development or even any recognition that there was a need for it. Because career-development support begins with training managers and professionals in the process of career management, which in turn begins with improving the person/job fit to the current assignment, it contributes to the individual's and the organization's effectiveness and vitality. Progressive technical organizations start career-development programs as an input to improved productivity and reduced turnover.

Effective career-development support for professionals needs to include several elements. All these elements should be built on a study of and a deep understanding of the reasons why professionals turn sour in the organization. Recent research (Raelin, Sholl, and Leonard, 1985) emphasizes the importance of this understanding and suggests that job design (discussed in Chapter Twelve) is more powerful in avoiding professional disenchantment than is participation, which I have previously stressed. The management of each organization must find out what is true in its organization.

Career-development support works best when it is organization-specific (culture-specific). Built on this understanding, there should first be policy support for career management and for those changes of jobs and careers which may result from its practice. Second, support systems should include training for both managers and professionals in the process of career management; the professional needs training in order to become properly assertive in self-representation. Third, management policies and practices should include requirements for the individual and the manager to sit down at least once per year and have a career discussion. This discussion is different from performance planning for the next year; its scope is broader and its focus longer-range. Discussion should provide the individual an opportunity to check out and supplement self-assessment from another's point of view. It should be an opportunity to hear the manager's perspective about opportunities, about what works and what does not in the organization, and about the particular skills and knowledge needed for career growth. Whatever the elements of a career-development support program, it must make the process of development and change acceptable and must not lock people into their jobs and careers. It must also support the individual in the risks of change.

For more information on career development for the professional and/or manager, you might look at *Personal Vitality* (Miller, 1977a) and its accompanying *Personal Vitality Workbook* (Miller, 1977c), at Raelin (1984) or Schmidt (1982) for the individual's responsibilities, and at Kaufman (1982) for emphasis on underemployment and the search for work.

Burnout, Obsolescence, and Retraining

Despite all that management and the individual can do to support individual development and to support career growth, individuals will burn out and/or become obsolete.

Burnout exists when the individual loses the sense of payout from life and work, is emotionally and physically exhausted, feels trapped, is demotivated, and feels powerless to change his or her personal career or life. Burnout is usually a self-assessment and includes such symptoms as interpersonal problems, loss of energy, difficulty in applying oneself, declining performance, and depression. Although any of these symptoms can occur alone without burnout, the presence of these symptoms in groups is usually a sign of burnout.

Obsolescence exists when the organization and the individual, previously having worked together successfully, cannot make a meaningful job/person fit. Obsolescence can occur as a result of: a loss of self-confidence, inadequate skill or knowledge, a failure to adjust and grow, personal or career growth away from the organization, a decline in energy, a loss of organizational acceptance, or a diminished need for the functional specialty.

Both burnout and obsolescence are diseases resulting from the interaction of the individual and the organization. The responsibility for their occurrence is shared by the individual and management. Prevention is more desirable than a cure. In reporting on an interesting recent study, Hall (1985, p. 282) says that certain types of task activity may moderate the effects of plateauing, a form of obsolescence: "this organization also provides a third type of career ladder, that of the project manager. . . . Project management work puts a premium on experience, which means that the skills and value of the generalist grow as he or she matures in the career." This is not true for the technical specialist, who is narrower and must run to keep up with the leading edge of technology. This suggests that we should look for aspects of work that delay obsolescence. It was this type of answer that I was aiming at in "Changing Job Requirements: A Stimulant for Technical Vitality" (Miller, 1972).

Burnout is avoided by lowering negative job stress. Cures for burnout consist of reducing pressures (but not of total disengagement) and of short-duration assignments (in which quick feedback and positive reinforcement can be obtained), followed by eventual change to a different assignment. Managerial nurturing is needed, providing a lot of positive support, but tempered with realism about the situation.

Cures for obsolescence essentially consist of finding ways to motivate individuals to adapt and change, of providing the retraining necessary to achieve a new person/job match, and of finding assignments that provide immediate utilization of the new skills. Motivation of the individual requires that the individual come to the conclusion that the discomfort of the current situation (obsolescence) warrants an investment in change; the manager's role may thus be to demonstrate some of the costs and pain potentially associated with staying the same.

Retraining, except in a few cases, has to be designed for the individual. In the early days of combating obsolescence, we thought there might be some more or less universal approach, but the more we learned, the more we understood that every case has its individual characteristics. In one study I asked managers to list those individuals who would not be able to find a new assignment if their job assignments disappeared tomorrow. As we looked at these people, we found individualized circumstances demanding individual treatment. I can think of several cases where group retraining was possible. One was at General Electric; faced with a new technology, GE developed a training program for a large group of engineers (Zukowski, 1983). These were professionals who would have been displaced, so the activity took place before the people were actually obsolete. It was a career-transition assistance program. Another case was at IBM, where we developed a training program for facilities engineers, a need we could not fill, and let engineers no longer at the frontier of their technological area apply for the program. Through a combination of a three-month program that took place at California Polytechnic State University and a three-month internal program, in a six-month period the professionals were retrained and placed in useful positions. This was done with several groups of about thirty each. These people, who were probably obsolete at their time of retraining, were sufficiently conscious of and worried about their obsolescence to volunteer for this career-transition program.

Selecting the Leader-Manager

Managers in R & D—in fact, managers of all professional activities, from social work supervisors to lawyers and from internal audit managers to nursing managers—anguish over the challenge and process of selecting managers. Or, by contrast, they do it very casually without thinking about the effects that a wrong choice may have on the individual's career and on the effectiveness of the organization. There seems to be no middle ground. Some managements come up with elaborate processes of assessing skills and potential, such as assessment centers. These are usually three-day simulations, with one-on-one observation of each person's behavior and performance on a set of standard tasks presumed to be part of management. Experienced managers are trained as observers and write reports on the individuals being assessed. The tasks include exercises with in baskets: The individual manager takes on a new job and has one hour to read and do something with a stack of mail. They also include meetings at which a proposal is debated and action decided upon. (Those interested in the process and the types of exercises should look at Frank, Sefcik, and Jaffee [1983].) When these sessions are used for selection, people who are considered managerial candidates are invited to the sessions. The session can be an intense and threatening experience for the candidate. One of the problems is that line management, upon receipt of the report, has to make the decision about promotion to management or not. The line managers have the recommendations from the assessment center and they have their own observations and experiences with the individuals as bases for decision making. The general trend in organizations is to use this selection process in functions where there is little chance to observe managerial-type behaviors; such would be the case in picking a manufacturing floor manager from workers in the department. The only application of which I know in R & D is used not for selection, but to provide the individual with career guidance information. I suspect the reason is that managers in R & D do have the opportunity to assign special leadership tasks and to observe behavior; they could, however, benefit from some of the training in observation and assessment that has been developed for assessment center observers. They are also dealing with professionals who are supposed to be self-managing and who should be articulate about their own career interests.

In R & D environments, the anguishing end of the selection process has most often consisted of setting up detailed requirements for promotion proposals (similar to but not as elaborate as the proposals for tenure used in academe) and/or the use of promotion review boards; in the better situations, incidentally, these same requirements and boards are used to review promotions on both ladders. Thus, they review and judge technical as well as managerial proposals. The intent of the process is to force the proposer to cover a basic set of information about the education and experiences the individual has had as well as a critical set of questions supporting the decision to promote. There are several problems with either or both detailed proposals and review boards. First, the most articulate communicators do a better job of proposing, in writing, and defending their candidates before the promotion board. Second, since the members of the promotion board also have similar people in their organizations, they may tend to block promotions for which they feel that they have better candidates; this obviously has both good and bad attributes. A third problem is that these boards often develop the image in the organization of being devices for blocking promotion rather than of making the selection process more rigorous. A variation of this process is to call the board review if and only if someone objects to the written proposal. Then the objector has some responsibilities for preparing a position on the reasons for objection.

The casual end of the selection-for-promotion process is exemplified by the manager who does the selection being essentially a king, nominating and approving. In this case, the tendency is to nominate and promote someone who has worked with the nominator, a known entity being better than an unknown. The complainers will call this the buddy system. Perhaps the worst case of the casual system that I have ever run across may be described as choosing the professional with the least negative votes. This procedure consists of listing all the potential candidates on a chalkboard and then having a group of managers sit around and cross off anyone they know who has made mistakes or done something wrong. The result, you guessed it, is to promote the person who has not done anything and about whom no one knows anything. Another technique used in some R & D organizations is open posting of opportunities. In this case, the individuals are responsible for asserting themselves as candidates. This presumably removes from management the responsibility for ensuring that all who should be considered are considered. It leads to forcing managers to become defensive because of the negatives of the many potential turndowns for an individual. It leads at times to managers defining requirements so tightly that only one person can actually meet the requirements.

My recommendation is a multiphase process; this represents a middle ground. It consists first of requiring managers to get together and define the roles, the requirements for experience and training, and the measures for success in management in the organization. After this is done, all managers are trained in their roles of identifying individuals' potential for promotion to management and higher nonmanagement technical positions. They are additionally trained in observing behavior and in assessing its applicability to a new set of tasks that have been described. Assessment centers or something similar are provided for professionals along with career management training. The information gathered in the assessment center is fed back only to the individual, not to management. The human resource function is charged with collecting assessments of potential for promotion from all managers annually. They are also charged with ensuring that when an opening is declared, the managers involved look not only at those people they have said had potential but also at those whom other managers have proposed have potential. Interviews are established, at which the selecting managers are required to discuss their criteria with their respective candidates and feed back to them individually why they were chosen or not chosen and how they can improve their potential for future selection.

Training the Leader-Manager

Ginzberg and Vojta (1985, p. 19) observe: "Clearly, the large numbers of young people who make such substantial investments in their education develop certain aspirations and expectations about their careers, which will exercise a shaping influence on their future behavior. We doubt that most large corporations have devoted adequate attention to this change in the values and goals of their junior and middle managers. And yet only by doing so will they establish a working environment in which they can effectively utilize their managerial personnel." Effective training of the leader needs to start with indoctrination into the roles of the manager. Broad management-development goals might be:

- Improving the leaders' understanding of the management process, thereby providing a conceptual framework for thinking about their management roles and for understanding how they can affect individuals' and groups' effectiveness, development of capability, and satisfaction from work.
- Changing the balance of managerial emphasis from an overemphasis on technical aspects to a more person-centered emphasis, increased human resource management emphasis, at conceptual, policy, and practice levels, so that the leader can become more effective at improving utilization, productivity, and the potential for achieving both individual and organizational goals.

- Improving the practice of management through skill training aimed at improving interpersonal communication, and thus improving the matching of people and work, individual performance, individual development, career management, and again contributing to the effectiveness in achieving organizational goals.
- Improving the satisfaction from work (psychic income) and the fun that leader-managers can achieve. Accomplishing this—helping the leaders to think positively about themselves as managers—will enhance attainment of all the previous objectives.

In principle, the training of the leader should be continuous. It should take place on the job and be reinforced by formal classes on a regular basis, and there should be a tie-in between the two so that the manager is required to practice some of the things learned in class. Top corporations are shifting toward this in part; according to Bolt (1985, p. 168), "Senior executives—including the chief executive officer—are not only mandating a larger role for management training and development but are also themselves taking part." It is important to note that this has long been a practice in IBM. I taught as a manager, and undoubtedly this is the source of some of my feelings. In my experience, most everything less than a week of formal training is less than enough. Some of the best programs have resulted from unique packaging, for example, using several weekends, or continued problem solving over an extended period with a catalyst (trainer), and sometimes that sort of shock treatment which results from immersing people in a totally changed environment. For example, I once conducted a successful program in twenty-below weather in a drafty old hotel where one had to build a fire to be warm enough to dress, but a friend who used a river-raft trip on another occasion overwhelmed the training and was less successful. In a related way, organizations should make use of extensive university-based management development, one of the prime advantages of which is that the leader discovers that other managers in other organizations are facing similar challenges.

The first and most important function of training is to help the professional turned manager with the transition process. One must deal with the need to change one's outlook, to find new psychic incomes, to combat loneliness, to let go of old approaches, and to examine oneself and develop an image of oneself in the role. This area of training is, I believe, one of the weakest in all R & D organizations. Training should include process, practice, and those concepts or principles that have practical application on the job. Transfer from the classroom to work is the key challenge and the key failure of most programs. Classroom experiences using real problems from the work environment, but tackled in the safe environment of the classroom, are one way of increasing the potential for influencing work behavior. Early training for the leader should cover the specifics, like how to conduct a performance evaluation interview, how to make a salary change, what managers are expected to do, and something about how to carry out the role. As the training progresses, the focus can shift toward concepts and principles and the improvement of specific skills. Still later, it is necessary to get into philosophy and the knotty issues of social responsibility and the organization's relationship to the public. Transfer to the workplace can be enhanced by having managers bring real problems to class, discuss ways of solving them, and return to the workplace to try out new ideas. All training should be enhanced by measurement and follow-up. In its most direct form, this means contacting the manager and asking what, if anything, was used from the class and how. It may mean asking the participant to go back and tell his or her manager what was learned. It may also mean following up with surveys and interviews.

Whatever training is designed for the professional turned manager, the following unique questions and aspects should be addressed:

• How can one achieve psychic income and fun in this new role? Since psychic income as a professional flowed from the work itself and the nature of the work has changed, what can one do to feel good about this work? If I do not like it or am not good at it, is there a safe landing?

• Since authority is granted for technical competence,

not managerial position, how does this affect the manager's role and the appropriate style?

• Because the typical scientist and/or professional starts with a negative view of management, how does one overcome this bias, what does it suggest about how the manager should manage, and what styles are appropriate? Not only must the bias be overcome in the relationship with those being managed, but it should also change internally for the individual as a manager.

• How does the manager deal with the fundamental belief structure that supports the idea that research and development cannot be planned, managed, and measured? When this is the requirement placed on the leader, how does one come to grips with it?

• Since educational preparation emphasized facts and denied feelings, how can the manager become comfortable with feelings as input to decisions and style choices?

• How does the scientist turned manager, who is probably uncomfortable in interpersonal relations, gain comfort in these relationships?

Summary

• It is important to the success of the organization to attract outstanding professionals who have appropriate preparation and characteristics and to hire them. Attraction depends on the image of the organization, and this can be developed through appropriately aimed public relations and by using the professionals of the organization to work at creating this image.

• The nature of the work and whether it is viewed as exciting and challenging can make a major difference in the attractiveness of an organization. If work is viewed as important on a technical frontier and paired with appropriate rewards, it enhances the organization's ability to attract professionals.

• Having world-class professionals as members of an organization helps attract outstanding professionals because of the career desirability of working with leaders. Integrating unique technical leader personalities and using them appropriately, however, can be a significant managerial challenge.

- It is important to support recruiting efforts with a continuing university relations program, thus assuring the university's representatives that the organization's interest is deeper than just hiring graduates.

- The organization's geographical location can affect its ability to attract people because the professional is at a point in his or her life where personal interests can influence location.

- Of the many recruiting sins, the most prominent one in R & D is giving the impression that one can come to work and continue to pursue personal projects without encountering organizational constraints and/or being in conflict with business goals.

- The screening, selection, hiring, and indoctrination processes should emphasize listening to the applicant and honest, timely, and clear communication, all things that can make a difference in the quality of the person/organization fit. Managements that understand this carefully manage the recruiting process.

- Environmental support of continued learning (technical and personal) and management support of individual development, training, and support in career management are all necessary in order to create QPL. Professionals make employment decisions on their assessment of an organization's QPL.

- Dual ladders make a difference in the professional's perception of the organization's understanding of the need for some individuals to grow as technical nonmanagement personnel and for others to grow by becoming managers. Dual ladders are in effect environmental statements that transmit a message from management to the potential recruit about management's understanding of the needs of the professional.

- Both burnout and obsolescence can result from prolonged and unrewarding assignment to an unchanging set of duties and/or mismatch of the individual with the work. One of the aspects of the environment on which the applicant will make judgments about the quality of a potential relationship is whether or not they see people who burn out and become obsolete in that organization. Thus, in recruiting it is important for management to understand the environmental image being communicated and try to make it one where individuals are seen as free to make assignment and career changes in order to maintain personal vitality.

- In R & D management tends to either agonize over the selection of the manager or make the process rather casual. After selection, most R & D managements have not done a good job at training and developing managers. Improving management practices through establishing criteria for selection, by clearly enunciating the expectations for managerial performance, and by making training more relevant and useful are necessary if R & D effectiveness is to be improved.

Chapter 10

Recognizing and Rewarding Effective Performance

Only if someone cares about what we do is our work important. One system through which an organization expresses caring and reflects value consists of establishing performance expectations, setting work goals jointly (in discussions between manager and employee), jointly establishing criteria for measuring success, and requiring managers to observe and provide feedback for improvement. Performance measurements can result in recognition, or lead to a lack of recognition, and can cause an increase in salary, or perhaps loss of one's job.

Both the organization and the individual need this performance management process. The organization needs it because it ensures that the work of individuals is oriented toward goals and thus helps improve productivity; while this need has existed over time, it is causing increased attention to appraisal now because "of the ever-increasing importance of human resources to what an organization can accomplish" (Baird, Beatty, and Schneier, 1982, p. xi). Individuals need it so that they can have goal focus, attain results, make performance improvements, learn and grow in capability, and achieve recognition and reward.

Management needs an appraisal process, a performance measurement, so that it can effectively relate pay to performance and provide an objective base for decisions about people.

(All judgments about people are subjective, but when done in a consistent way, they tend to be seen as more objective.) A trend that causes management to heighten its current attention to appraisals is the trend for government to look over managers' shoulders and judge fairness. The courts have also gotten into the area of deciding about the validity of appraisals; they suggest that appraisal systems will be valid only when several managers, seeing the same performance, rate it the same. When managements do cause pay to respond to performance, they expect that it will motivate employees to achieve. But good performance management systems are difficult to design and tough to manage fairly. Ginzberg and Vojta (1985, p. 13) cite several weaknesses: "The individual or individuals who make the appraisals, especially immediate supervisors, are never free from conflict . . . performance appraisal systems focus on assessing a wide range of factors that cannot be objectively determined or quantified. . . . A supervisor will hesitate to mark an employee 'unsatisfactory' if he thus initiates a personnel review that could eventually result in the employee's dismissal. . . . Every supervisor recognizes that his evaluation and the feedback he provides to the person assessed will affect the latter's future work, attitudes, and behavior. Many supervisors trim their evaluations to this reality." So the leader feels caught in a no-win situation.

Despite these problems, the individual wants an appraisal of performance in order to be recognized in pay and position on the basis of effectiveness and achievement. This is one basis for another problem (one specific to performance management in R & D): Especially in research, professionals expect that their pay will reflect their educational preparation level, the ability and knowledge they brought to work; when they are hired, this is the basis for the offer amount. Many expect maintenance of this status difference throughout their work careers. Because of this belief, and because education level and seniority are the easiest bases for determining salary, an analysis of pay in research organizations will generally show the greatest correspondence to degree level and years of experience. By contrast, the salaries in a development organization will to a greater extent reflect achievement after the first few years. For five or so years, the entry degree has, and should have, the greatest impact on salary. Offsetting this, when creativity or innovation takes place, the professional with good self-esteem, even in research, wants recognition. In a type of activity in which discovery, creativity, and innovation cannot be exactly planned, or sometimes cannot be measured except in the context of history, this conflict is between the need for security and the need to gain through risk taking. Security is represented by the need for status associated with degree and seniority, and risk is associated with a salary that responds to accomplishment and to responsibility level. In varying degrees, this conflict exists in both research and development. It is thus one of the problems that management faces in creating a quality work environment, QPL. The measure of the effectiveness of performance management, recognition, and salary systems is in the attitudes of the members of the organization.

Despite these conflicts, good management of human resources requires that there be a process for planning, feedback, and appraisal of performance. Only through such a process can the individuals and the organization grow in capability, and only through such a process can management ensure that the employees it rewards and retains are ones who pursue organizational goals and achieve. Performance management is the basis for achieving improved productivity and for weeding out the inadequate performer. Top performers do not want to be part of an organization that is populated by those who do not perform. Appraisal is the basis for selecting the key performers, ones on whom you will bet the scientific future—ones you will trust to be leaders, both technical and managerial.

Most managements get hung up on the design of the form, the piece of paper used to regularize the process and record the data, and in addition, who uses the form, who sees the form, and how its use can affect the employee. Too much attention generally gets paid to the number of points on the rating scale, how many factors to rate, whether there is a summary number representing the overall appraisal, and the wording of the form. Too little attention gets paid to establishing the philosophical basis, the shared need for it, and the employee and managerial responsibilities associated with performance management. Even if the personnel department did not create a system, I believe that managers and employees would come up with a relative equivalent, for it is necessary to provide assignment definition and goals, improve performance, and stimulate development of capability. Nash (1983, p. 243) notes: "One of the fundamentals of performance psychology is that setting goals activates behavior. It increases performance by focusing the person's efforts on specific goals. Many research studies have shown that setting hard goals results in better performance than setting easy goals or no goals at all." Yet leaders in R & D, and often managers in other parts of the organization, believe that they are doing performance planning, feedback, and appraisal for someone else, usually feeling that it is for the benefit of the personnel department. For my discussions, I shall use the term *performance management* to include: performance planning; managerial observation, assessment, feedback, and coaching, all of which should occur on an ongoing basis; the annual appraisal of performance, including its discussion and how its data is used for counseling and other purposes; and the related recognition and salary rewards.

Increasingly, work in R & D is accomplished by teams rather than just by individuals working alone. This raises questions about team formation and tasking, team behavior, team characteristics, and recognition and reward for teams. If it is not possible to separate the performance of the individual from the performance of the team, then management is faced with a serious difficulty, which is that almost all salary systems and most recognition techniques are directed to individuals.

There is one more confusion that should be addressed. This has to do with the difference between an annual appraisal discussion and the planning of the next year's work activities and career discussions. Certainly, the next year of activity is part of the career, but many organizations suggest (or insist) that in this same discussion there should be review of longer-range interests, goals, and opportunities. There is a problem in this, for in the appraisal interview the manager is cast as a judge. In a career discussion, the manager should be a catalyst for the individual to do personal assessment and make personal decisions about career and life. I believe that appraisal interviews and career discussions should be separate events because I feel that many employees and many managers cannot make the necessary shift in perspective in one sitting.

Recognition, which in reality includes many forms of feedback, is often thought of in narrow terms with respect to the organization. Managers have come to think of recognition in organizations as primarily a change of status. This means promotion, the expectation of special perquisites, and an increase in salary. The basis for such changes should be accomplishment and an assessment of the effectiveness of the individual in applying skills and knowledge to attain the goal, for, as Jansen and Von Glinow (1985, p. 816) observe: "The reward system comprises the related set of processes through which behaviors are directed and motivated to achieve individual and collaborative performances; the set of processes comprise goal setting, assessing performance, distributing rewards, and communicating feedback." Thus, there should be a strong relationship between a salary system and the performance appraisal. Many discussions of differences in feelings about performance management systems are related to how tight and direct this relationship should be. A performance management system for R & D that overcomes as many of the difficulties as possible and contributes to a positive work environment, QPL, is proposed near the end of this chapter.

R & D Is Not a Sandbox

A management that chooses to establish, staff, and fund a research organization generally does so (or should do so) because it believes that creative professionals will, in the long run, contribute the ideas and concepts that will fuel the company. Similarly, it establishes a development organization to pursue specific programs and projects (whether based on research creativity or not) that will lead in the near future to marketable products, systems, or services. Thus, R & D is not a frivolous undertaking. My definition of a sandbox is a place where the purpose is play (and good work should be play), but play that has no value beyond the instant in which it exists and that has no potential for affecting the organization or finding a useful application after it is finished. Let us look at research first.

Managements are guilty of creating the false image that research is disconnected from the business. This is due in part to the recruiting practice of promising individuals, especially scientists, that they can pursue their research in the organization, but it is also due to several other factors. First, managers do not know how to manage the unplannable and unpredictable. Second, general managers are often unskilled in creating that special balance of freedom which is loosely but meaningfully tied to the goals of the organization. Third, they may create a confused image by being unclear in specifying or indecisive about using the ideas created in research. Sometimes this is justified because the creativity is outside the current business scope, and sometimes it is justified because the associated technologies necessary to make the idea useful are not available, but sometimes it results simply from not understanding the potential of the idea. Fourth, it appears that some managements seem to put much of their emphasis on selling the stockholders, the stock market experts, and the world on the idea that just having Nobel laureates, a spectacular facility, and a funded research effort is in itself enough. These are some of the reasons why some people and some scientists look at research as a sandbox. Creative performance planning, with feedback (counseling) and appraisal, is one of the key elements in creating the effective bond between the researcher and the organization, but this is not easy when managers often do not know what the results of research may be and may not be in a position to judge quality results accurately when they see them. Yet my hope is that, through using creative performance management as one of many tools, leaders of research can ensure that it is not a sandbox.

In development, the issues seem clearer. Although some marketing people and manufacturing people look askance at the luxury facilities and loose rules in development as indications that the people in development are only playing, the environment is more closely tied to the reality of the business. Usually it is possible to plan the development of a product because the

innovations necessary are limited in number and possible to
base on some known science or technology. Thus, people in development are philosophically more willing to accept the need
for management of performance and appraisal. I believe that
this is because the end cycle of the program is a product; the
end cycle of an individual's work can be predicted and measured. The end cycle of a team project can also be predicted
and measured, but it is harder to relate rewards to an individual's
accomplishments. In the culture of development, success means
getting your product to the market and having it be a success in
the hands of the customer; consequently, the salaries and positions of people in development are more likely to reflect their
accomplishments than their pedigrees. Creative performance
planning is necessary in order to make this environment real and
fair and to ensure that the work is goal-oriented.

Why Professionals Believe That Appraisal Programs Cannot Work

Professionals believe that their work cannot be planned
or measured because it is the work of creation—and creative results cannot be predicted, scheduled, or even assigned a value in
advance. In the extreme, this is true, but not all professional's
work is of that type. True scientific breakthroughs are usually
accidents resulting from intense study and experiment—but in
unpredictable ways. The work of setting up the accident is plan-
nable, orderly, and (up to the moment of the accident) predictable. Another scientist reviewing the work of a scientist can,
within the limits of training and experience, evaluate whether
the plan of attack (the logical sequence of exploring alternatives) has been laid out as a scientist should pursue a goal. Thus,
while the day of the project or program breakthrough cannot be
predicted, the work of the individual scientist can be assessed
for its quality and evidence of intuition. It is in this translation
from the overall to the specific that it becomes emotionally
convenient, a way of avoiding risk, for individuals to take the
position that their work is not like the work of others and thus
cannot be planned and measured.

Another basis for the difference in opinion lies in the fact that the research professional should be self-managing. If this is true, then the work is not really assigned by the manager. And this is indeed true in almost all research work, for the individual makes decisions and choices; not everything is specified by the manager. What varies is the range of freedom for decision making. Conceptually, therefore, the use of an appraisal program based on work objectives ought to be useful, especially if we can get the individual to participate in establishing the measurement criteria as well as the plan for activities.

With engineering, programming, and other professionals, the rationale is somewhat different than that of the research scientist. The usual reasons given to explain why appraisal programs cannot work are (1) that the work changes too many times during the year, and thus the paperwork of keeping objectives up to date is overwhelming; and/or (2) that my supervisor does not really understand the technical nature of my work.

The first reason has some merit. In a rapidly moving technical area, it is true that the direction of the work changes at a rapid rate. But it is also true that to manage such a change, the goals must be changed and documented as a normal part of pursuing the work. Thus, the excuse that the appraisal program creates the paperwork is not valid; it is the nature of the work itself that creates the need for keeping up with documentation. The difference is that in the normal work process, engineers and technical managers would probably get away without documenting the changes. This results in a fuzzy basis for measuring results. It is sometimes done with intent because of insecurity. This is one of the situations typically uncovered in an audit.

The second reason carries over from the belief system of the scientifically trained person—that the only person who can judge one's work is someone with the same training, experience, and interests. This applies to both scientists and engineers, but I feel that it is built on the wrong premise—a belief that managing is just making technical decisions and handling some administrative issues. I have seen this carried to great lengths by scientists, engineers, and programmers when they use it as a rationale for not following the direction of management. Because that person up on top is not trained in their specific discipline, they feel ethically justified in not following that leader's direction. Again, there seems to be no real fundamental reason why the process of setting goals and measuring individual progress with respect to those goals is not a valid approach. If professionals and managers would focus on the prime purpose, the improvement of capability and performance, I believe that much of the quibbling would disappear.

The humor of the controversy about appraisal becomes evident when you observe a group of scientists or engineers engaged in the process of designing an appraisal program. Because they are measurement-oriented, on any specific factor they often come up with rating scales that allow ratings to the second digit beyond the decimal point. Surely, a person who does not believe that anyone can judge another's performance is beyond reason if he recommends it be done to two digits beyond the decimal point! Yet when it is suggested that the total performance can be reduced to one summary figure, a shorthand for sorting and dealing with large numbers of people so that managers can deal with them as categories in order later to deal more effectively with individuals who are out of alignment or who have been misassessed, they object violently. They miss the whole point!

Nash (1983, p. 227) points out that "The fundamental problem in appraising the individual is psychological. People regard appraisal as a threat. They know appraisals can have negative affects on salary increases and promotions. A poor rating can injure self-esteem and discourage subsequent performance. Everyone wants to be evaluated as performing above average. People hunger for feedback but want to hear only good news. They want to be complimented, not criticized." Creative leaders must offset this basic psychological fact. First, they can do it by involving professionals in the design and day-to-day implementation of the program. Second, they can do it by training managers to emphasize the positives, for the aim is improvement and growth; we learn more from what we have done right than from our mistakes. Third, they can do it by being honest and forthright up front about the uses of the data and about who has accessibility and for what purpose. Lastly, they should not avoid dealing with inadequate performance, but should handle it in a process disassociated from the annual appraisal. The annual appraisal can become the basis for the individual's right to influence his or her job and its design which is earned through satisfactory or better performance.

Talking About Work:
The Need for Language and Process

It would seem that talking about a task, a piece of work, would be a very easy thing to do, but it is often difficult. The problem seems to be that our talk about work focuses on two aspects: the results we want, and how the work is to be done. These topics are necessary, but we also need to develop the language and the process to talk about all the many characteristics or elements of work that make the match between the individual and the work a good match. These work characteristics range from how long it takes to get some sort of feedback on task results to the kind of support one can expect from management and others in doing the task. Chapter Twelve covers this subject in detail because the match is vitally important in creating an effective psychological work contract, in ensuring effectiveness, and in gaining psychic income. For our purposes now, it is sufficient to recognize that the basis for planning, measuring, feedback, and appraisal must be an understanding between two people about the work and about the relationship of the individual to it. The danger in technological activities is that both the manager and the professional will get diverted and talk about technology, programming, or science, not the work and the characteristics that contribute to a good or poor match.

Improved Performance:
The Purpose of Performance Management

Performance management is the process of agreeing on what is to be done, planning in a broad way how to do it, observing how it is done, feeding back these observations (coaching), and measuring and assessing the performance. The logical foundation of the process is the careful matching of needs to capabilities.

The aim of the manager's observations of the individual

at work is thus to gather data that will be helpful in improving performance (otherwise, what good is it?). This the basis of all coaching. It works in athletics. In sports events, even the fans believe that their feedback, their cheering for the team, affects performance. I believe that it should work in other endeavors. It is easier to do in athletics because almost all the activities being observed are physical. It is harder to do in a field in which the majority of the activities are intellectual, in which the results are not immediately apparent, and in which all the interactions between individuals are not as observed or observable as they are in athletics. The manager's lack of knowledge about the employee's performance is, according to Reed and Kroll (1985, p. 51), "primarily constrained by time and distance.... Henry Mintzberg found that the average manager spends 37% of his or her time dealing with employees, but only 9% of this at their actual work sites." It is harder to do where the manager does not assign all activities and individual professionals are free to choose both goals and means. Since we expect the professional to be self-managing, the professional makes many of the decisions about what, how, and when to do things.

Despite the difficulties of measuring performance of the professional even in the field of science, open communication between two people about expectations and measures has been shown to improve the performance and growth of the person. For example, if you wish to increase the probability of growing a new Nobel laureate, hire one, and have others communicate regularly with that person and observe that person at work. Over and over, we see evidence that breakthroughs occur in the laboratories of scientists or engineers where there have been other breakthroughs. Thus, just because it is difficult, leaders should not shy away from trying to improve performance through observation and feedback in R & D.

Improvement in Capability: The Purpose of Feedback

Another purpose of the performance management process is growth in individual capability. Feedback is essential to learning. In fact, researchers in biofeedback have shown that the human can learn to influence aspects of bodily function, previously thought not to be controllable, when regularly provided with more specific feedback. When we do not know the results of our actions, there is no way to make corrections or improvements. In the world of work, there are two major sources of feedback most of the time. Especially in the crafts, or where the results of our work are observable to us, we have our own observation as a source of feedback; however, much of the professional's work in high technology and R & D is so complex in its interrelationships, so indirect in the source of feedback, that the observations and input from others become very important. Observations of others are the second source. These may come from the manager, peers, or others in the organization who see the results of what the individual does or have to base their own work on it. The observations of the manager and colleagues are important in improving capability because they provide a reference base for experiment and change.

Reference to the literature on coaching in organizations almost invariably provides a negative image because the emphasis seems to be on improving unsatisfactory performance. "The first step in the coaching process is to get agreement a problem exists" (Fournies, 1978, p. 135). In my experience, the coaching of the unsatisfactory performer is a small but necessary part of the coaching that the manager or leader should do. Coaching is fun when, like the coach on the football field, one is trying to take an already good or outstanding performer and help that person become even better. We never talk about the basketball coach dealing with unsatisfactory performance; that coach is dealing with team members who are already a select group, selected because they stood out in performance! My coaching activities in industry were more like those of the basketball coach than of a correctional officer, the typical image held by management. I had fun helping the good performer become even better. Coaching also takes place as a positive event between leaders and teams. The coach lowers the threshold for improved performance most often by helping the individual gain a better self-image, and/or to reach the understanding that with a little fine tuning of one's actions one can do an outstanding job. Coaching is a major and important managerial activity, so please join me in eliminating the negative aura. Coaching is what a peer or a manager does when helping another person understand him- or herself, by providing feedback, mostly positive, and thus helping the person rise to greater heights.

Appraisal Forms, Processes, and Systems

Johnson (1979, p. 21) observes that "The appraisal form, intended to be a useful personnel tool, often ensures that nothing really productive comes out of the appraisal process. This may be true because of the defects in the form itself, problems in how the form is used, or misuse of the form by the appraiser. Yet there are ways to get around a bad form, conform with organization policy, and have constructive appraisals." If every manager and employee had perfect communication about the planning, executing, observing, and feeding back of observations, measurements of performance, and recognition, there would be no need for a form or a process. Appraisal should go on all the time, not in the negative sense of finding fault, but in the positive sense of feedback for improvement. In fact, prompt feedback increases the chance that we will learn. If it is prompt, the probability that we will associate what we did with what happened increases significantly. Daily feedback does not happen, or at least it does not happen well enough. Here, therefore, are some of the reasons for having a performance management process and form:

- To remind manager and employee of the need for and mutual value of the performance management process. When it is properly executed, both the organization and the individual gain. The existence of a system makes an environmental statement; it shapes the values and thus the culture of the organization. It says that this organization cares about the individual's contribution and growth.
- To ensure that managers and employees will work at goal-oriented activity, focus on improvement of performance, and work to improve capability.

- To provide a vehicle for training—for teaching the process to managers, professionals, and other employees.
- To provide individuals with a structure (usually a function carried primarily by the form) and policies that ensure consistency and fairness of evaluation and reward across the organization.
- To make the performance ratings reasonably valid so that actions relative to salary, change in organizational rank, selection for further development or responsibility, and promotions can be made with fairness. Reasonable validity means the ability of one evaluator to replicate another's rating.
- To ensure that, at a minimum, one formal feedback-appraisal session between the manager and employee occurs with some frequency, usually once per year. Documentation of this interview on a form, in most cases signed by the employee, serves as a record of this discussion, an entry into the organizational memory about the person.
- To provide documentation for decision making about people, both for internal management, control, and consistency and, unfortunately (in our litigious era), for defense in the case of outside audits and court cases. Such defense is becoming more important because of the increasing frequency with which management must prove what actually happened.

The form carries the brunt of communication about the intent of organization's management in having an appraisal, an interview, and a record, and the form presents the rating system. Rating systems vary in content: some list traits like assertiveness; some call for an assessment of general behaviors and skills, such as promptness and presentation ability; and others are based on what is called management by objectives (MBO), which stresses performance in terms of mutually agreed-upon goals. Historically, systems tended toward the trait type and managers filled out extensive checklists. Today the trend has been toward MBO types, with the most sophisticated using behaviorally anchored rating scales (BARS). BARS define the differences between levels of performance by using descriptive statements of behavior that have been tested for their ability to differentiate (by having had many managers sort statements into rating categories). Those who need more information on BARS are referred to Baird, Beatty, and Schneier (1982, pp. 56-65); from the same reference (p. 118), one can get a feeling for how others do it. For example, their analysis of forms shows that quantity of work was a category used on 56 percent of the forms for rating nonmanagement people and that only 28 percent of the forms used judgment as a category in rating them. Managers rating technical professionals ranked the traits to be in the following, descending order of importance: dependability (1), quality of work (2), and communication ability (3); among those ranked the least important were relations with public (12) and relations with others (15). I strongly recommend Baird, Beatty, and Schneier (1982) as one of the best and most complete references for those who set out to design or redesign a system or to train others in appraisal processes. Most appraisal systems (and thus forms) are some combination of traits, skills, and specific performance ratings. While it is possible to design forms with long lists requiring checks or short entries, the trend has been toward shorter, more open forms using essay-type entries. This trend has been caused by a desire to get away from some of the past tyrannies in forms.

Since I have indicated that the form is the source of many of the difficulties with appraisal systems, it is important to list some of the problems created by the content or design of forms:

- Covering too much; having too many subjects or categories.
- Including personal characteristics, such as attitude or tact. There are high-order abstractions and represent the most difficult (if not impossible) areas for coaching and counseling; furthermore, they change on the part of the individual.
- Using loaded words about behavior, such as *questionable* or *abrupt*, or wording items in such a way as to set up a negative tone, thus inclining the manager to find faults instead of good things.
- Forcing a comparison of performance between several employees when the objective is to rate the employee's perfor-

mance against personal objectives in order to improve the individual's performance.

- Mixing performance and potential ratings.
- Using rating scales that call for too fine a differentiation, such as a ten-point rather than the most common five-point scale.
- Using scales to differentiate aspects which are generally not differentiable through observation or which humans are incapable of judging.
- Encouraging the manager to store up incidents and "surprise" the employee at the end of the year rather than to cover these things in the daily feedback, where they should be covered.

I believe that a system for managing performance on a shared basis between employee and manager is of value. I also feel that the move toward assessing behavior against specific job goals is a move in the right direction. It causes the manager to coach for improvement on subjects about which something can be done rather than to beat up the employee over something that cannot be changed. It helps the manager escape the trap of dealing with some of the most emotionally loaded areas, such as personal traits, when the best that can happen is that the employee turns off the figurative hearing aid and blocks the input. Nevertheless, there are some fallacies in MBO. Here are four of six items suggested by Sayles (1979, p. 135):

1. Looking at results encourages subordinates to engage in behavior that may be destructive to organizational relationships. A subordinate may benefit but the coordination necessary to meet overall organization goals suffers.

2. Such an emphasis encourages excessive competition for scarce resources, such as space, personnel, parts, maintenance facilities, and leads to neglect of the unmeasured aspects of a job.

3. It is difficult to pinpoint the cause of source problems. Looking at results simply does not give one enough information. . . .

5.   Many times good performance is not identified
     —only failures.

Appraisal Discussions and Career Discussions:
The Differences

Many systems combine a host of tasks on one form, requiring the leader to assess performance against the prior plan, to document and plan future goals, to assess potential for growth, and to discuss and document career expectations and plans. Like some of the tyrannies of the form just discussed, this forces the manager to do several necessary things with the employee—but it encompasses too much at one time and calls for a shift in perspective and role on the part of the two participants, which is difficult if not impossible. Mixing these topics also probably increases the potential for misinterpretation of what was said. For example, can you really believe that I have a sincere interest in helping you grow and prosper after I have just listed all the things you failed to do in the last year?

I remember a story told me by one of my mentors. Late one afternoon he had received a one-hour phone call from his boss, the CEO, in which for the total hour the only things discussed were the manager's failures. He went home to tell his wife that he had been fired. She asked whether those exact words had been used. He said no, but that one could draw no other conclusion from the interchange. The next morning he went in to wait to be relieved and turn over the keys, so to speak, to the replacement. At about eleven the next morning, the CEO called and told him that he had just given him a one-third increase in salary! It is extremely difficult for the individual to make sense out of such an exchange.

The *appraisal discussion* is an evaluation of past performance against plan. It is retrospective, narrow in focus, and judgmental on the part of the manager, and the manager is very much in charge. The *career discussion* is a forward look, exploratory and broad, and is nonjudgmental on the part of the manager, for the manager's role should be that of a catalyst; in general, the employee is in charge. I *strongly recommend that these two conversations be separated in time.* Both the employee and the manager need to have the appraisal as a base line for looking at the broad future, but if they have just done it, they will tend to regress into the appraisal mode. The advisable separation is about a month. The only argument against this separation seems to be that the leader feels it will take more of the leader's valuable time, but there is nothing more important that the leader could spend time on!

Characteristics of Assessment and Reward for Teams

Technical and business projects are becoming more complex. They require that the leader bring together individuals with different kinds of expertise and skills and orchestrate their working together on a common goal. As Quick (1976, p. 91) says, "Although people have been assigned to work in groups, teams, and departments for as long as there have been organizations, the thought of a work group as an entity, a body that exists with an identity, has not until recently been taken seriously on a wide scale." The key difference in today's managerial perspective is that we have begun to understand the formation of groups and the behavior of individuals in the group, to look at group behaviors as a whole, and to see team building as a managerial function. Teams as concepts will be discussed in Chapter Eleven and team building as a function of the manager in Chapter Twelve. The focus here is on performance management and reward of teams.

The tasking of a group is similar to, but not the same as, assigning a task to an individual. Arriving at an agreed-upon definition of expectations of what the task is becomes more difficult because several people's perspectives must be melded. As the manager must encourage self-management in the case of the individual, the manager must also strive for the group to become self-directing. In the former case it is clear who is to become self-managing: it is the individual. In the latter case, however, a leader from within the group must evolve into that role and will probably emerge only after some activity. The group may even have more than one leader for there are several leadership roles within a group. One role is task-oriented, another takes care of the psychological needs of the group, and still another may have to do with mustering resources, assistance, or knowledge. These roles may be carried out by the manager tasking the group, or they may be carried out by those leaders who emerge from within the group, or they may be shared. In any of these cases, tasking the group includes sorting out these roles. Thus, the first step in carrying out performance management—establishing objectives jointly and in broad terms deciding how these objectives are to be accomplished—is more difficult with teams than with an individual.

Once that step has been accomplished the manager must decide how to assess the results and how to identify whether the contributor is an individual, a subgroup within the team, or the team as a whole. Most often the manager is not present for the majority of the team debates and activities and must therefore depend on reports from group members about activities and contributions (which may be distorted by the reporter's own psychological needs). The results of a task group or team are generally evaluated by a community of managers, not only by the manager to whom the group reports. In a sense, therefore, the manager neither writes the team's appraisal nor evaluates it in any way parallel to the discussion with an individual, since evaluation flows through many communication channels by a diverse group of managers from several parts of the organization. The manager loses some of the control that is present in the one-on-one situation when a team is chosen instead of an individual.

Group recognition and reward, which at this point is primitive and limited, is also often out of the hands of the manager. Some forms of group recognition include: acceptance and implementation of the team's recommendations, dinners (often including spouses), certificates or other symbolic award trinkets, and sometimes group awards or bonuses. If the task of the group is broad and has potential for affecting the entire organization, the shift in control over performance management from the original manager to management in general is great. If the task of the group is defined within the functional or programmatic responsibilities of the manager, such as a product program in a development laboratory within the product area of the manager, the initiating manager may retain more of the performance management role. Even this can be diminished in some organizations by the matrix form of organization (discussed in Chapter Eleven). For the most part, the manager who chooses to use a team or group must realize that performance management in all its aspects is diffusely delegated, for better or worse, to a broad collection of members of the management group.

Daily Appraisal and Feedback

One of the dangers in appraisal programs is that managers and employees will think that the annual appraisal is enough. On the contrary, it is immediate, daily feedback that supplies the stimulus for growth and change. The closer the feedback to the event, the greater the chance that the individual will associate the two. There is no substitute for the impact that attention from the leader can have on performance. There is a desired symbiosis to be achieved from frequent communication, especially between a technical leader and a professional. The emphasis should be on the communication—the exchange and the feedback—often this is accomplished by just playing back to the professional what the professional has voiced, rather than restating what is on the written appraisal. It obviously is of greatest value when there is mutual trust and respect in the relationship.

Appraisal, the Annual Event: Purposes

It would seem that the prime purposes of improving performance and stimulating growth in capability could be accomplished simply by using a system that ensured a daily communication about work in a meaningful, caring, and open style. There are two problems with this idea. First, no one has discovered such a system, and second, managers do not generally provide the kind of daily communication that is necessary. Therefore, managements turn to the annual appraisal to make an environmental statement of intent to provide the individual with the feedback necessary for improving performance and assessing capability. The performance management system that includes an annual appraisal can also ensure that communication occurs at least once a year on the subject of employee performance and improvement because the system includes a follow-up and measurement of the manager's own performance in this area. A system providing follow-up also ensures some consistency in what is discussed, through the use of a standard form, and that the conversation has taken place, through the requirement for the employee's signature on the form.

The annual appraisal is intended to ensure that information about an individual's performance and contributions is entered into the corporate memory, as opposed to being maintained only in the minds of the two individuals. This is something that daily communication cannot accomplish for lack of documentation. Conducting annual appraisals, according to an established procedure and supported by training, adds rigor to the system. It provides a defined unit of human resource management action that can also be used to measure the manager's performance. It can provide needed emphasis on human resource management functions of the manager (such as coaching) and can make an environmental statement about the importance of the leader's human resource management activities (as opposed to technical management) in the R & D environment. The documentation provides both a reference for actions on salary and change of status and a trail for audit and control purposes. Since the appraisal form often calls for a summary evaluation, usually a single numeral, it also provides a shorthand for gross sorting of people as an aid to analysis of salary by group (or level, or year of degree), when there is a need to find a top performer list as a basis for selection for some opportunity and other similar functions. The summary evaluation provides the manager with a quick reference trail when the manager must address potential changes for the individual, such as a promotion up the technical ladder in response to demonstrated increased capability and technical maturity.

Because the collection of the data provides management

with ways of looking at groups and classes of people, there is a potential danger that many managements have experienced. Built on the rational concept that all people are not alike and that a population should tend to show a normal distribution of appraisal ratings, top management has looked at and attempted to manage appraisal distribution. There is nothing wrong with the rationale that a normal curve should result when applied to large populations, but who is to define what a large enough population is, especially given that R & D managers are dealing with a highly selected slice of a total population? Motivated by the need to force managers to deal with the small percentage of inadequate employees, managements have attempted to define an appropriate rating distribution skew. Again, if the size of the group is large enough, it is reasonable to assume that a skew toward the better assessments should exist in a highly selected group of professionals. But managements have applied skew criteria to small groups, like ten employees. This is not only wrong; it is illegal.

Other Uses of Appraisal Data: Problems

One's performance should be judged against one's capabilities and assigned goals. This is fine for the prime purposes of improving performance and increasing individual capability (as previously discussed); there are, however, other organizational needs for which data about individuals can be useful. These ancillary uses, while necessary functions, are the source of many of the difficulties with performance appraisal programs.

For example, it is necessary periodically to rank and compare people in order to choose which person is best and most valuable; this could be the basis for choosing who should be moved to another job because of reduction in work or loss of contract, or perhaps who should receive the highest pay in a class of employees because of his or her value to the organization. Since most organizations have a performance appraisal summary number, this would appear to provide the necessary data for gross comparisons. But remember, the appraisal was of that person compared to objectives set for that person on the job, not of performance compared to another employee. One person might be doing very well at what one manager considers an easy set of tasks, while someone else is doing only reasonably well at what another manager considers a difficult set of tasks. A comparison of the two persons would be unfair in this case. Or both sets of tasks might be equally difficult, but one of the two jobs might be much more important to the success or failure of the organization. These needs for interpersonal comparison have led managements to ask the manager to consider other people and assignments when coming up with an overall appraisal of an individual, even at times to suggest that there are appropriate proportions of A's, B's, and C's that the manager can have in the group. This is trying to manage the distribution of ratings as just discussed. This is unfair since it has a high probability of distorting the feedback that the manager and employee need for the prime uses of appraisal. The solution to this dilemma is to perform the ranking as a separate function.

Another example of a supplementary use that may cause trouble is a necessary part of most salary programs. It is generally felt that pay should reflect performance; however, as I indicated earlier, there are other determinants of pay. Some of them are: university degree level; years of experience; responsibility level (usually reflecting managerial position); professional level (staff classification based on acknowledged technical expertise); the size of the impact the individual can make on profit or loss; and to whom the individual reports (for instance, headquarters staff may be paid more than location staff). Thus, if salary is tied rigidly to performance in a particular classification, it may cause distortion of relative position in some broader conceptual framework.

The most dangerous ancillary uses are those which are not open, preannounced, and agreed upon. That is, if the individual feels that this data may be seen by or used by others in the organization in a manner that he or she does not understand, this will undermine the confidence in and/or credibility of management, the system, and the organization. The most important message to carry away from this discussion is that ancillary uses should never be allowed to detract from the prime purposes of performance improvement and individual growth, and that any ancillary uses should be open, not covert.

Performance Management: A Two-Way Process

Another issue on this subject is the fact that most discussions of appraisal and most programs in organizations are built on the mistaken assumption that appraisal is something the manager does to the individual. While the manager is cast in the role of a judge by the organization, if the activity is one-way, it will not improve performance, probably not change behavior, and may cause real dissention in the organization. People can be helped only when they are open to being helped or coached, only when they feel that they need help, and only when they respect and trust the helper-coach. It is often the case that the performance of the individual is being directly affected by the performance of the manager, in which case it will be discovered and corrected only if the manager listens. This is particularly true in R & D organizations, where the authority of the manager flows from technical and managerial competence, not from position. One strong source of objections to appraisal in R & D organizations is built on that distrust and lack of respect of managers discussed in earlier chapters.

A necessary solution to this challenge is to make it a two-way process in which both the individual being appraised and the manager-appraiser have responsibilities and functions. Some things that could make it a shared responsibility are:

• Empowering the individual to ask for the appraisal rather than having some system or manager schedule it.

• Requiring both parties to prepare for the discussion, with each one assessing from his or her perspective what has happened since the last discussion.

• Expecting the individual to comment on those actions of the manager which detract from or support good performance on the part of the individual.

• Training both managers and individuals for their roles. Programs in active listening and discussions of the Johari window might supplement specific training in the use of the forms and the performance management system and might reinforce the intent of the program. The Johari window was developed in 1955 by Joseph Luft and Harry Ingham to provide a model for analysis of and awareness of interpersonal relationships in the communication of personal information between two individuals. It divides a square into four segments: public, blind, unknown, and private. A two-dimensional matrix is thus formed, ranging from "known to others" to "unknown to others" and from "known to self" to "unknown to self." Thus, the *blind* area may include data about self that is unknown to the individual but known to others; the *unknown* area, data unknown both to self and others; the *private* area, data known to self but unknown to others; and the *public* area, data known both to self and others. For an exercise that will lead to understanding the use of the Johari window, see Pfeiffer and Jones (1974, pp. 65-69).

- Publishing the expectations in an employee handbook.

Creating a Positive Culture for Performance Management

High-technology R & D organizations, as well as others, need a breakthrough in establishing and managing a performance management system. The issues discussed, as well as others not discussed, are sufficient to make most appraisal and counseling systems work poorly, if at all.

Many managers do performance management with the feeling they are doing it for someone else and thus do it because they feel they have to. Some managers give appraisals in a style that turns the employee off rather than assisting the employee. Often even those that generally do it well fail to listen to the employee. Some fail to do the day-to-day coaching and then drop surprises in annual appraisals of the wrongs they have saved up. Many managements use the appraisal results for ancillary, and unannounced, purposes.

On the other side, many employees, both professionals and others, also keep the system from functioning properly. Individuals come to the appraisal process with wrong expectations and attitudes, expecting either a kiss or a spanking rather than a

useful exchange, and are thus quick to misinterpret the manager's intent and stop listening as soon as they hear a critical
word. Some individuals feel like nonparticipants in the process,
almost like victims, and go into appraisal discussions expecting
to be victims. Others question the competence, and sometimes
even the need, for the manager to provide instructions about
work or to make judgments about their performance. Many employees expect the system to remember the positives and forget
the negatives; incidentally, a good system should forget both
after some time (such as five years), since people change and
should be allowed to change.

On both sides, the problems result from: a poor culture
base; an improper or incomplete understanding of the process,
its importance and value; poor training; and mistrust of each
other in the roles of manager and employee.

The breakthrough needed requires creativity on several
fronts. Here are some of the areas in which management must
be creative:

• On the philosophical base for performance management: what it is, why we need it, and the roles of the participants.

• On the way the performance management system is introduced (if there is no system currently) or on the way that
change is introduced (if there is a current system that is functioning poorly).

• On the process itself, including the associated forms,
instructions, and data storage and retrieval systems.

• On the training of the participants, both managers and
individuals.

• On the day in, day out discussions of, use of, and support of the system once it is installed. Managers tend to destroy
systems through the attitudes they project when they talk
about and use human resource systems.

The Nature of Recognition

Performance improvement and capability enhancement
will occur to some extent simply as the result of improved communications about work between leaders and individuals. But

the ultimate result of assessment in the eyes of the individual is recognition and reward, both from salary and other aspects. To be effective both in stimulating performance and in creating an image of a quality environment (QPL), recognition and reward must meet several criteria. When we apply our energies to some activity, we do so with the expectation of certain results, based on prior experience and our view of our skills. If we get more results (that is, we are for some reason more effective), we are pleased. If we get less output, we are displeased. Both these feelings are internal. Reward and recognition represent something beyond the results. *Intrinsic* reward is that sense of well-being which comes when we like our results, when we are pleased; this is what happens when we look in the mirror after an exercise regime and notice the slim waist and muscles. *Extrinsic* reward and recognition comes from other people and the system; in the exercise example, extrinsic reward comes when others comment on our loss of weight or how good we look. Another layer of reward comes when we go to the store and find that we look better in the new clothes and the salesperson confirms this. The important point is that the recognition and reward must, as the results had to, match with some expectations that we have in order for satisfaction to occur. What I have generally described here is called the expectancy theory of motivation; it is more fully covered in Katz and Kahn (1978).

To understand what this means in the management of R & D, we should think in terms of the characteristics of and expectations of the professional (discussed in Chapter Three). A couple of examples may put it in perspective. Too much recognition, that which is out of keeping with our own assessment, is not motivating and makes us suspicious; such would be the case in R & D if the manager were overly solicitous and gave a large salary increase for what the individual considered to be a small contribution. Or the reverse would occur (as it frequently does in R & D) if the individual felt that he or she had made a large contribution to the organization's income (amounting, say, to millions of dollars) but had not had any unusual salary increases or change in status. Some of the best corporations have systems for revisiting and reassessing contributions in the light of history, since often the time of evaluation is not reflective of true value. Both IBM's outstanding contribution and outstanding patent award programs require periodic reassessment of awards and provide for additional payments if the value of the contribution or invention increases over time. Often the inventor of a key concept is recognized several times over the years as the dollar impact of the invention becomes more evident. (Such was the case with Bill Goddard, a friend and co-worker, who was one of the early inventors in disk storage.) Good recognition fits the expectation range of the individual, is commensurate with the accomplishment's value, and is delivered as soon as it can be after the actual activity.

In awarding recognition, managers are trying to accomplish two things: to be fair in acknowledging the value and quality of a contribution, and to do this in a way that lowers the threshold for the individual to be self-motivated. *Motivation* can be defined as an inner striving, supported by the individual's values, needs, wants, and drives; it is an energized state that moves the individual to action. It is represented (and evidenced) by energy applied toward achieving a goal. Inherent in our concept of motivation is the fact that it is selective functioning, goal orientation, and encompasses learning for improved capability. For the individual, motivation is generally accompanied by a feeling of pressure, or stress, that is reduced by the goal-oriented activity.

Creating a Good Salary System for R & D

A good salary system for R & D pays professionals, managers, and others in accordance with the concepts for good recognition, as cited above. It provides the manager with techniques and a mechanism for bringing one's worth to the organization and one's salary closer together. It provides incentives for the individual professionals to increase and maintain their capabilities.

A good system is one that management and employees can be open about. This does not mean that it is necessary to post individual's salaries on bulletin boards (to which I am opposed), but it does mean being open about the factors used in determining salaries. The individual is entitled to know how much of a salary change is dependent on personal performance, how much reflects a change in the value of the dollar or reflects the organization's acknowledgment of its overall improvement in productivity, and how much represents a change in the perceived value of the individual to the corporation. The individual is entitled to know the relationship between a given performance evaluation and a salary change and is entitled to know what the organization does to ensure that it is paying people properly relative to other organizations.

A good salary system provides reward techniques for both team and individual contributions. It provides the manager with a multifaceted reward kit. That is, I envision a good system as one which considers salary, one-time dollar compensation, perquisites, if any, and benefits as one total compensation package.

A good salary system supports the manager and the personnel function in performing all the classical salary functions. For example, providing data that helps ensure that an individual is paid properly relative to others who perform similar work, who have similar experience levels, and who are in similar job classifications indicates that the organization values the individual in proper comparison. I consider such a system to be a vitality-enhancing system.

Proposed Specifications for an R & D Performance Management System

What follows can be considered a script for changing a poorly functioning performance management system into a model system for an R & D organization. This outline has several dangers: First, it is like prescribing for an illness without ever seeing the patient; this is wrong for me to do. Second, no matter how universal it is in concept, it must be tailored to the culture of the organization for it to be effective. Third, once it is on paper, it is static and unchanging, yet organizations are continually evolving and changing. I have nevertheless decided to take the risk. With these caveats, here it is:

1. Establish performance management as a shared responsibility between employee and manager—the goal being improved performance, which benefits the employer with results and benefits the individual with increased satisfaction and growth in capability.
2. Communicate this philosophy throughout the management chain and the professional chain. Encourage discussion and definition of the process, both within and between the chains. It is important in an R & D organization to deal with the tough issues—the unpredictability of results and the difficulty of measuring the results of creative activity and knowledge work.
3. Establish a joint (management and professional) committee to survey what has been done and to specify the broad changes or new system for the organization. Any viable system must meet certain criteria:
    *   It must be easily understood and require minimum administration and paperwork. The form should be simple and should match the sophisticated needs of the organization. The form or forms should be useful, but it is a mistake to make the form the major focus of the discussions and system design, for a form is a dependent variable, not the driving variable.
    *   It must assure fairness; that is, there must be safeguards and there must be enough training to ensure a reasonable consistency of approach and standards among managers.
    *   It should be owned by the management and the professionals, not by the personnel department. Personnel can handle the paper, the training, and the checks and balances.
    *   Its prime purpose should be to stimulate the growth and improve the performance of the individual and/or team.
    *   Secondary uses of the information, such as to drive the salary system, should be spelled out and should, to the extent possible, be open.
    *   Rating scales should not have more than five values, and the scientists should resist the thought of taking results to decimal values!

- Either the manager or the professional should be able to initiate the process, but there should be an administrative safeguard that ensures at least once-a-year documentation and discussion.

4. Performance appraisal concepts and systems should be compatible with the recognition and salary systems. Systems should complement each other in ways that create a feeling of an integrated culture and QPL.

5. Implement the program with extensive communication and training.

6. The program should include techniques for periodically reviewing whether assessment, recognition, and reward goals are being met and whether progress is being made in achieving understanding and a sense of fairness. It is probable, for example, that forms should be changed every three years or so, just so that people do not get in a rut and fill things out for the sake of doing so, on the same basis they did the year before.

Summary

- The performance of professionals, scientists, engineers, and creative individuals can and should be measured against jointly set goals. In addition, both parties should agree on results, how they were achieved, and how they should be measured and discussed. These agreements are necessary, both for the good of the organization and for that of the individual.

- Performance management includes the joint setting of objectives, joint agreement on objectives and measures, ongoing feedback and coaching, appraisal and measurement and its feedback, and the wrap-up of these processes in appropriate recognition and salary. It is a necessary process for managing an organization and ensuring the development of the individuals.

- Performance management is a day in, day out process. It is punctuated by annual sessions between manager and employee, which are discussed and documented.

- There is a difference between performance appraisal and career support. I strongly recommend that appraisal and career discussions be separated in time so that the individuals have time and space to change their roles and outlooks.

- The tasking and assessment of team performance, along with the appropriate recognition, are more difficult than dealing with the individual. In some sense, when the leader chooses to use a team, the performance management is in part delegated to a broad and diffuse group drawn from the management team.

- Appraisal is of little value without feedback and discussion, for it is through feedback and discussion that we learn. Development of capability and improvement of performance are the prime objectives of the process.

- The form or forms should not drive the process, but should be a simple, easy way to document what happens, thus reinforcing learning.

- The many ancillary uses of appraisal data are the source of much of the distrust and many of the problems with appraisal systems in all organizations. These uses should be open, agreed on beforehand, and kept to a minimum.

- A viable, usable, performance management system must be built on a philosophical base that is designed into the culture of the organization. Both the individual and the manager should have responsibilities.

- A process for introducing or improving the performance management system was presented. In itself, it represents a good summary of the principles that should be used in developing or changing a system.

Chapter 11

Designing Productive
R & D Organizations

Bonoma and Slevin (1978, p. 102) say, "Next to staffing the organization, the most important function of a manager is to design that organization so that people work together effectively," yet how many leaders or managers feel that way? Sure, we might quibble as to whether organizational design is the number two function, or number four, but it is an important function and it is not just done once and forgotten—it is a continuing role. Writings about structure of organization as a means of improving control and effectiveness date way back. The Bible refers to Moses and his management problems. Much later, Henry Fayol, a French industrialist, laid down the requirements for command and readdressed structure by coming up with his "bridge," in which he determined that one leader should manage five managers. He was searching for the ideal span of control. Still more recently, as reported by Peters and Waterman (1982), we have been through a period of emphasizing organizational structure as the factor in effectiveness and productivity. Structure (organizational form) alone will not solve effectiveness problems, but it is a creative tool in the hands of an innovative leader. Through its appropriate use, the manager can teach values and establish some dimensions of environment, emphasize function, improve communication, sharpen focus, gain commitment, and make work easier. Organizational boundaries can, in the best case, add rigor to the transmission of information and, in the worst case, impede the transmission of data and the movement of people.

In designing the organization, the leader must first have decided about the mission and goals. The next step, before determining which organizational form to use, is to identify those things which one hopes to accomplish with the design. Is the purpose to improve the focus on some new area of activity? Is it to divide the work so that it can be encompassed and given proper attention by some number of leaders? Or is it perhaps to tailor the activities so that they are more nearly in balance with the strengths of a manager? I suggested in Chapter Two that R & D organizations are *ad-hocracies,* which means that they are high in a dimension called differentiation—that they are populated with many professionals, with different fields of interest, pursuing sometimes seemingly unrelated activities. Dynamic and fast-changing organizations need to be high in this dimension of differentiation and in their ability to adapt and change; adaptability energy is what I call vitality. The other dimension is *integration,* which means that activities are tightly associated with each other, controlled and coordinated with direction from the manager. But here we have a problem, for integrated organizations are more effective and more productive than are highly differentiated organizations. One of the differences between research and development and the remainder of the organization is in the appropriate level of differentiation. Research organizations are highest in this dimension; development organizations, because of their mission to develop a product, move toward integration, but stop short of the integration appropriate for manufacturing, for example. Differentiation is established primarily by the diversity of the professionals hired. How much and what to integrate requires understanding the subtleties of design impact on behavior. The leader must decide what aspects to integrate; should it be information exchange or decision-making authority?

In R & D, there are basically two forms of organization and mixtures of the two. In the programmatic form, structure responds to projects and programs with the idea that product focus is the most desirable emphasis. Programmatic organizations are typical of developmental organizations. Field-of-endeavor (discipline) organizations group chemists together because of their scientific base and put physicists in a different group. The structure of field-of-endeavor organizations tends to resemble that of departments in a university. Discipline forms of organization are more typical of research; here, the most important emphasis is thought to be the collegial support of those with similar backgrounds. Nurturing of learning in the specialty is best accomplished in the field-of-endeavor organizational form. Support of the learning of how to get useful things done (that is, the applications made) is best done in the programmatic organization. Combinations of the two, called matrix forms, try to gain the best of the two forms in one; one structure is overlaid on the other, and a given person or group has two managers emphasizing different aspects. A further organizational complexity typical of R & D has to do with the organization of the support functions necessary to facilitate the work of the professionals. One form calls for centralization of such functions as procurement, model shops, design services, records services, and financial and personnel support. The other form decentralizes as much of these functions as possible and gives each of various groups its part of these functions.

I have raised a few of the issues of design in order to highlight the importance of this topic for the manager. The chapter will proceed by developing some of these ideas and suggesting some concepts critical to the adaptive and control aspects of R & D organizations.

Structure: The Classical Concepts

Until very recently, managers operated according to the belief that there was one right organizational structure. All one had to do was to find it. Much time and energy (both in the theoretical and practical sense) has been spent trying to find the one right structure. Some forms of organization have been pursued with missionary zeal, yet we have examples that teach us that any structure can be made to work by people who wish and need to make it work. Thus, one of the leader's functions, regardless of the organizational form chosen, is to gain agreement on the usefulness of the form and thereby gain the commitment to make it work.

Field-of-Science and Programmatic Forms. In research, the classical structure is based on the discipline, or field of science. This falls generally into the concept of a functional classification for other parts of organizations, such as marketing or manufacturing. Thus, for example, a research organization will have a chemistry group, a physics group, a life sciences group, and a materials science group. Each of these will normally be led by a person trained in that discipline. Some of the difficulties in communication, misdirected allegiance, and lack of cooperation can flow from this differentiation by discipline. For example, at the next management level above the discipline group, the leadership of a physicist who has been promoted to direct several different discipline groups will only be accepted reluctantly by the leaders and professionals in the life sciences group. Discussion and comment about the qualifications and field of interest of the person on top is a consuming game in some R & D organizations. In organizations in which insecurity and feelings of powerlessness run high, if one group has a representative with its background in the key leadership position, it is one up on the others.

In development, the more classical form of organization is programmatic. Thus, an organization is formed in the early conceptual period of a product or system, grows with the need to develop the product, and lasts until the death of the product. Development organizations thus tend to follow the product cycle. Organizations in which products go on and on are relatively stable; thus, while the recent reorganization of General Motors' development activities into a large-car organization and a small-car organization was traumatic, there has been a Buick organization, with Buick model–associated subgroupings, since the inception of the car. In organizations with rapid product displacement, specific organizational groups and structures are short-lived. Such is the case in the computer industry, in which the change of technologies and products formerly supported about a three-year cycle in the days when large computers were the prime output. Now, with personal computers displacing themselves almost monthly, I suspect that the life of an organization is even shorter.

In both research and development, because it is usually not economically feasible to have each group have all its own functions, there are normally central service functions. In research organizations, typical service functions are both technical and nontechnical. Service organizations include functions like computer services, engineering and equipment support, facilities management, finance and budget, and personnel and education. In a development organization, the service functions might include a materials laboratory, a testing laboratory, a chemistry laboratory, instrument services, facilities management, finance and budget, and personnel and education. In both organizations, this classification of a support function tends to set up second-class citizenry. It can be the basis for friction, ineffectiveness, serious differences, and a feeling on the part of the service group of not being appreciated.

Consequently, in most laboratories there has been a constant centralization versus decentralization struggle over these functions. This struggle has been further exacerbated by accounting practices that charge these functions to projects or basic science groups either as an overhead or a direct charge. In either case, the attitude becomes that they are a *burden* and even sets up feelings that they are nonproductive. The argument supporting decentralization is that unless they belong to us, they will be ineffective. It is further enlarged to include the concept of the need for association with the results for psychic income. There is some strong truth here, in that it is much easier for the model maker to feel a part of the team that built the product if the model maker reports to the leader of the product team. For the purchasing professional or nonprofessional, for the personnel specialist, and for the financial support specialist, association with the mainstream of organizational function is even more difficult. As a result, attempts have been made to decentralize these functions. The argument for centralization is that there will be a waste of time and energy unless we centralize, since no function needs these support activities 100 percent of the time, or that waste will occur through poor supervision of these functions, and that learning and peer support will be improved if we bring these people together. Both arguments have some validity. When managing many of these functions, I would change from a decentralized to a centralized form periodically, as I mentioned when talking about stimulation and vitality.

Matrix Forms. A recent fad has been the use of a matrix form of organization. It was thought to provide the best of both worlds, both function and program bases. The intent was good, for it was created to attack one of our major challenges, the implementation of new technology. As Leonard-Barton and Kraus (1985, p. 102) observe: "For all the dollars spent by American companies on R and D, there often remains a persistent and troubling gap between the inherent value of the technology they develop and their ability to put it to work effectively. At a time of fierce global competition, the distance between technical promise and genuine achievement is a matter of especially grave concern. . . . Those who manage technological change must often serve as both technical developers and implementers."

In the matrix form, all people, except project and program leaders and staff, belong to discipline or functional groups for the purpose of developing their expertise and it is the discipline manager who supplies the nurturing, caring functions of management. They are assigned to programs on an as-needed basis and are managed by a program manager with respect to that program. The promise of the design was that effectiveness would be improved by easing the flow of people from one project to another and that a constructive conflict would occur at the intersections of the two lines of management, making for a sharpened attack on problems. The design also promised an improved interface with the customer, in that the program manager would be seen as the customer's representative; this single, goal-oriented interface was seen as more desirable than an interface with a manager who had conflicting and multiple goals. In most cases, however, the complexity and conflict have outweighed any gain and have resulted in a proliferation of staff functions in order to ameliorate and adjudicate differences.

Back at the bench, the professional is confused! Had the matrix been implemented differentially, viewed as an experiment, and flexibly interpreted, it might have had value. Had it been implemented with the understanding that structure does not solve everything, it might have had value. Implemented monolithically, viewed as permanent, and interpreted inflexibly, matrix has been a disaster.

It is important to give some more attention here to the problems of the matrix form in order to understand both the power and the weaknesses of attacking effectiveness problems through structure. The intersections of the matrix are points of conflict—and the need is to manage agreement at these points. Harvey (1974) identifies six aspects of this paradox: (1) private agreement, person to person, on the nature of the problem; (2) private agreement, person to person, on the steps to be taken to solve the problem; (3) failure to communicate desires or needs and beliefs to one another accurately; (4) collective decisions based on invalid, inaccurate, or partial information cause action contrary to what they want to do and perhaps contrary to the intent of the organization; (5) counterproductive actions elicit frustration, anger, irritation, and dissatisfaction; and (6) the organization's members do not deal with the basic issue, the management of agreement, and thus the cycle of conflict and counterproductive action repeats itself. To my knowledge, no management implementing a matrix form dealt with this last aspect of the matrix.

In reporting on a study of the matrix at Thompson Ramo Woolridge (TRW), Kingdon (1973) commented on the fact that technical professionals, assigned to project and program management roles, felt that the matrix contributed to technical obsolescence for the manager. It took the technical person away from the frontier and from those studies which help maintain up-to-date technical knowledge. (Note how this ties in with the concept reported in Chapter Nine that project management might mitigate the effects of obsolescence because it requires generalized, not specific, frontier technical knowledge; here we have two sides of the same coin.)

The human side of the matrix has been left to chance,

which has thus contributed to the failures. In discussing the human side, Lawrence, Kolodony, and Davis (1977, p. 54) point to the fact that "individuals who have spent all their time in traditional organizations . . . cling to the myth that the formal power a boss has is what gives him influence." Managing in matrix organizations requires a new concept of management, new beliefs, and new types of support. These same authors (p. 58) say: "A matrix organization includes matrix behavior, matrix systems, and a matrix culture, as well as a matrix structure. After years of working with a matrix, some organizations find that they no longer need the contradictory architecture of the matrix structure to accomplish their goals. Instead, they revert to the simpler pyramid for their structural form, while at the same time retaining the dual or multiple perspective in their managerial behavior, in their information processing, and in the culture of their firms."

A contributing editor to *Research Management,* Wolff (1980) reports on the Research Institute's May 1979 special-interest session on matrix management, citing five caveats for those who would implement matrix: (1) beware the culture shock in implementing matrix, (2) understand that some people simply cannot adjust, (3) understand the need for a team commitment and manage it, (4) setting priorities can be a problem and top management should be prepared to step in and set them, and (5) matrix may be a fad.

In summary, I recommend that managements consider the matrix form only if customer demands support an increased need for a specialized program interface, and then only with heavy emphasis on the human side of the impact. Remember, I stated in Chapter Three that *any* management that *feels* like management is distasteful to the professional—and matrix means a lot of management.

The Creative and Innovative Design Outlook

In my pre-IBM experience I saw an organization eliminate a whole layer of management. It did so after it found the layer to be noninvolved in the issues facing both the higher and lower levels of management. Among other things, this elimination brought engineering management closer to the top. From my early experience with this type of organizational change, I realized that organizations and the charts that portray them are not sacred and unchangeable. This came as a shock, for at that time my educational preparation and experience as a professional had been totally in engineering. I was in my first semimanagement job as the technical program manager for telephone instruments design, with two design technicians reporting to me.

My early experiences in organizational design at IBM put me in touch with two further, important thoughts about structure. First, it was IBM's practice, on an overall basis, to change mission, focus, and title at such frequency that no manager could gain anything by creating a fiefdom. It would soon be lost. No individual could gain anything in the long run by building protective walls around individual or managerial territory. Loyalties were built with IBM, not with the subunit, because of this change rate and the individual's need to find security in something. Second, when there was more than one obvious organizational form that could be applied, the practice was to try them all. Often managers oscillated forms to gain the best of both approaches. As an example, in the struggle between having a central model shop or separate model shops for each group, I would go back and forth on about a three-year cycle. In the centralized phase, I would have the leaders try assigning centrally managed people, for technical guidance, to the projects or areas. In the decentralized phase, model-shop management would become more of a coordinating function, trying to ensure utilization and researching new equipment. There would also be a small (by comparison with the other mode) central shop with some of the most specialized or complex equipment to provide for training of new model makers.

I further enhanced this creative outlook by experimenting on my own, observing more of what was being done in IBM, and reading about and visiting the experiments of others. For example, one of the interesting and productive approaches was to take part of a manufacturing organization and part of a development organization, and in effect form a company within the company. This would provide an integrated team focusing on one product. It helped overcome many of the differences that normally occur at the time a new product is introduced into manufacturing. It helped in making those necessary design changes which make the product producible at a price and a schedule. After things were running well, the organization was dissolved and the groups went back to their parent organizations.

At one point, in an attempt to create vitality in IBM, laboratory management experimented with changing the size of the basic group. At another time, I tried improving the personnel service to the functions by assigning resident minipersonnel managers to sit with and work with subunits of three hundred or so. At other times, fellow leaders and I have made extensive use of temporary organizations and task groups. In commenting on designing the innovating organization, Galbraith (1982) says: "It is my contention that innovation requires an organization specifically designed for that purpose—that is, such an organization's structure, processes, rewards, and people must be combined in a special way to create an innovating organization, one that is designed to do something for the first time" (pp. 5-6). "Because innovation is destructive to many established groups, it will be resisted. Innovation is contrary to operations and will be ignored. . . . Managers have tried to overcome these obstacles by creating venture groups, by hiring some entrepreneurs, by creating 'breakthrough funds,' or by offering special incentives. These are good policies but by themselves wil not accomplish the goal" (p. 25). I would add that structure itself should be included in the things with which managers experiment.

The message in all this is that it is important to free the thinking of managers about organizational structure. One must experiment with structural change as a means of creating vitality and effectiveness.

Choosing What to Change

Upon identification of a malfunction in an organization, the manager can review the possibilities for correcting it through structural change. Here are some of the problems for which I have seen structural change prove useful:

- When the process that needs to be controlled occurs in

more than one unit, especially when the measurement of results is done in a separate unit, one should consider the possibility of putting all aspects under one leader. This should mean that feedback can be used to increase learning.

• When there are problems in transmission of data across organizational boundaries, ask first whether the boundary is intended to be a checkpoint for accuracy and quality. If it is, try to fix that. If it is not, consider eliminating the boundary.

• When the organizational structure has simply been in place so long that there has been no stimulus for a fresh approach, consider change. Such a change will usually stimulate vitality and improve adaptability capability.

• When the organization has been in place, or under attack, so long that people have dug in and are spending most of their energies defending and protecting their positions rather than pursuing their work, consider a change.

• When personalities, backgrounds, and experiences seem to be acting as blocks for fresh activity, consider a change.

• When changes in technology, business emphasis, or goals require a new focus or new emphasis, consider a change. Creating a new unit with a new leader, if it specifically highlights the new goal organizationally, can stimulate innovation and can build better bonds between individuals and goals.

• When a task group has defined a new challenge and convinced management to pursue some new direction, consider a change of organization. Implementation of change is assisted by creating a new organizational entity with a single focus and goal.

It is important not to use structural change as a crutch to avoid making the hard decisions. In one research organization, for example, this occurred over many years. When two strong scientists had differences that negatively affected the performance of the organization, management set up two laboratories and let each of these scientists do his thing. Early in the exploration of conflicting ideas such an approach could be of value, however, in this organization management failed to make a choice about the correct course of activity and thus allowed the scientists to develop followers and their differences to deepen. This type of difference becomes embedded in the culture of the organization and resists reconciliation and healing. Management's actions with respect to structure (and other things) can create an organizational schism that may not heal, even after the original protagonists are gone. It is important in R & D to use the emotional connection between the professional and the idea or project in positive ways. Managers must not let it permanently damage the effectiveness of the organization.

The Importance of the Vision of a New Organization

Most organizational changes, whether policy changes, process changes, structural changes, or changes in direction and goals, fail because those who must change their beliefs and behavior do not understand how they will gain from the change. This results from a failure on the part of the leader to articulate the dream, the vision. A failure to communicate it, and through participation to get others to share it and buy it, means built-in resistance to change. The following comments set forth several requirements for success in introducing change. (More principles are covered in Chapter Thirteen.)

First, create the dream. People respond to images of a better set of working conditions. This has been demonstrated by the growth and use of principles elucidated in "inner" tennis and "inner" golf; that is, when individuals in a sport can create a picture of themselves achieving success at the task, this has been shown to have a strong positive influence on outcomes. I believe this is also true in achieving organizational effectiveness. Creating an image of success helps bring about success. A leader should thus propose change in the form of a vision that embodies how things will be better as a result of the change. If members of the organization buy that vision, and the leader holds to it, the probability of success is greatly enhanced. One of the ways to ensure this is to have those participate in creating the design for change who must personally change and take actions to implement the change.

If we assume, instead, that the change design is the leader's, then the second step is to communicate the dream. Using several channels and modes of communication can assist in its transmission. For example, setting up groups to tackle the problems of implementing the change and to propose actions ensures discussions and improves understanding of the change. Communicating simultaneously both in a direct mode and through the several management layers ensures that the message will arrive two ways. This provides the opportunity for the message's accuracy to be checked. Setting up a requirement for feedback ensures a check on what got through.

People who own the change will work to make it succeed. If it belongs to the leader, the followers may or may not support it. If it belongs to the followers, they will ensure that it happens. How can leaders gain a sense of ownership for those who must change? Ownership occurs when the individual sees a personal gain. To achieve this, the leader must get into the shoes of that person and help that individual create reasons why the new condition will be better. If managers do this, the change will happen.

Management Layers: The Impact on Vitality and Effectiveness

A goal-oriented, committed, capable individual is the most effective organizational unit if—but only if—the function can be performed by one person. Errors in communication are confined to the biases of one individual. Errors in perception are confined to the view of one individual. Since we assumed commitment, there are no alternate or conflicting goals to dissipate energy. Learning is enhanced, providing that the individual is open to feedback and change, because the circuits are short and direct. However, the work of organizations requires more than one person. For most activities, the viable organizational unit is the small group or team. This is the reason for having an organization and for working to design these effective groups and create the leadership for them.

Interpersonal communication that is accurate and well-understood is difficult to attain, and attaining agreement is probably just short of a miracle. Agreement depends on shared perceptions, experiences, outlooks, and goals. Within organizations, we attempt to achieve this by dividing people into groups or units that have common goals and are of a size to make communication reasonably probable and effective. Clarity of communication is affected by the number of human links in the communication channel. Most of us have participated in that party game in which a message is passed around a circle and have discovered the message distortion that occurs. It follows, therefore, that the flat organization with the minimum possible levels from top to bottom is the most desirable organizational form for effectiveness in communication.

Minimizing the layers ensures a broader span of activities for each leader, and a broader span provides the opportunity for experimentation and greater freedom. Thus, vitality is enhanced by fewer layers. Vitality is adaptability energy, and organizations with fewer layers are more adaptive since they are more differentiated. But remember, there may be a loss of control or integration in this mode. We are back to the balancing act.

One of the aspects of an organization that causes us to have multiple layers is the limit to the diversity of and to the physical number of meaningful contacts that one individual can have. Here are four basic ways to improve the individual's span and to resist the addition of a new layer:

1. Provide the individual with capital equipment that improves time management, the numbers of possible contacts, the accuracy of the data transmitted, and other aspects of communication. Such devices range from helicopters to cellular phones in autos and include computers in data nets.

2. Add staff to support the leader. This solution, specifically in technical organizations, allows sharing of the technical leadership responsibility, but does not add another layer, and is intended to avoid removing the opportunity for contact with the leader on nontechnical matters. This role is filled by a technically trained nonmanagerial professional, who, through providing technical leadership, can be trained and tested for future leadership; this staff aide does not assume the hiring, rewarding, or firing functions of the man-

ager. In the best case, this additional staff improves effectiveness. In the worst case, it adds to confusion of messages for the individual, provides two bosses, and may not be a rewarding activity for the staff technical person.

3. Consider the use of committee leadership structures. The leadership in such a case is shared among several people, but another layer is not added. Large corporations, such as Du Pont and IBM, have tried this structure at the very top so that the CEO functions can be shared in a corporate office.

4. Consider the use of the self-designing systems approach to organizational design. Self-designing systems (Weick, 1977, p. 38) involve "arranging and patterning" by the participants; "must contain provisions for and support of the continuous evaluation of ongoing designs; typically focus, not on the designs themselves, but on the process responsible for the designs; wrestle chronically with the stubborn reality that specific adaptations often restrict subsequent adaptability"; and are "often hard to separate from implementation."

Multiple layers, which are necessary for integration, control, and limitation of span, reduce flexibility and vitality—yet small groups seem to be essential for good management of professionals. One manager for seven professionals seems to work out as the average in most successful R & D organizations, but such small groups virtually force a deep, vertical structure. Thus, the leader in R & D organizations is on the horns of a dilemma. There is no clear answer, no one right answer (which is one of the reasons why the matrix looked attractive to R & D leaders). Nevertheless, functional or discipline structures do seem to be able to provide for the clearest pursuit of basic science or technology. For this reason and because of collegial support, the scientist is most comfortable in this type of organization. It provides the maximum interaction between people with similar training.

However, no single form of organization is ideal across a total organization. The search for an ideal form, I believe, is one of the errors that managers as designers or organization designers as specialists make—they like the appearance of an organizational picture that has all the parts duplicating the patterns of the other parts. Rather, most successful R & D organizations are a combination of forms in an attempt to fit form to need; they shift forms periodically in an attempt to make the organization respond to some change in goals, technology, or business emphasis.

Temporary Task Groups, Systems, and Teams

Most of my activities and/or positions in the latter half of my IBM career grew out of task-force (task-group) assignments. *Task groups* are temporary systems established to tackle an emerging challenge to the organization or a challenge not yet out of control. The task-force assignment provides an opportunity for variety in assignments and for growth in a new direction, a chance to experiment without unhooking oneself from the security of position, and a transition activity that aids one in moving through the evolution of assignments and careers. Therefore, from the individual's perspective, temporary assignments are good.

The task group also provides management an opportunity to define a new challenge or experiment with a new activity or direction without committing to permanent change. It comes into existence when management identifies a new challenge, and it ceases to exist when it proposes a solution to the problem. Thus, task groups add to the adaptive capability of the organization. Task groups also provide for participation—a more open organizational structure. Task group activity broadens the individual's involvement and builds commitment to evolutionary change on the part of the team members. In many ways, the organization's ability to encompass change is strengthened as the result of the choice to use the task group.

This type of activity is especially needed and valuable in high-technology and R & D organizations, for it is here that leaders and professionals are unsure about what needs to be done. The potential for synergistic creativity is high in a task group. Task groups help define direction in new areas. It is also true, as mentioned earlier, that one of the key factors for achieving a good fit between the professional and work is a sense of autonomy and control—and the task group, which is largely self-directing, provides this. Task groups are effective in enhancing participation, spreading the involvement in direction and goal setting to new people.

Temporary systems are in a broad sense an extension of the task-group concept. Usually a *temporary system* refers to a temporary, or transitional, organization in which the roles are well-defined. This is different from the task group, in which the roles are usually not well-defined until the group defines them. A temporary system is usually established for the purposes of pursuing the productive work of the organization; by contrast, a task group is usually established for defining the future rather than performing an executing-implementing function. A temporary system might last months in a rapidly changing organization; it might last years in a slowly changing one. It ceases to exist when the basic organization adapts to the change or when the issue that caused it to be formed disappears.

Teams may be formed in ongoing organizations as subsets of groups, as groups, and as cross representation between groups. The word *team* connotes a special relationship between the members that creates effectiveness in achieving a goal. Schein (1985, pp. 164–165) sets forth four stages in team development (he uses the word *group*): "*Stage 1: Confrontation of dependency/authority issue.* The group, in coming together as a group, must deal with the issue of who will lead; who will have how much authority, power, and influence; and who will be dependent on whom. . . . *Stage 2: Confrontation of intimacy, role differentiation, peer relationship issues.* . . . Assumptions governing peer relationships will be the next major cultural layer to be formed. *Stage 3: Confrontation of creativity/stability issues.* . . . When everything was a first effort, creativity and innovation were valued; but as success mounts, creativity can become itself a source of disruption and anxiety. . . . *Stage 4: Confrontation of survival/growth issues.* As the group matures and continues to interact with a dynamic external environment . . . the question arises of whether the group serves important functions and should survive or whether it should allow itself to die." In the case of the team that forms in the task group, the proposal for organizational change made by the team often provides the opportunity for life, after the death of the task group itself. In the case of a team that fulfills an ongoing need, the issue of continuation should win out.

Team effectiveness can be improved through team development, an activity in which the team focuses on its own formation and processes and learns to learn together, which I shall discuss in Chapter Twelve and which is covered in Hines (1980). If managers expect their teams or groups to be creative, it will only happen if the organizational norms about groups support innovation and creativity. If they support conventional solutions and traditional approaches, then organizational norms may sabotage the manager's goal in setting up the task group or team; this is well-covered in Blake and Mouton (1985). There are those, too, who question the idea that teams are effective. This may occur when the individual feels that personal contribution cannot be identified or recognized (an issue raised in Chapter Ten).

Group Size: Effects on Vitality and Effectiveness

The main effects of group size on vitality and effectiveness seem to be:

1. The availability or lack thereof of a variety of assignments for the individual that contribute to vitality and learning. The small group usually provides the greater multiplicity of tasks, as does the small, high-technology start-up company.
2. The clarity or lack thereof of goals, with small groups providing greater clarity in the overall sense, but simultaneously providing space for the individual to be self-directing.
3. The homogeneity or lack thereof in the tasks that make up a job assignment. Here, again, we have a dilemma, for

homogeneity supports the development of a clear image of role and identity. This is necessary and good, yet (per item 1) variety is important for vitality.

4. The speed or lack thereof with which something can be agreed upon and accomplished. Usually, from the perspective of effectiveness, this favors the small organization.

5. The length of communication lines, with small organizations having shorter communication lines internally but perhaps requiring an increase in the numbers and length of lines externally. Again, as the organization designer, the manager must find the appropriate compromise that fits that particular organization.

There are undoubtedly some rational limits to the range of group size. Most effective organizations seem to have arrived at an operating range for the size of the basic organizational unit. It tends to be smaller in organizations composed primarily of professionals and larger when the work is formatted and routinized.

One R & D organization with which I am familiar has as one source of its problems the fact that it has not decided upon and enforced a suitable range. The basic group unit in that organization has ranged in size from three to three hundred. Obviously, at the large end there has been a shadow, or semi-acknowledged, organizational structure. This means that there has actually been another layer of management, one whose managers have not been trained or recognized as such, and that the person at the top still retains the unwieldy responsibility, at least on paper, of managing and evaluating the entire group. Failure to define the appropriate range makes the selection, measurement, training, and reward of leaders difficult because there is no possibility of a standard of reference and because in reality there are different levels of responsibility within one category, that of first-line manager.

For vitality and effectiveness, there are no rules about the right group size. The size depends on:

- The nature of the work

- The nature of the people
- The need for differentiation, adaptability, and creativity
- The style and personality of the leader
- The culture and history of the organization
- The need for integration, control, and uniformity of action
- The size required for critical mass

Critical Mass

In nuclear science, the necessary mass of substance to create a reaction is called critical mass. The concept is useful in thinking of organizations. When you have the right numbers of people with the right backgrounds, action takes place. Too few or the wrong mix will most often mean that the desired result evades the group. Unlike nuclear science, we cannot create an equation and come up with the numbers. Deciding how many people of what kinds is one of the leader's most challenging tasks. The number is not an absolute number but a relative one; that is, under certain styles of leadership and with certain kinds of personalities in the group, the number creating effectiveness may be larger or smaller. The number is also affected by the culture of the organization within which this activity is to take place. Nevertheless, the concept is useful. In attacking organizational design, the leader should try to identify the necessary critical mass. It may be useful to use a task-group approach to discuss and determine what this number is. In most R & D activities, the critical mass remains a matter of opinion and usually one on which the manager and management disagree.

A number greater than critical mass does not shorten the time to results. In fact, too many people and the wrong mix may mean that the friction and ineffectiveness caused by their presence will eliminate the possibility of success in goal achievement. Thus, in the organization in which management wishes to pursue a certain scientific goal, the leader must carefully experiment and must listen actively and openly to the members of the group. Even in scientific organizations, the natural human tendency to think that more is better sometimes distorts organizations. The most successful high-technology organizations, like

IBM, seem to have a knack of always having a few less people on the project than everyone thinks are necessary.

Some Last Thoughts on Organizational Design

Gone are the days when one right organizational design should be pursued or is possible. Gone are the days when organizational design should be left totally to some expert in organizational design, as was done in most large organizations in the 1950s. Now is the time for the leader to step up to the challenge and realize that organizational design is a leader's responsibility, although this does not mean that the leader cannot use the assistance of someone who has seen many different designs or has studied the theories of organizational design.

Organizational design is not something that is done and forgotten, as was once thought to be the case; it is an ongoing, iterative activity. Nor is it a matter of replicating a particular form across a large organization; it is adapting the structure to fit the function and needs of the time. J. W. Lorsch, a researcher who focuses on the problem from a human resource point of view, argues that organizational design is best done from a situational perspective; Lorsch (1977, p. 14) says: "In sum, the organization designer must create a structure, rewards and measurements, and other elements compatible with the external environment, strategy, tasks, organization members, top-management style, and existing culture. This may seem like an impossible task, but it really resembles an architect planning a house." Lorsch is reinforcing my opening point: Structure cannot alone solve problems; it must be used with full understanding of all the other elements, and these must be balanced with it. Good structure will not override a poor matching of individuals and work any more than a good matching of individuals and work can occur without an appropriate structure.

For the leader in R & D, here are some special thoughts to review:

- Structure can affect creativity. If the leader opts for integration and control, which is sometimes very necessary, then the probability is that adaptivity, creativity, and innovation will be depressed, for they tend to thrive under differentiation.

• It is important to keep the goals in focus. If the goal is creativity, as it is in research, then I would opt for the higher differentiation. If the goal is to turn out a product, as it is in development, then the solution seems to be to move toward integration, but not so far as to stifle innovation.

• Structure can affect vitality, and vitality and adaptivity energy are equivalent in some respects. Therefore, when an organizational design is under consideration in R & D, it is important to ask what will be the effect on vitality. In doing this it might be a good idea (by way of a checklist) to refer back to the specifications for vital organizations presented in Chapter Six.

Summary

The reader who has been following this discussion is as well prepared to deal with recounting the novel organizational concepts as is the author. There is no R & D organizational cookbook. There is no one right way, but together we have uncovered some concepts that can be reiterated:

• Any organizational form can work if the people want it to work.

• There are three basic forms: functional- or discipline-oriented, programmatic, and matrix. Functional organizations are truest to scientific pursuits. Programmatic organizations are best for single-purposed goal pursuit. Matrix organizations are complex, create a culture shock and a need for new behaviors, and are hard to manage; when instituted with appropriate attention to the human aspects of the organization, a matrix will probably evolve back to a pyramidal structure when the new behaviors (such as team thinking) are institutionalized. A matrix must be used sparingly, and only when external or internal forces strongly support the need for it.

• Support organizations in R & D tend to be viewed as second-class. Thus, they provide psychic income for their members with great difficulty. Design improvement can change this if it allows the support professionals and others to be seen in others' eyes as part of the mainstream function.

• To experiment with different organizational approaches

is desirable. The leader should try to develop a creative, innovative design outlook. No organization is sacred, sacrosanct, or perfect. In fact, the thought that organizations should form symmetrical patterns, with replication of the same form, is obsolete and probably counterproductive.

• There are specific conditions for which organizational change may be useful.

• Temporary task groups, systems, and teams are effective organizational techniques to assist in adapting to new needs and goals.

• Larger numbers of layers of management tend to lengthen communication lines and thus affect communications effectiveness. Choosing the right number of layers depends on balancing the needs of communications effectiveness with the need for differentiation or creativity.

• It is important to have a dream, a vision of the value of the changed structure, and to communicate it in order to secure the commitment to change from those who are affected by it and must implement it.

• The use of task groups and temporary organizations can aid in implementing change because by letting the group define the change, the leader broadens participation and support.

• It is important for the leader not to let any one organizational form persist so long that the majority of the energy is used in its defense rather than in the pursuit of goals.

• Organizational design is an ongoing managerial task.

• Group size affects vitality and effectiveness. Small groups have many, but not all, of the votes in favor of vitality and effectiveness.

• In R & D organizational design, it is important to define the critical mass—that number of people with varied talents which results in the explosion, the creation, the innovation.

Chapter 12

Matching Individual
and Organizational Needs

When individuals come to work, they bring needs and capabilities that they wish to match with the needs and capabilities of the organization. The effectiveness, or productivity, of the individual in pursuit of the organization's goals and the satisfactions the individual can gain from work are a function of the quality of the fit, or match, between organization and job on the one hand and the individual on the other. If the leader did nothing else but concentrate on continually and iteratively addressing this match, the leader would be concentrating on a major purpose for having a manager. The manager's role is to interpret the goals of the organization, break down these needs, and assign them to appropriately prepared and skilled individuals and teams. Motivation of the individual is dependent on the self-motivation that is achieved through a good fit and through recognition and reward for achievement.

In a study of job unrest in an R & D laboratory, Oliver (1981, p. 75) reports that when professionals were divided into *internals,* those who believe that "most of what happens in my life is the result of my own actions and initiatives," and *externals,* those who believe that "most of what happens in my life is the result of powerful forces outside myself," they gained insight into individual differences in the amount of ambiguity the individual could handle in the job/person match. If the internal was matched with ambiguous job requirements, it was a better match than for externals in the same situation. Externals required more structure. This example demonstrates the importance of understanding the person and the job and working to achieve a good match. A poor match not only leads to ineffectiveness but can also lead to job and career unrest. Oliver's thesis is that career unrest should not be looked at in its negative context, but rather as a source for creativity for both the manager and the individual. Orchestrating the work of a group adds an additional challenge; it requires dealing with team goals, team development, and team recognition. Matching the team and work is easier if both the manager and the individual professional have worked on the person/job fit and understand individual needs and capabilities.

Typical needs of the individual are for challenge, achievement, and recognition. In a sense, there are no typical capabilities since they relate to the special qualifications of the individual. Typical needs of the organization are for goal achievement, which can be accomplished by individuals who have the right skills and knowledge. Typical capabilities of the organization are to provide the equipment, facilities, and work environment that can make goal achievement possible and result in output for the organization and in recognition and satisfaction for the individual, psychic income. Sometimes needs are matched with needs, and other times with capabilities. For example, the individual's need for reward and recognition is matched with the capability the organization has for recognition and reward. The capabilities of the individual professional, knowledge and skills, are matched with the organization's needs for skilled work to be performed. But the individual's need for achievement is matched with the organization's need for achievement to meet its goals.

At different levels in the organization and in different functional areas, both the role of the manager and the role of the individual are changed by expectations inherent at that level and/or in the culture. For example, at the highest levels in the structure, the individual takes more of the responsibility for specifying the match. This would be true both for the professional who is a fellow and for a manager at the vice presidential level. At lower levels, the manager takes more of the responsibility. In the case of an entry professional, much of the responsibility for the match is with the leader because the individual does not yet know the organization and is not yet self-managing. In R & D organizations, because we are dealing with a highly professional organization, more of the responsibility falls on the individual than it does in manufacturing, for example; expectations are shaped by the special cultures of the organizations, and in manufacturing the culture usually supports a more directive style of managing. The negotiation about match or fit is, or should be, truly a shared responsibility. In high-technology organizations, a main feature of the matching challenge is rapid change. Both the individual manager and employee change, the technology changes, and the organization's requirements and the nature of the job change. Change comes at such a rate that a perfect job/person match is only a matter of the instant. It is probably the aspect that keeps the excitement and challenge level high in these organizations, since a prolonged perfect match would probably be demotivating.

Improved matching depends on training managers, professionals, and (to a lesser extent) others in the matching process and on providing them with the appropriate vocabulary to deal with the issues. The normal ways of talking about job assignments are not specific enough to be helpful with respect to job characteristics. For example, when did you or your manager ever talk about the nature of the feedback you could expect and the time delay in receiving it? If the individual needs specific physical evidence (the computer screen confirms entry of data) concerning accomplishment, and we all need some, a match with a job where feedback comes to the organization rather than to the individual would be difficult. Many professionals complain about the fact that they seldom receive feedback at all when they provide information that a manager takes to management for discussion and decision. Not knowing either what the reactions were in the meeting or the key factors that affected the decision deprives the professional of the opportunity to learn and contributes to a feeling of powerlessness.

In this chapter, the concepts useful in matching are presented with their unique vocabulary and are woven together to assist the reader in using the principles. These are covered through discussion of a tool that I have used to assess person/ job match, to teach the principles, and to provide the manager with a guide which assists in the negotiation over match. The chapter ends with a sample implementation scenario.

A Key Role of the Leader: Matching People with Work

In an organization, the manager is assigned a part of the overall goals, as well as specific objectives within those goals, to manage on behalf of the organization. This means that the leader has to: interpret the needs of the organization; determine what people, money, time, and facilities are necessary to carry out these objectives; gain the necessary support from higher management; and then divide the work appropriately among people with different capabilities, needs, and motivations. It means listening to and getting to know the people so that their needs and capabilities are understood and developed to improve the match.

In essence, the manager must match the needs and capabilities of the organization with the needs and capabilities of the individual. This means matching people and work, and it sounds easier to do than it is in reality. This match can be somewhat ephemeral on both sides, since work and people are in constant change. Both manager and professional usually have difficulty in understanding and communicating their needs and capabilities well enough to facilitate the match. The elusiveness of a good match is especially high in research, where the search is for an unknown and the tendency is to rely more on the individual's hunch about direction. The effectiveness of the unit being managed is to a great extent the result of the quality of this matching process. In an R & D organization, the responsibility for this matching process is shared between the individual professional and the manager. For the others, the nonprofessionals in the organization, the manager takes more of a directive role. These employees also have a responsibility for assisting in the match, but it is less than for the professional. Their responsibility is smaller because the individual's capabilities make less difference in matching with formatted and routine work than they do in matching with creative and innovative work.

A perfect match, if achieved, is only perfect for an instant in a vital, dynamic, and changing organization. A perfect match moves the performance of the individual and the organization toward greater effectiveness, but the continuation of a perfect match over an extended period may eventually erode vitality because it eliminates a piece of the challenge. If, for example, the individual does not have to learn new things because the capability needs of the job are well matched to the capabilities of the individual, then one of the factors of quality work has been eliminated. This is somewhat theoretical, because in the work of R & D perfect fit virtually never happens. We need only go back to the story about the magnetic-head designer (discussed in Chapter Four under Conflicts and Problems) to see this challenge. In one sense the engineer-designer, once he learned how to design magnetic heads, was perfectly matched with the task of designing magnetic heads. For the manager assigning him, he was the best, quickest, and most assured route to the desired end result. Yet something went wrong. This repetition of the same process soon became demotivating to the individual and raised the need for variety and the need to explore other activities. The design of another magnetic head, however challenging technically, did not meet one of the criteria of QPL, good work; it failed to stimulate learning and growth. It sacrificed vitality for effectiveness and the achievement of short-term organizational goals. This is one of the reasons why I suggested, when discussing vitality and effectiveness, that they must be pursued in a balanced way. Thus, the value of the emphasis on matching, of the search for a good person/job fit, is in the process more than in the actual achievement of the good match. To focus on matching causes the leader and the professional to consider aspects and take actions that otherwise might not receive attention. They must talk about work in a meaningful way, which improves the adaptation to change (remember that vitality is adaptability energy) while continually seeking effectiveness. Learning how to manage toward a good work/person fit is one of the managerial techniques for achieving the twin goals of vitality and effectiveness.

In research, more of the work is individual work than it is in development and in other parts of the organization. So the emphasis on individual matching is appropriate. In development, and some research, much of the work is done in teams. So we must supplement our understanding of person/job matching with an understanding of team/job matching. In team/job matching it is equally important to understand the needs and capabilities of the individuals, but we have added a level of complexity to the matching process and introduced the nature of team behavior as an additional variable. The leader must not only match individuals with work but must also match individuals with each other in order to achieve the synergism desired in team effort. This requires assembling groups, teams, where the capabilities of the individual members supplement and complement each other. This parallels the challenge of recruiting and selecting for the function, but it is more difficult because of the need for close-knit work relationships. Interpersonal chemistry becomes an important criterion for a good match of team members, yet it is difficult to define and to predict. Thus, the need for understanding and the need for the professional to communicate about personality and personal work style, habits, and desires must be added as important elements in the matching process. In team building, more of the responsibility appears to fall on the manager than it does in the one-on-one matching that is shared with the professional—yet at the same time, we have counterpressures represented in the self-management and operational struggles within the team (which were introduced in Chapter Eleven).

Needs and Capabilities: What We Match

Both the organization and the individual present needs and capabilities at the interface where matching must occur. It is important to note that this statement implies, as indirectly expressed earlier, a responsibility on both sides. The manager has the responsibility for interpreting the needs and capabilities of the organization, and the individual has the responsibility for presenting and interpreting his or her own needs and capabilities. Clarity in understanding and in communication is important. In R & D, however, the understanding of the organization's needs is often unclear, and the individual's understanding of personal needs may also be unclear. This adds to the creative challenge for both leader and professional.

Typical needs the organization presents are represented by: goals to be achieved; skill and knowledge needs required by the work; work relationship needs, such as the requirement for teamwork and the work-flow sequences that specify the order in which things must be done; needs for understanding of what is happening within processes or events, represented by organizational learning and the building of organizational memory; needs for new concepts and technologies on which to base products; needs for products that fit customer needs or create new customer needs; and needs for innovation and new features for existing products. Typical capabilities presented by the organization are: work-process understanding, systems, and facilities; financial capability; reward and recognition systems; educational and training facilities and capabilities; management and organizing skills; values and culture, which shape and characterize the work environment; structure, which assists the goal-setting and matching process; and for R & D, contact with and interpretation of the marketplace expectations.

Typical needs the individual presents include: the need to match personal goals with the goals of a larger enterprise; the need for a purpose that is tied to the receipt of income; the need to be needed; the need to utilize personal skills and knowledge; the need for achievement; the need for recognition and reward; the need for collegial support and stimulation; the need to find a work environment which is compatible with the individual and which provides opportunities for the desired psychic income; and the opportunity to learn, to grow, and to have a career. The individual brings capabilities, which include: skills and knowledge related to the field of specialty; interpersonal skills, including the ability to work with and communicate with others and the ability to operate as a member of a team; the ability to be self-motivated and to commit one's energies; the ability to learn and to grow in capability; and the ability to pass on knowledge and experience to others, as in documenting research, in providing technical leadership, and/or in teaching the less experienced.

A 1985 survey of 6,159 nonstudent members of the Institute of Electrical and Electronic Engineers with a 46 percent response provides an overall picture of what some engineers feel are important aspects of work. Langbein (1985, pp. 1–2) explains: "Respondents were asked to indicate which aspects of their job have an important influence on their level of job satisfaction. The most popular response is working on an interesting project. Next, in descending order of popularity, is having authority commensurate with one's responsibility; participating in decision making on issues that affect one's work; receiving recognition when it is deserved; adequate compensation; an effective supervisor; compatible colleagues; job security; working independently; opportunities for continuing education; having a comfortable workplace; and adequate clerical help." Many of these items will be reflected in our discussion of the elements to match.

This matching of needs and capabilities is described and pictured in Miller (1977a, p. 345) and is described as a human resource function of the manager in Miller (1979, pp. 94–107); the picture adds a dimension by showing that this matching takes place in an environment that can aid or impede the matching process. The discussions of culture, climate, and environment in Chapter Seven should help in this understanding, and later in this chapter elements of environment specific to this topic will be covered. In the picture one can also see that there are external influences that can affect match and matching probability. Typical external influences include: those cultural values in society at large and in the community where the organization is located which relate to work and appropriate work expectations (the culture of a university town, for instance, would be different from that of a rural farming area); societal attitudes about the value of the activities of the enterprise, and whether or not they are seen as contributing to the quality of life; family pressures and expectations (in a dual-career household, for instance, these would be quite different from the historical model of the male at work and the female at home); and the events of the day in the world, the country, and the community. In the latter case, the actuality of the Soviet Union and the United States agreeing to reverse the arms buildup would most certainly affect the matching potential in a war-related equipment design organization. One of my client relationships has been with the Los Alamos National Laboratory, where one can see and feel the change in the internal environment based on the morning headlines from Washington. Another aspect of internal influence should be noted: The individual, or individuals as a group, occasionally go outside of direct negotiation to influence the negotiation and match. This would be the case when the employees decide they need third-party representation. Such is the case when individuals influence their legislators to change laws governing the enterprise and its freedom to engage in certain activities. Equal opportunity and job safety legislation are representative of this type of action. Considering the changeability of individuals and the change rate of technology, this prospect or possibility of external influence increases the enormity of the challenge to both manager and professional.

The search for improved matching leads us to the subject of work design and work redesign, sometimes referred to as job enrichment. Hinrichs (1978, pp. 154–155) warns of some problems with job enrichment: "The fact that there was a theoretical base for job enrichment—Frederick Herzberg's motivation-hygiene theory—also increased the attractiveness to organizations of a motivation technology. . . . By the mid 1970s, a number of organizations were beginning to express some disillusionment with job enrichment. . . . More reasonable commentators, however, were able to point out why there were serious problems with some so-called job enrichment programs. . . . Some of the reasons given for the problems with job enrichment were that: the concept was misapplied; . . . little, in fact, was done to change the content of the work; there was inadequate support for the changes from senior management." As we pursue this topic of matching and job design, we should be mindful of these warnings but also understand that in the case of R & D management we have a powerful tool for improving productivity and personal psychic income. Evaluating this tool, Raelin, Sholl, and Leonard (1985, pp. 37 and 41) say: "Our view is that job enrichment can be used to deal with cosmopolitan professionals who have a tendency to fall into deviant behavior. . . . Managers of cosmopolitan professionals should design challenging and varied job responsibilities and should evaluate professionals on performance. . . . Management needs to understand, however, that some role conflict and resulting deviance among professionals is a structural fact of organizational life. The liberal use of enrichment combined with selective deployment of participation strategies will provide substantial benefits for the professionals as well as the organization. And after all, professionals are worth holding onto, since they are among the organization's richest resources." Raelin, Sholl, and Leonard thereby underscore the power of the techniques discussed in this chapter for retaining professionals. For a clear understanding of the quotation, it is important to recall that cosmopolitan professionals are those who relate strongly to the profession and the field, as opposed to the organization.

The Context in Which We Match: Other Influences

The matching of people with work takes place in an organizational environment that influences the process by supporting the search for a good fit or by working against it. Sometimes environments do both, sort of helping and hindering at the same time. For example, a work climate that endorses freedom of choice of assignments and encourages rotation of assignments is supportive of the matching process. By contrast, an environment that makes the manager the owner of the talent and builds impenetrable borders between groups impedes the effective matching of individual skills and knowledge with the needs of the work. One laboratory organization tried to achieve the best of both worlds by policies that shaped the environment. It had a policy that a manager could resist a request for transfer of an employee to another group (where the employee's talents were needed or where there was a promotional opportunity) for three months, and no more. This was an attempt to ensure support of the manager's result-oriented goals but not to trap the individual permanently. Another of its policies protected the individual's right to return to the prior assignment for up to six months after transfer. The intent of this policy was to lessen the individual's risk during the change by assuring return to the prior assignment, where the individual was presumably successful. A third policy protected the individual's performance appraisal rating, gained in the prior assignment, for a period of time so that the individual was not fearful of being immediately and harshly appraised on a new set of tasks about which the individual was still learning. These policies were more important in their cultural impact, in the tone they set in the environment, than in their actual use; that is, they seldom had to be invoked.

Having discussed what is to be matched and the overall environment affecting matching, I now need to discuss influences on the match and some of the effects that these may have. Some factors affecting a match are best thought of as having a mediating affect, and I shall call these mediators. Influences on the match include:

- *Climate and environment.* (Discussed in Chapter Seven.)
- *Task characteristics.* These are mediators. An example is autonomy, the amount of freedom the individual has to be self-directing.
- *Values and norms.* These include both those expressed by the organization's culture and those inherent in the individual. A conflict in values between the individual and organization affects the probability of a good match. An organizational norm that supports group action toward improving the match would impede both the manager and the individual in pursuing the match one on one.
- *The individual's strength of needs.* This is a mediating factor. It includes the importance to the individual of belonging, of creating a personal identity with the job, and of monetary income.
- *The organization's strength of needs.* The development or-

ganization that must create coatings but lacks a coatings expert has a strong need for one, but its need would be less strong if many of its professionals were knowledgeable about coatings and it desired only to add another professional. If the individual has strong needs to pursue personal research, this will provide the basis for conflict with an organization that has strong needs for project-oriented activity. In the extreme, when an individual reaches a level of discomfort no longer justifying the gain from the relationship, that individual will demonstrate deviant behavior or leave the organization.

- *The individual's outlook and self-image.* These have obvious effects on the match. If the individual comes to the task with the idea that it will be fun, that the challenge is exciting, and that success is possible, the prospects for a match are good. If the individual's self-image is one of inadequacy or the challenge seems overwhelming, the prospects for a good match will be poor.

- *Managerial style.* This can be considered another mediating factor affecting the match. (It is discussed in Chapter Eight.) In a program in which a group of professionals were discussing matching, one professional spoke up and asked whether it was possible to have one factor change and thus turn a good match into a poor one, or vice versa. My response was that while one factor could have such an effect, an individual usually reacts to a combination of factors. The questioner had had this match deteriorate on one job, and only the manager had changed. The individual who feels strongly about self-management but has a tendency to feel inadequate would react strongly to a manager whose style was close supervision.

- *The individual's expectations.* These are important mediators. I remember that when my son was looking for his first professional job, he did not know what to expect from the job. All his work experiences had been at part-time jobs as a busboy or a baggage handler, and what one expects and gets from such jobs is quite different from what one can expect and receive from a job as a professional.

• *The individual's capabilities.* These constitute another mediating factor. If the individual has the skills and knowledge required by the job, this will contribute to a good match. If the individual does not have the skills, this will contribute to difficulties in matching. A slight mismatch of capabilities, however, can increase the challenge and the chance for learning, which can improve the character of the match. Many mediators and characteristics have both good and bad attributes, and matching requires that these be balanced.

I am sure that there are other mediators, but this list should transmit the concept and the need for understanding them in pursuit of good job/person fit.

Discomfort (dissatisfaction) with a job is a function of the difference between our expectations and what happens. If we expect freedom but feel that we receive detailed instructions, this will feel like a mismatch. We can improve the match by changing our expectations. Working to achieve a match is an iterative process because these factors are changing over time as a part of the change of individual and job.

Different Responsibilities at
Different Levels of Management

The immediate manager (the manager of the nonmanagement professional) is driven by short-term goals for results. This means that the focus on the matching process will be governed by short-term goals and considerations. This was the case with the manager of the engineer who designed magnetic heads (described in Chapter Four). It is the responsibility of higher levels of management to take the longer view.

Management can legitimately expect upper-level managers to put more emphasis on the long-range development of the individual's and the organization's capabilities. This means that the upper manager should intervene in the job assignment process whenever a change of assignments will strengthen capabilities in the long run and not interfere too greatly with short-term goals. Thus, part of the blame for the error in the case of the magnetic-head designer falls on the manager's manager. That leader should have seen the conflict between the needs of the individual and the needs of the organization as expressed by the immediate manager.

Another function of upper-level managers is to look across organizational boundaries and facilitate movement, to offset the parochial views of the leaders of subunits. For example, an upper-level manager might see that combining two previously separated functions into one unit would make it possible for the manager for the new unit to offer a variety of experiences that neither manager can now offer. This change would contribute to the long-run increase in individual and organizational capabilities and thus to vitality.

Upper-level managers should also provide a safe place for the individual to express personal needs when the individual feels that these are not being understood or appropriately met by the immediate manager. Some organizations have effectively institutionalized this support by instituting skip-level interviews. This annual (or more frequent) practice makes it permissible in the environment to talk to one's manager's manager without others feeling that one has broken a cultural norm. In these interviews, many of the individual's problems with fit and career needs come out quite naturally.

The Role of the Individual

If as individual professionals or managers we do not represent ourselves at the interface where matching takes place, then our manager is left to guess about our needs and capabilities. A manager who personally needs high risk and high challenge, for example, will tend to assume that those working in the organization also need high risk or high challenge. Consequently, the individual is responsible for making sure that his or her needs and capabilities are understood, for providing feedback on aspects of the assignment that support or do not support a good match, for negotiating in a way that contributes positively (not just from a you-adapt-to-me perspective), and for exhibiting a willingness to compromise some of the time for the good of the organization.

Professionals who learn and grow in the organization learn several lessons in the pursuit of their responsibilities in matching. For example, I remember the advice of a manager when I felt that I had been wronged by the organization, which had chosen someone else for an assignment that I wanted, felt I needed, and felt I was best-prepared to pursue. My manager's advice was to understand that management was aware that I was disappointed and additionally to understand that they were watching my activities. The suggestion was to show management that I could rise above this loss and continue to perform in an outstanding fashion. How we take our losses and failures is an important input and influence in the matching process. Over the years of my professional and managerial experience, I learned that by doing what the organization needed, I earned an increased opportunity to influence the character of a future assignment. It was as if performing what the organization needed was like making a deposit in a savings account, which would earn interest and which I could later invest in my own way. Taken in the long view, in the early part of my career I did what I was asked to do, and in the later part of my career I told the organization what to ask me to do. It worked!

Team Building and Matching

Many projects in R & D require more than one person because they encompass a range of technology beyond the capacity of one individual. Some projects require more than one person because of the magnitude of the work to be done in a limited time frame, some because the needed breakthrough requires making new connections between previously unconnected ideas and disciplines, and others because the skills required are not normally found in one individual. All of these reasons require that a team be formed and that the members of the team work together in a complementary, supplementary, and synergistic way. How, then, does the manager go about building a team?

Team building is a combination of selecting people with both the right technical skills and the right interpersonal capabilities. It is a process of helping a group of people share its

342   Managing Professionals in Research and Development

leadership and roles in a way that takes advantage of the differences in individual capabilities and of helping the people learn
to learn together how to work together effectively. With professionals, this is best accomplished by making them participants
in all these activities, for as they participate, they become owners of the goals and the needs, and commitment follows. Matching requires that team qualifications fit the goals, in the perception of the team members, as well as in reality, which is only
revealed in pursuit of those goals. It requires the manager's continual monitoring and appropriate catalytic intervention. It requires feedback from the manager by way of letting the team
know that it is viewed as a team, that the expectations and the
interest are high, and that it is making progress in the eyes of
someone else.

Team development, sometimes called team building, is a
process or set of processes, borrowed from other activities, that
accelerate team learning and improvement. As Dyer (1977, p.
41) describes it: "Team development is an intervention conducted in a work unit as an action to deal with a condition (or
conditions) seen as needing improvement. It is vital to the success of the program that it be the result of a good diagnosis of
the need of the work team; depending on the need, different
team-development designs may be appropriate. It would, for
example, make little sense to conduct a team-development program designed to improve trust and communications if the
problem is a lack of clarity of job assignments or one of general apathy and lack of innovation and energy." Dyer is a useful
reference for the manager who feels that a team-development
challenge may be impeding the organization's effectiveness. In
my own application of the concept, I start with interviewing the
members of the family group of team to discover what the
problems are. (My process is discussed in Chapter Thirteen.)

The Unique Challenge in R & D

What makes the matching process different or unique in
R & D? Here are some of the aspects that create a special challenge and make it difficult:

- The relationship between the individual and the nature of the work is more unique, more individualized, potentially stronger, often emotionally based, and related to the extensive investment in preparation that I have discussed. Thus, the quality of the fit takes on a higher importance for the professional in R & D than for others whose preparation leads them to more formatted work.

- The professional expects to be self-managing and is especially sensitive to a managerial style that feels overly directive. This factor makes it especially difficult for the manager, for to appear too directive in seeking an improved person/job fit may destroy the very fit that the manager is trying to achieve.

- Although teams are needed and used, much of the work is still individual. A shifting of roles within a team can help adjust and modify the match. For the individual on an individual assignment, role shifts may not be possible. Sitting at a desk and being expected to create is potentially one of the most stress-producing situations. At one stage in my own career, I had such an assignment, and I found myself pacing the floor, seeking repetitive and noncreative jobs to offset the pressure.

- The work in R & D, by the very nature of its unplanned and unplannable aspects, can be specified in less detail. Thus, it is not always clear what is being matched to the individual. Assignments are, in part, specified in the process of doing them.

- The rate of change of jobs and tasks is greater than in other activities because the work is tied to the very technologies that the professionals are discovering and pursuing. Thus, the iterative and continuing process of working toward a match has more iterations and the potential for dramatic change in the nature of the work is great.

- Those expectations from work which the professional brings to the work are stronger in influence and more specific than those brought by most people who work. Expectations rise with the level of education. The R & D professional tends to be the most highly educated in an organization.

- The match is affected by a natural conflict between the goals of the scientist or engineer and those of the organization, which has schedules and results goals. This is related to the conflict between the organization's need for output and the professional's desire to do it right. For the researcher, doing it right often means taking more time to find out why something happens. For the development professional, doing it right means polishing the product.

The Unique Challenge in High-Technology Organizations

Most of the challenges for R & D discussed in the previous section flowed from the nature of the professional and the nature of the work, the search for the unknown. In high-technology organizations, an additional complication in matching people (especially professionals) with work is that the rate of change in the technology is often very fast. This means that the nature of the work is changing at an even greater rate than is that change which results from the normal unplanned character of research and (to some extent) of development. This makes a good match even more elusive.

The pace at which high-technology organizations tend to work is fast. Often the only lead they have over competitors is a few months in the marketplace, and thus the pressure for quick solutions and fast processing of information to get the product to market is intense. This falls more on the development professional than on the research scientist because of the development professional's relation to a product or service. The pressure raises the general project- or program-related stress. Under a higher level of stress, individuals become more critical of small evidences of mismatch, tempers flare, communications are incomplete and/or inaccurate, and all these tend to change the work environment. In one sense, they make the work exciting and transmit a sense of importance to the individual; this is good stress. In another sense, they may contribute to individual overload and stress-related problems; this is bad stress. The responses and outputs resulting from a match have these twin possibilities of good and bad stress and their effects. As a response, there can be performance activity by the individual, which is the result of good stress. Another possible response is anxiety and general stress or emotional and negative behavior, the results of mismatch. Outputs follow responses and can be negative or positive. One result might be accomplishment, which is positive. Another might be poor health, which is negative. In matching, management is trying to set up creative tension, but not too much of it.

A further challenge to matching in high-technology organizations comes from the fact that often the leader of such an organization is the person with the dream, the idea, and has a strong personality. Meshing with and matching with this person presents special difficulties and definitely affects the person/job fit. This is why we have defections during the development of young technology-driven industries, as in Silicon Valley in California. Defections occur when individuals (and often a group of professionals later) decide that they are fed up with the leader's style or feel that the leader has sold out to the business interests or is on the wrong technological track. They move out and start another high-technology organization. To a very great extent, the thrust and progress of high-technology organizations depends as much on the personalities of the individuals involved as it does on the concepts or the technological base. Clashes of personalities are a normal characteristic of the work climate in high-technology start-ups and can have a profound effect on the manager and the professional who are in search of a good person/job fit.

Balancing the Goals of Vitality and Effectiveness

The twin goals of vitality and effectiveness contain many secondary goals for the manager and the professional. Goals of higher utilization, enhanced individual development, improved psychic income, improved results, beating the deadline, and winning in whatever competition they feel they are part of are examples of the intertwined goals. The relative emphasis placed on each of these goals by upper management, by the manager, and by the professional all affect the potential for good fit, the approaches to be used in gaining it, and the quality of the fit. The quality of the fit directly affects the individual's motivation and thus the results. Manager and employee are faced with a tough balancing act, and to a great extent they are not conscious of the goals or pressures they are balancing. Some of the goals and pressures are explicit and external. Many are implicit, or hidden, for they are part of the individual's self.

It is again desirable to return to the case of the magnetic-head designer. The engineer's goals in this case were to learn, to achieve, to experiment with different activities to find the right one, to produce for his manager, and to receive recognition and reward. Over time, the experimentation with different activities became more important to the individual and the other goals relatively less important. By contrast, the goals of the manager were to produce results, to gain personal recognition and reward, to match people and work for effectiveness, and to retain qualified professionals in the group. Notice the absence of vitality as a managerial goal. The young engineer's search for the right career and for maintenance of vitality became the dominant goals. Two things contributed to the eventual failure: The manager did not keep the twin goals of effectiveness and vitality in balance and did not really listen to, and accept, the employee's needs. A match that was initially appropriate deteriorated over time.

Consequences of a Poor Match

The consequences of a poor match, although by now apparent from preceding discussions, are worth recapping here:

- Low motivation for the work
- Low effectiveness and productivity
- Loss of necessary psychic income for the individual
- Diversion of the employee's energies to outside activities in search of psychic income
- Negative stress and stress-related problems or illness
- Interference with the work of others
- Disproportionate use of the manager's time trying to fix the match
- Poor morale and attitudes among others in the group because the dissatisfaction tends to spread

- Loss of learning, development, and growth for the individual
- Lowered vitality and loss of organizational capability
- Loss of the employee

These examples should be enough to motivate both the manager and the professional in their search for a good person/job fit.

Job Elements: The Necessary Vocabulary

One of the problems in improving the job/person match is that most managers and professionals have lacked the vocabulary, the checklist of job elements, to focus their attention on the real issues of matching. A typical element is the feedback, the evidence, that one gets that something has been accomplished. Two aspects of the feedback are important: the nature of the evidence and its timing. First, the best evidence is real in the sense that the individual can relate it directly to what was done. This type of evidence is most normally associated with craft activities. When we make something, we have physical evidence. We can see it and touch it. This allows us to develop our own internal recognition for the accomplishment. Others can see it and touch it and as a result provide us with acknowledgment related to their own experience. This is external recognition. Second, it is easier to relate feedback to what we did when it comes quickly. Good feedback comes in a form that we can identify in a time period that allows us to relate the feedback to what we did. In the real world of R & D work, professionals seldom gain the feedback in the prompt time frame just described.

For my own work, I have developed an assessment tool that I call "Assessing Person/Job Fit: Job and Career Redesign." It is to be used by the manager and the professional as a guide, and I have used it experimentally in assessing groups to identify job-fit difficulties affecting a whole group of professionals. I have also had the opportunity to interview professionals about the job characteristics or elements that need to be matched and about which ones are most important to them. As previously indicated, I found the need for autonomy (self-management) to be one of the most important elements. Katz and Kahn (1978, p. 394) also voice this belief: "Self-expression and self-determination within the organizational role make possible intrinsic job satisfaction. The basic conditions for such self-expression are the variety, responsibility, and challenge of the job, as the research literature attests. Changing job design to provide for job enlargement and job enrichment has generally been accompanied by more intrinsic job satisfaction." These authors support my contention that if the manager and the professional can be taught to identify important elements, such as self-determination (self-management and autonomy), and can redesign the job to improve the match, then both satisfaction, which they cite, and productivity, which is the other important goal, will be improved.

In research work, the feedback or evidence of accomplishment is sometimes slight, negative, and/or delayed. The person pursuing the goal of increased knowledge about a reaction in physics or chemistry may work for long periods with no evidence. That individual may get negative evidence for long periods. Some personalities can tolerate this, but others cannot. So matching is enhanced by understanding one's needs for concrete evidence of accomplishment—positive evidence and prompt evidence. Some well-trained scientists cannot stand research because of this mismatch and they do not discover this type of mismatch in the university because the university environment provides benchmarks, evidence of accomplishment. For the development professional, this particular element of evidence of accomplishment and its promptness is usually better. A product, service, or system is real, for it can be touched and seen. Product cycles are normally short enough that the feedback comes in some reasonable time. Yet, even here, I have seen product projects that were testing the frontiers of ability go on so long that they failed to provide sufficient satisfying evidence to match people's needs. IBM's Selectric typewriter was such an example. The concept was some fifteen years in development before there was a producible product.

To pursue the matching of people and work, it is necessary to identify the elements or characteristics of work that need to be matched. Some of these characteristics are identifiable for all people, but individuals put different priorities on them and these relative needs change over time. For example, our recent experiences change our tolerance for risk. If an individual has worked on projects that have a high risk of failure and has succeeded, the individual will probably be willing to accept another high-risk assignment, but an individual who has failed on a recent high-risk project will probably have a low tolerance for risk on a new project. Some of the elements or characteristics are very personal and probably not shared by others. As an example, the fit of the work with personal goals is very specific to the individual. If the individual's goal while working for an organization is to prepare for a career outside the organization, this will shape that individual's needs in a way not shared by other professionals.

Here are some of the characteristics or elements currently used in my experimental form that identify the vocabulary, the set of elements about which the manager and professionals should talk when considering job redesign:

- Discretion, autonomy, and control
- Opportunities for learning and discovery
- Wholeness
- Closure, results, accomplishment, and/or impact
- Promotion
- Challenge, risk, uncertainty, and excitement
- Span, depth, or size of responsibility
- Trust, acceptance, and/or respect
- Understanding of, participation in, and impact on organization's mission and goal setting
- Freedom and support in developing professional relationships outside the organization
- Manager-supervisor relations
- Environment, climate, and culture
- Meaningfulness, worth, and social purpose
- Feedback
- Personal growth
- Support, facilities, backing, and cooperation
- Newness, variety
- Utilization of capabilities, skills, and knowledge

- Recognition and reward (psychic income)
- Opportunity to make a creative, artistic, scientific, or technical contribution

- Salary or compensation
- Social and collegial support
- Working conditions
- Life balance

Job Redesign Concepts for Improved Match

Hackman and Suttle (1977, p. 98) write: "Whenever a job is changed . . . , it can be said that work redesign has taken place. . . . work redesign is used to refer to any activities that involve the alteration of specific jobs (or interdependent systems of jobs) with the intent of increasing both the quality of the employees' work experience and their on-the-job productivity. This definition of the term is deliberately broad. . . . It subsumes such terms as *job rotation, job enrichment,* and *sociotechnical systems design,* each of which refers to a specific approach to or technique for redesigning work." Once the manager and professional have identified the elements that need to be matched and have determined that the organization and individual do match in some cases but not in others, what can the manager and/or the professional do? Sometimes it is possible for the two parties to negotiate a different relationship on a specific element, and sometimes it is not. For example, if an individual works on a paced assembly line, that individual may find that because the activity is being controlled by the pace of the line, that individual is frustrated by the lack of control over the work. This is a requirement created by the technology, the design of the line, and the individual's assignment. It is improbable that any amount of individual negotiation with the manager will be able to change this condition. That individual must determine whether it is a sufficient discomfort to require a change of jobs. On the other hand, if the individual is a professional working on a development project and that professional finds that the manager is specifying activities so tightly that it leads to dissatisfaction with the lack of control over work, that professional can probably negotiate with the manager and gain improved freedom to control work. The ability to redesign an element is thus not always within the control of manager and professional, but the chances of having that opportunity are considerably greater in R & D than in other parts of the organization.

Improving the match on any specific factor is thus a process of determining the fact that there is a mismatch, determining the intensity of the discomfort, and then seeing if there are ways in which that aspect of the job or the individual can be changed to improve the match. One may find that the things one has to do to improve the match are too costly or too difficult for the gain that will be made. If, for example, there is a mismatch in skills needed for the work, it is possible to redivide the work, thus changing the skills needed from a particular individual. Or it is possible to retrain the individual to develop the skills. Or it may be possible to invest in capital equipment that changes the skills needed to do the job. For some characteristics, there are multiple ways of improving the match.

Four cautions are important for those leaders who would redesign to change the match. First, all factors are not amenable to change. It is fruitless for the manager and employee to struggle over some factor embedded in the technology of the job. As an example, if one must use a nuclear reactor to perform one's experiments, no amount of negotiation will change this. Second, when the manager changes the match on one factor for an individual, the manager may worsen the match for someone else. It is a dynamic system, and unless managers change the goals and requirements of the job or invest in capital equipment for a change, the manager may, in changing it for one, just shift the discomfort to another individual professional or nonprofessional. Third, the leader must make sure that the individuals involved have identified the discomforts as well as the current comforts and are all taking part in the process of change. Assuming that someone else has discomfort with the match on a given factor because you, the manager, would, may lead you astray. Lastly, check to see that the job redesign activities have support both in the organization's culture and in the national culture. Discussing certain elements important in the match may be dangerous in some cultures because it means discussing something that is out of bounds for the manager, something manager and employee should not talk about. For example, in our own culture there are rather tight restrictions concerning the manager's talking about life outside work and its impact on the quality of match between person and job. The cultural support for talking about these issues must be present if the process is to succeed.

A Self-Assessment Concept for Improved Matching

Let me now discuss matching in terms of a concept that has practical and immediate application for both manager and professional. Some of the job elements that must be matched have been identified in the preceding sections. The list presented in "Job Elements: The Necessary Vocabulary" may not contain all of the elements, and it may include elements that are not important aspects in a particular match of person and job, but the leader and the professional can use it and their own creative thinking to develop a checklist for discussing the match. For each element, it is necessary to determine the quality of the match. This is done by first asking the individual what expectations the individual has brought to the job relative to that element and then asking oneself what the job delivers on that element. If there is a mismatch, it will show up in a failure of the job to provide the relative amount of that element the individual expected. A sample item from my questionnaire will demonstrate what I am talking about:

> *Manager-supervisor relations.* The quality of management, the style of the manager, and the ability for the manager and the individual to communicate openly are all critical elements in gaining satisfaction from work. Some may thrive under the manager's guidance and support, and others may be irked by it. Some individuals require a close personal relationship with the manager, and others do not want it. On this factor, assess what you need from your manager in an overall sense, and indicate the degree of delivery you feel that you get from

the job relative to that expectation. (*Note:* For *expectation,* the numbers mean: (5) I need a lot, (4) I need quite a bit, (3) I need some, (2) I need a little, and (1) I need very little. For *delivery,* the numbers mean: (5) I receive a lot, (4) I receive quite a bit, (3) I receive some, (2) I receive a little, and (1) I receive none or almost none. An expectation of 5 and a delivery of 3 would result in a difference of −2, a failure of the match by two points on the individual's subjective evaluation of need and fulfillment.)

Expectation	*Delivery*	*Difference*
(5) (4) (3) (2) (1)	(5) (4) (3) (2) (1)	( )

One feature of this approach is that the individual must assess each factor in two ways. First, the individual assesses (measures) the expectation, or need; this is an attempt to recognize that different people bring different expectations to work, relative to specific factors. Second, the individual assesses the delivery of each factor; this requires the individual to assess how the need for that factor is being met on this job. Mismatch is indicated by the difference between the need and delivery numbers. It is left to the individual to estimate the relative values of the discomfort. It may be that a mismatch of 1 on a factor like control and autonomy represents much more real discomfort than a mismatch of 2 on span of responsibility. It is probable that the manager and the individual should choose to try to improve only one or two of the factors where there is sufficient discomfort (mismatch) for action at any given time. No one can really tell in advance what the effect will be of a change on a given factor.

A Possible Implementation Scenario

It is important in closing our discussion of the creative matching of people with work to present some further ideas about how the manager and professional might implement these concepts in an organization. The steps are relatively straightforward:

1. *Determine that quality of match is an issue.* This is done by questionnaires and interviews that attempt to search out the key issues impeding effectiveness and vitality in an organization. If it is determined that person/job mismatch is a major source of discomfort, then consider proceeding to step 2.

2. *Enlist the support and commitment of all involved.* In order to change, people and organizations must identify the discomfort, or hurt (more about the hurt factor in managing change in Chapter Thirteen), and must then be convinced that the investment necessary to remove the hurt is compatible with the improvement.

3. *Indoctrinate managers and employees in the principles of person/job matching.* Some type of seminar or workshop is of value to help people understand the information in this chapter and perhaps become aware of job-improvement efforts in general.

4. *Establish the human resource policies and programs needed to support the effort.* If it is really necessary to make an improvement because real discomfort exists, but if there is no technology for job redesign or no mechanism for transfer to another assignment, then there is little use of embarking on the program. If the manager and professional discover that the match can be improved with training or investment in capital equipment but find that they are blocked, then there is little use of embarking on the program. Management must assure that there is support, not blocking, inherent in the human resource policies and programs of the organization.

5. *Provide the tools.* Using the concepts presented in this chapter, provide checklists or tools (written documents).

6. *Require person/job-fit discussions.* Some method of follow-up and measurement must be designed so that people recognize the importance of utilizing these person/job-fit concepts to improve effectiveness, productivity, and vitality.

Remember that what we measure in an organization takes on importance because we measure it.

7. *Create ongoing open discussion about results and other ideas for improvement.* It is important to support any change with reinforcement of accomplishments and with continuing attention.

Summary

• Matching people and work is a key responsibility of the manager, but it is shared with the individual. Improving the match is important in achieving effectiveness, productivity, and vitality.

• A perfect match is almost unachievable, or is at best achieved for but short periods. If it were to be achieved over a long period, it would probably deplete vitality. The value seems to be in the things that the manager and individual do to improve the match—that is, in the process of job redesign.

• Values, goals, skills, knowledge, work mode, and recognition needs are but some of the job elements or characteristics to be matched. Both the individual and the organization bring needs and capabilities to an interface where matching should take place.

• The quality of the match is influenced by the organizational environment, culture, and climate as well as by characteristics of the individual and the job.

• The output of a good match is effective (productive) effort which does not diminish vitality and which hopefully enhances it. A good match should result in desired output for both the organization and the individual.

• For professionals, the important focus is on individual matching, since in R & D much of the work is still individual in nature. Attention should be paid to team matching where teams are used, but here the process is more complex.

• In R & D and high-technology enterprises, there are some special challenges to the matching process, such as the lack of definition of the work and the rate of change in what is done.

• It is possible to identify job factors that individually

and collectively affect the quality of the match. Once these are identified, the individual can determine whether for each factor there is a match or a deficiency in match between expectations and delivery.

• Once a mismatch is identified, many factors can be modified by job and assignment redesign, but some factors are not amenable to negotiation and change. The manager and the individual should concentrate on changing those one or two factors over which they have control in order to see whether this change improves the overall effectiveness and sense of satisfaction.

• There is a structured way of assessing the match between person and job that utilizes a checklist of job factors (elements) that can lead professional and manager toward change (redesign) of the most important factors.

Chapter 13

The Final Challenge

Implementing and Managing Change

In this book, I have presented concepts for improving the effectiveness (productivity) and vitality of R & D organizations. To put these messages to work for you in your organization, you must manage change.

People and organizations change when they hurt. The hurt factor can be the positive discomfort that comes from achieving goals and needing to replace them with new goals. It can be the negative discomfort of ineffectiveness, friction, distrust, negative interpersonal competition, poor communication, the lack of a team, and/or impending or actual failure. It can be a present hurt or an expected future hurt. Although it seems negative, organizations and people will be more motivated to change by discomfort than by satisfaction. Motivation is necessary for the individual and organization to mount the energy investment necessary for change. Thus, in implementing change, the hurt factor is always positive in its effect.

R & D organizations can hurt in several ways. They can hurt because they seem to have run out of technical challenge and/or because they lack technical direction; because of ineffective internal operating practices; because of mismatch or goal conflicts with other parts of the organization; because they feel

357

unappreciated or unneeded; because of inadequate leadership, poor quality staffing, trying to operate at less than critical mass, and/or inadequate funding and facilities; and/or because their product has been beaten in the marketplace or is disliked by the customer. External disapproval or criticism in the scientific community or in government is also a source of discomfort. Hurts can be technical, organizational, financial, product-based, process-based, and/or people-based.

The leader must stimulate interest in change, create a vision or dream of the improved condition, and elicit the energy necessary for managing change through to fruition. Since the leader and the consultant may share some roles, the consultant is often staff to the leader. The consultant, acting as a catalyst, can help the organization identify and define its hurts, assist in the process of planning change, and help people in the organization live through the pain or trauma of change. The leader often makes a tentative identification of the discomfort and then turns to others for confirmation or to check the diagnosis; the leader may also turn to others for assistance in gaining agreement and commitment to change. But in the end it is the leader who must shoulder the responsibility and be seen as the creator of the dream factor, the picture of tomorrow—the goal for the organization and people.

Once the dream has been created, or sometimes during its creation, there must be participation by those people who will be affected by the change and will implement the change. It is through this process that these individuals buy the goal, own it, and commit to it. These same individuals must define the action plan and specify what must be done, in what sequence and by whom. Sometimes another person may assist the manager as a process catalyst in these stages of goal definition and action planning. One mode for such assistance is through interviews in which the participants define the issues, issues which the other person or consultant then uses to create a planning or a team-building retreat. In the retreat, while moving toward the goal of change, the individuals learn to learn together and to master the power of team synergism.

For the change process to be effective, there must be

measures of progress, benchmarking of achievement, communication of accomplishment, and immediate recognition and reward for positive actions toward the change. All reinforce the process of change. Measuring how well the change is being achieved also provides the necessary data on which to base course corrections, the changes in what is being done to implement the change. Measuring the change and acknowledging and documenting accomplishments also enhances the benefits from change, because it makes an environmental statement declaring that the organization values this activity.

The last two sections of this chapter review and summarize the messages of this book and provide suggestions for putting the book's ideas into practice. I will have achieved a part of my goal if, at this point, you are able to identify several ideas or processes to introduce into your organization. The book will have been helpful if you have gained some insights into how to design, build, and implement positive work environments, climates, and cultures—work environments that create QPL by supporting effectiveness (productivity) and vitality, individual growth and achievement. I will have reached my ultimate goal if you implement changes that improve the effectiveness and vitality of your organization, improve the psychic income for professionals and managers, and assist in achieving your R & D goals.

Managing Change: Concepts

Managing change is increasingly becoming a more important managerial role. As Harris (1985, p. 42) affirms: "One thing is certain: namely, that not only the way in which we work but also our very notions about work are changing. Tomorrow's work not only will be different but will be constantly changing." The importance of managing change is increasing because the pace and frequency of change is increasing. It is most true in R & D, the source of many changes. It is necessary, therefore, for each manager to develop a perspective on the subject, to learn something about how change takes place, and to learn some techniques for implementing change. Change results from a desire for a better condition or process and from active learning from what one has done. But since change represents the unknown and the untried, each of us is somewhat fearful of change. The status quo represents safety. Change represents risk. Change is synonymous with growth and learning. Despite this, all change is not good. Whether a change is good or bad depends on whether it helps achieve an improved condition—the measurement of which is sometimes open to argument or is at least not discovered until considerable time has passed—and whether the improved condition has been appropriately specified and envisioned in the first place.

• The first concept about change is therefore that change in itself, while tied to learning and growth, which are positive, is not in itself good or bad. It is the results that count. Achieving good results means that there must be a vision of the new improved condition. The dream translates into goals, and goal setting is important in making progress—but also significant is the planning for implementation and the process of achieving change.

• The second concept is therefore that there must be a desired goal (discussed in a following section, The Dream Factor). Neither of these concepts will work, however, without the desire for change.

• The third concept is that the desire for change comes from some form of discomfort, which I call the hurt factor. As I see it, my hurt factor is related to (is a sort of precursor of) Kurt Lewin's concept of three overlapping stages in the change process (Hackman and Suttle, 1977, p. 20): "The first involves the *unfreezing* of the existing structures of the existing ways of functioning, thinking, or behaving. The second stage is the actual *change* to new structures and procedures, or new ways of thinking and acting. The final stage involves the *refreezing* of the newly acquired characteristics and behaviors." The hurt factor identifies the need for a discomfort, its identification, and its acceptance by those who will have to implement the change. In organizations, individual change follows this cycle, but organizational change is normally a group process and requires the discomfort to be shared by more than one person.

• The fourth concept is that the manager, as the agent of

change, can often help the group identify the discomfort and thus help them feel it. The manager needs to be a change agent, a catalyst, and in some sense a stimulus for action. Often, however, the manager and the members of the organization are, in effect, in the middle of the forest and unable to see more than the surrounding trees. This is where the consultant (internal or external) comes in—as an aide in furthering the process of identification, in translating the discomfort into a dream, and in managing the process of change.

• The fifth concept is that in problems of the organization, a third party, sometimes an outsider, is often useful in the change management process. Like your doctor, trained in listening and in diagnosis, someone not involved in the middle of the problem can often pinpoint the cause and cure. Kilmann (1984, p. 22) suggests that "External consultants are needed most when top management wants to collect information about problems the membership experiences, particularly if these problems involve the way the organization is managed."

• The sixth concept is that the participants in the process must buy in: they must own the problem and the solution. Getting people to buy in, to take on the problem and the solution as their own, most often results from participation.

• The seventh concept is that change is best managed as a participative process. Kirkpatrick (1985) describes the three keys to successful change as empathy, communication, and participation. Only through participation can the individuals feel as if they are a part of the process rather than feeling that something has been forced on them.

• The eighth concept is that the starting condition must be established through measurement and that measurements must be taken along the way to determine whether or not progress is being made. Progress is sensed (felt, experienced) only when one has a starting point against which to measure change. Benchmarking, measuring, and feedback thus become important factors (elements) in the change management process. When there is measurement, the organization demonstrates that what is happening is important; then there can be recognition and reward.

• The ninth concept is that the change process must be

reinforced and aided by recognition and reward for contributions to the process. This is basic—as basic as the concept of participation.

The Hurt Factor in Managing Change

In managing change, the motivation to invest energy in the process of change must come from somewhere. Changing usually means additional work. In the short run, it makes whatever we are doing more complex, more time-consuming, more confusing, and perhaps more energy-absorbing. Change may even temporarily rob us of the fun, the psychic income, associated with the work. It is important, therefore, to build this motivation for action on a strong base. The base is the discomfort, the hurt.

Discomforts are of several varieties. One type of hurt is the pain of failure. This can occur at the individual level or at the organizational level. For example, a research organization that has set a goal of a technical breakthrough is hurting when it finds that after years of investment of time and money, it has not achieved the goal. If it were a sports team losing games, the manager would be fired. The quick fix in organizations is the same. It is seldom the real cure in industrial organizations, though it sometimes seems to be the cure in sports activities. The challenge is to take this discomfort and transfer it to motivation, for a longer-lasting change. The process is most often one of asking the participants what they feel is wrong, feeding this back anonymously, and using the group to create actions that will eliminate these problems. This is the team-building process (which I will describe later on in the chapter), a process that encourages the buy-in.

Present hurts include: failure to achieve a goal; goal confusion and disagreement; leadership inadequacies; inappropriate management styles; discomfort in interpersonal relations; communications failures; distrust of management; energy-wasting friction with other parts of the organization; negativism, which feeds on itself; and a general loss of interest in and motivation for work. These are but a few of the possibilities. They may be felt more or less intensely by different individuals in the group or organization. Present discomforts are easiest for the manager and the organization to deal with, because they feel them now. Even those who do not currently feel them can have their sensitivity to the discomfort enhanced by talking about it. The trap, however, is that discomforts that people can express are often secondary effects, not the prime causes. They are like the headache that one complains of to the doctor; the headache is the result of something else, not the real problem. Only by increasing trust, the comfort in saying what the participants really feel, can these hurts be translated into real causes and thus form the basis for a goal and an action plan.

Future hurts present even more difficulty. This is because the pain is in the future, not yet felt, and a sensitivity today must be created for a future that will be worse. This is necessary if one is to find the motivation to try to avoid that future. An example, drawn from my IBM experience, will demonstrate the challenge. As previously stated, I spent a portion of my IBM career on the issue of technical obsolescence, or, in the positive sense, technical vitality. When we first tackled the subject, it was present and therefore real. This was in 1957, when we could see that engineers did not have the necessary educational base in solid-state physics to deal with transistors. It was easier to gain the support and the energy to do something about it at that time than it was the second time, in the early 1970s, when there was no dramatic technical change and no major surface evidence of obsolescence. To gain attention, we had to ask questions of the manager, such as "Would you be able to find an appropriate assignment for a specific person if his present assignment ended tomorrow?" If the answer was no, then future obsolescence was the problem. Obsolescence was in effect redefined from something evident today to something that would become evident tomorrow. If, through this exercise, the manager came to see that there were numbers of people who might be a problem tomorrow, then it was possible to elicit energy today to do something about those people. Another hurdle had to be overcome, however. The typical manager feels that when his or her people are no longer useful, they can be transferred to other managers. Managers feel that they will always be able to find another person with the right knowledge and skills. Somehow, it is necessary to convince managers that managers themselves, not the organization, are responsible for the future effective use of the individual who is becoming obsolete. The major technique used at IBM was the inclusion on a managers' performance appraisal of measurements covering aspects of people management. The manager had to see that people management counted as much as schedule and goal achievement. I do not feel that this approach was totally successful, but I do feel that it was on the right track. The reader should think of this story as exemplifying techniques for dealing with future hurts.

The Role of the Leader-Manager in Managing Change

The manager is the team leader, the catalyst, the focuser of irritations who helps the group manage change. Most often, but not always, it is the manager who sees the need for change. Even if the need for change bubbles up from the bottom of a seething cauldron of discomfort, the manager must be convinced of the need, for the manager's backing is as essential as is the commitment of the group. The manager must first gain sufficient agreement about the discomfort to cause the group to want to change and to invest energy in changing. This must be some sort of participatory process in order for the need to be shared at the critical-mass level. That is, while organizational and cultural change are not up for vote, there is a power base necessary to effect change. This power base requires that the proportions of the group who wish to change outnumber (at least in influence) those who do not. Even with the power on the side of those who wish to change, it is possible for a disruptive personality to sabotage change. Troublemakers, whatever their motives, can disrupt change just by intensifying the turmoil, enhancing the doubts, and sapping in useless debate the energies needed for change.

Schein (1985, p. 299) summarizes the leader's role nicely when he says: "When we are dealing with social systems (as opposed to biological units), there is no such thing as spontaneous change or mutation. There are no cosmic rays hitting the social genes to produce unpredictable changes. There is always someone inside or outside the system who has a motive to make something happen. The actual outcome may be a complex interaction of the forces unleashed by the different intentions of different actors, but the outcome will never be random and unpredictable. The only difficulty may be that events and interactions are so complex that it is not practical to try to unravel them."

Once the hurt has been identified and agreed upon, then it is necessary to decide what to change and how to change it. At this stage it is important to examine the relationship of culture, of norms, to what is to be changed. If values are to be changed, these must be changed before the activities or processes are, for without cultural support, the change will fail. There is a high probability that changes will require a focus on the human resources values and policies that make up the culture. Tichy (1982, p. 72) observes: "The technological, economic, and demographic changes of the 1980s are pressuring organizations to use more effective human resources management . . . the long-run competitiveness of U.S. industry will require considerably more sophisticated approaches to the strategic role of human resources management." Tichy's article can be particularly helpful in sorting out strategic, political, and cultural aspects as the leader participates in deciding what and how to change. It is important to give priority to changes that can be changed by the group. That is, some things are beyond the group's control, and choosing to change those things will involve other forces, take longer, and usually be less likely to result in success.

After the choice of what to change, then it is necessary to build an action plan. Michael (1982) identifies six different techniques, each with its own focal point, symptoms of need, types of changes to be made, type of control, continuity pattern, and change agent. An analysis like this is useful in choosing which techniques to incorporate in the plan. Again, the manager should be a major force. Action plans should be defined in a participatory mode. Energies will be applied when all involved own the plan. Implementing the action plan calls upon the manager's normal managerial skills. A key role for the manager is to provide the measurement of change, the feedback of accomplishment in a way that reinforces the change, and recognition for the contributors. The manager needs to increase the relative comfort in the process of change, since change creates fear. Comfort can come from positive reinforcement and group recognition of the little things that have improved. Things planned in the action planning phase often do not work. As a result, it is necessary for the manager, much like the pilot of a boat, to implement course corrections. Since the change process is deeply rooted in participation, the style used in course correction should continue to be participatory.

To bring the manager's role into focus, I will use an example built around a decision to make a change based on one of the ideas of this book. One of this book's ideas is that vitality and effectiveness can be enhanced by choosing them as strategic goals to be paired with the need for results. If you, as a manager, have decided that this is a good change to integrate into your organization and its culture, where do you start? You need to follow the steps I have just been discussing: gaining agreement first, and following it with decisions about what to change, an action plan, measurement and follow-up, course correction, recognition for contributors, and rewards for accomplishment. Many changes are lost because the manager and the people feel that the change has been made but fail to recognize and provide the continual reinforcement necessary to ensure lasting change. It is too easy to fall back into the old ways. Here is a brief outline of possible steps:

- Engage the organization's members in some sort of assessment of the current conditions that elicits problems or poorly functioning aspects.
- Create participatory discussion of the issues or problems, and gain agreement on the need for a change.
- Assist and guide the group in an exploration of things that could be changed. At this point, you might introduce the group to this book or to other books on change, especially

cultural change, such as Kilmann (1984), Schein (1985), Miller (1977a), and Hackman and Suttle (1977).

- Try to include a vitality and effectiveness strategy as part of the ideas for change.
- Form a task group to discuss ways of changing values, beliefs, and policies—the culture—in such a way as to focus on vitality and effectiveness. Task force results should enhance these qualities and provide suggestions for instituting the cultural support of the changed behaviors that are necessary to improve vitality and effectiveness.
- Manage the implementation of the ideas from the task group.
- Follow up on, measure, report on, and recognize accomplishments in the direction of the goal of weaving vitality and effectiveness into the fabric of the organization.
- Arrange for periodic revisiting of the topic—reports and anecdotal stories about what is different, or a new task force review, or any other ideas—to ensure continued management and organizational attention to the change process.

The Role of the Consultant in Managing Change

The internal, or sometimes external, consultant may be the change agent, catalyst, or aide to the leader in fulfilling the manager's roles. The other party (catalyst) must be invited to be a participant by the leader. Having identified a discomfort, management sometimes needs or wants confirmation of the problem. Managers often feel that they know what the problem is, but sometimes it takes another person to discover and/or verify the real problems. The other person can assist in diagnosing, confirming, and defining the hurt factor. It is then up to the leader to decide on a strategy for attacking the problems. When the distrust of management is high on the part of those being led, it is often better for the consultant to play the role of the change agent. When management trust is high and the manager can devote the energy and time, it is better for the other person to be an aide to the manager and have the manager pursue the role of change agent.

After defining the problem and creating the vision, the

consultant may assist in designing a strategy and devising tactics for managing the change process. Process consulting is usually a key role of the consultant. The goal of the consultant should be to assist in managing the process so that, by the time the change is implemented, the consultant will no longer be needed. Consultants leave the organization stronger, able to stand on its own feet, not weaker and needing continual use of the consultant as a crutch. Similarly, my goal as an author is to provide ideas and concepts, process consulting, and leave you able to go ahead and apply these concepts on your own. Of course, I realize that the prescriptions of this book are general and that the successful change of an organization, your organization, must be culture-specific. Your problem definition, your desired improved condition, the dream, and your implementation scenario, must all fit your culture, climate, and/or environment. Not only must your approach fit your culture, it must also fit your management style.

Often the consultant is involved in the design and use of diagnostic and measurement devices. One of these devices may be structured interviews, in which the consultant's value lies in the fact that it is easier to talk to the outsider, who is not embedded in the politics of the organization. Interviewing is useful in gaining definition of the problem, in searching for ideas for change, and in the continual follow-up and nurturing of the changed culture or organization. Other devices may be questionnaires, opinion or attitude surveys, or specifically designed surveys to get at the heart of the unique issues or problems. As an example, the concepts of job elements (described in Chapter Twelve), which are aimed at discovering mismatched factors between expectation and delivery, have been used for group diagnosis. Devices, in this sense, may also be measurement systems, integrated into the counting and reporting structures and systems of the organization. An example might be the modification of a personnel data system to account for the time that an individual has been pursuing the same activity. Such a measure would be useful in managing vitality when there is a need for variety. Measuring vitality can indicate the individual's ability to encompass the new when it is necessary to do so.

The consultant's role may be the classical role of providing an interested, but different, perspective for members of the organization. For example, I find that much of my time is spent in going to a manager's or professional's office and just being a good active listener. Through the process of listening, an outsider can assist managers and professionals in gaining perspective, working through difficulties, letting off steam or other pressures of stress, and/or considering alternatives without becoming embroiled in the politics of the organization or tipping their hand to the rumor mill. Listening may be supplemented by advice. The advice may be strategic, tactical, or process- or goal-related. I have spent hours listening to managers discuss the alternatives of organizational design. I find that the line between listening and giving advice is a fine one. Often neither person is conscious of the origin of an insight. In this sense, the outsider is a catalyst for thinking through complex organizational issues. My experience tells me that the best advice I give is remembered not as my advice, but as an idea owned by the receiver. Sometimes it takes many seasons for these seeds of advice, once planted, to grow to maturity and produce. So in putting the ideas of this book to work, you have some time.

The Dream Factor

Dreams, like values, are the stuff of which motivations are made. The manager who would motivate members of an organization to invest in change must create a dream, a vision to be translated into a goal. The dream may lead to new organizational values and culture, but in introducing the dream, it is better to deal with the improved experiences that people will have. The vision is the picture of the future state, which will be better than today, a place where work will be more fun, for example. The dream is a fictional description that is so desirable that people want to be part of it. They can see a personal gain.

As I write this, my wife and I are planning a European vacation. We have created a set of expectations about the trip—a dream, a picture of what will be—to which we can relate. We are caught up in building that dream, embellishing it with side trips to see friends, a visit to Stratford-upon-Avon to see Shakespeare's plays, and explorations of other particularly wondrous things we wish to see. We are already solving little problems, investing energy in solutions to the nonavailability of hotel space and the holiday schedules of friends. Even more consideration must be given to the problems we will leave at home. We invest in these solutions to maintain and extend the dream. We are managing change. I am well aware that this change appears more desirable than some that must be made in organizations. It is simple, by comparison, but it makes the point of the normal use of a dream factor.

(I can tell you now that the trip was a success, but we had another change to manage that we underestimated—meeting all the commitments we had at home after two and one-half months away.)

Failure to understand the need for the dream, and/or failure to articulate it and communicate it, has been a contributing cause of unsuccessful change in organizations. Sudhalter (1980, p. 84) refers to the process as "penetrating the purple haze, acquiring the skills of innovation, creativity and awareness." Not only does the dream provide the picture of the goal, and thus the basis for motivation, but it also provides some compensation during the pain of change. It is that something that makes all the pain worthwhile. In this sense, the dream is not just articulated and communicated, bought into, and left. It must be nurtured and maintained in order to provide ongoing comfort with change. The dream comes into being not all at once, but more like the picture in a jigsaw puzzle. It takes shape piece by piece. So one of the manager's functions is the measuring and feedback (described later). It is this measuring, taking stock of how much and what aspects of the change have been accomplished, and providing some feedback about them that provides the nurturing and maintenance of the dream. The ultimate result, like the jigsaw puzzle, allows you to compare it with the picture on the box. There must be a comparison of the dream with the results.

I will again use one of the messages of this book to build a story regarding dreams. In describing culture, climate, and environment, I made the point that one can design environments and that this process can have an ultimate effect on culture. Another important message in the book is that managers and professionals must focus more and better attention on the matching of people and work, the tailoring of job factors to ensure effectiveness, productivity, and vitality. Suppose you wish to influence this matching process in a positive way. You want to have your managers and professionals understand the concept and do a better job of matching. The dream might be articulated as follows, after the hurt has been identified and agreed upon:

> *Statement of the dream.* We are aiming for a quality work environment in which individuals share the responsibility with management for working toward a good job/person fit so that the organization improves its effectiveness in achieving goals and the individuals share in the benefits through improved psychic income. I see this as a work environment in which the individual shares needs and capabilities with the organization on a regular basis through job-matching discussions with managers. I see this as an environment in which the manager shares the needs and capabilities of the organization with the individual. I see this as a place where people are encouraged and supported in growth of capabilities, and where the organization responds positively to their changing needs. In short, it will be a work environment in which people are not forced to fit jobs and jobs are not forced to fit people, but where we negotiate and iterate for the best fit, over time, so that both the organization and the individual benefit. We will be creating QPL.

Communicating the Dream Through Participation

I have just presented a sample statement representing a dream. For the dream to be effective in motivating people, they must have heard it and bought it as their own. As Culbert and

McDonough (1980, p. 60) say: "Each time people enter a new work situation they engage in the implicit process of *aligning* personal values, interests, and skills with what they perceive to be the task requirements of their job. They seek an orientation that maximizes self-pursuits and organizational contribution." Alignment is their term for gaining *congruence,* which has been the term I have used. The best way to do this, with professionals, is to have them participate in the process of defining and articulating the dream. If they have taken part in its definition, then they own a piece of it and they understand it. This carries over to the management of change, the process of making the change. Four assumptions underlie participative programs (Kirkpatrick, 1985, p. 16): "People who do the work are the best qualified to improve it; decision making should be pushed down to the lowest level possible; worker participation increases both job satisfaction and commitment to company objectives; there is a vast pool of ideas in the work force waiting to be tapped."

In the introduction of the concepts of technical vitality at IBM, participation was used in the R & D organizations as a tool in communicating the concepts and gaining commitment. While the overall task group, the laboratory committee, had defined the dream, new task groups of managers were formed to work through the issues and articulate the goals (Miller, 1977b). In one sense, this was repetitive, since the groups rehashed ideas and concepts that had already been discussed by the overall laboratory committee. Previous committee discussions had not convinced this new layer of managers, but their own discussions did create understanding and commitment. These management committees created groups of goals and began forming action plans relating to different aspects of the professional's work life. The goals and the action plans became the content of the dreams, which could be articulated and transmitted to the broad group of professionals. The members of the committees were the people who went on to implement the changes.

The Necessity for Individuals to Buy In

Goal congruence, an alignment, a compatibility of the individual's goals and the goals of the organization, is necessary to gain the motivation and full energies of the individual. Each person needs to feel that, in the process of pursuing the goals of the organization, they are pursuing their own goals. This is why it is necessary for the individual to buy in to the goals for change.

I can remember a case of organizational change which was more painful than it needed to be and which was not as successful as it should have been. It was a case where organizational design was to be changed for the purpose of making that laboratory more compatible with its customers' perspectives as well as improving communication with its customers. The leader failed to articulate the dream, communicate it, and gain the organizational members' commitment. Rather, the changes in organizational concept, the intent of which was so obvious for the leader, were imposed, in the eyes of individuals, on the organization. Members of the organization never bought the leader's goal. Consequently, for several years, this particular organizational change was the cause of so much griping and negative energy that it became, in turn, the cause for almost every other organizational failure.

As I have suggested several times in this book, the most useful technique for gaining goal congruence, for achieving buy-in and ownership of goals, is participation. Not only must this occur at the broad organizational level, it must also occur at the one-on-one level where the individual and manager share goals and negotiate assignments so that there is congruence and thus a payout for both the organization and the individual. Agreement concerning the broad context of organizational goals is necessary if organizational change is to occur. In general, individuals will oppose something they do not understand. This is true when individuals feel that they are not respected by management because management has failed to explain the rationale behind the actions it has taken. It is again true when individuals suspect that there may be an ulterior motive, a reason for not explaining the rationale to them. That is, individuals tend to suspect that that which is not explained has a negative base, that there is some kind of cover-up. In general, individuals will go along with something they understand even though they do not totally agree. This is especially true if management has, in their eyes, gone out of their way to demonstrate respect for the individual, especially the professional, and for the professional's need for an explanation. In general, individuals will enthusiastically support and work for something they own as their own goals, so it is to management's benefit if it can achieve the buy-in. Participation to achieve a buy-in on goals must start with agreement on the hurt factor. If all agree on the statement of the problem and if all have helped to forge the solutions, then all have skin in the goal. Groups will support and work for the goal, because not to do so means a loss of face. If individuals fail at something they have agreed to, they cannot blame the failure on someone else. The next section, on team building and planning retreats, describes a process for achieving the level of participation necessary for agreement on problems and commitment to solutions.

Team Building and Planning Retreats: An Implementing Tactic

Over and over, I have managers ask me, "Why is it necessary to go through some process called team building? Why is it necessary to invest money in getting away from the workplace? Why is it necessary to take the time to discuss the problems and work out group solutions; is that not the leader's function?" The necessity rests in the rationale just presented, and I shall enlarge on it in this discussion of team building.

For some reason which I do not totally understand, normal functioning in an organization does not usually teach members of a group the advantages and "how to" of working together in an improved way. Perhaps it is because the focus is on results, not learning. Perhaps they are too immersed, too close to the issues. Perhaps it is because of the pressures that drive them, rather than allowing them to drive. For whatever reason, once a group has defined a hurt, or even is in the process of defining the hurt, it is often desirable for it to engage in a team-building, or team-development, event. Harris (1985, pp. 243 and 248) says: "Team building is a behavioral science technology for achieving many of the preceding characteristics in work groups. [The preceding characteristics were a list of positive attributes of effective teams.] It is best accomplished by a trained consultant, either an internal or external resource. . . . Teamwork and its development can be utilized at all levels of the organization—literally a way of managing." Simply described, a team-building event consists of: gathering of data; feedback of data to the group, in a nonwork place, with time to digest it; discussion of the data and agreement on what it means; discussion of solutions and action plans; and, finally, return to normal functioning with a commitment to change. Usually, team-building events are of two to four days' duration and take place at a facility away from the workplace. By taking the group away, it is possible to escape the cues and constraints of the workplace, which support the old way. The group is aided in this process by a catalyst-leader who is an outsider to the group, who ensures that the focus is on problems, not people, and who gently nudges them in the process.

The results of team building are several. Most important, the group learns to learn together. They learn that they can supplement and complement each other in solving shared problems. They learn that their problems are not all someone else's fault. They usually come up with several things they can do to improve their functioning. Almost invariably, they finish the session with positive feelings and a feeling of power. It is, incidentally, a good way to counteract the feeling of powerlessness that I addressed in the Preface. The fact that they live together, work together, and have unhurried time to focus on real issues contributes to the magic of the event. With proper reinforcement, this positive, constructive outlook can be brought back to the workplace and continue there. From this, you should be able to see how it can be an excellent launching pad for change. It is but one of several implementing tactics.

In a period of change, several tactics are useful. One of my favorite techniques is to take two minutes or so at the end of every meeting to focus on what could be learned from what had just been discussed. Another technique I have used has to do with freeing up people to encompass new ideas at the beginning of a meeting. I call it unlearning (Miller, 1977a). It simply consists of giving everyone the opportunity to state, at the start of the meeting, all the preconceptions, all the biases, that they carried into the meeting. By getting these off their chests, they are free to think anew. It is closely related to (if not the same concept as) Kurt Lewin's unfreezing, referenced earlier in this chapter. Another technique, already mentioned, is the formation of task groups, which take on the tasks of researching the problem, defining the problem, proposing a solution, and communicating to the organization. Another is to form temporary organizations, of which quality circles are an example, that take on some change management functions.

Still another technique is the planning retreat, used frequently in R & D organizations. It is in some ways similar to the team-building retreat. Usually, before the event, there are assignments to individuals or subgroups to research some issue and be prepared to report at the planning meeting. The actual meetings vary in length from half a day to several days. They are usually led by a member of the group, or the manager, and thus differ from team building, in which the leader is often an outsider until relatively late in the process, when the leader can review and join with the group in some of the solutions; the reason for this in team building is that the leader is sometimes a block to open communication about sensitive issues. In the case of the planning retreat, the result of discussions is a strategic plan, a tactical plan, and often a near-future action program. Planning retreats are more useful, after the problem and the dream have been defined, as a base for the implementation of change.

With these ideas, you should be able to come up with other tactical approaches that combine in a fresh way the concepts of participation and of freedom to think.

The Action Plan

If changes are to be made, the manager must find a way to convert ideas into action. Since the manager cannot, and should not, take all the actions, implementing them requires a plan and an assignment of activities. Kirkpatrick (1985, p. 72) emphasizes that "Changes in organizations can (and do) begin anywhere—in management structure, in technology, or in people. In the final analysis, however, changes in the *behavior of the individuals who cause the organization to function* must occur. These necessary changes cannot be left to chance. Indeed, they must be planned for with careful concern for implementation and reinforcement." The plan should provide a way of tying issues to actions. A plan should also provide a reference base for measurement of progress. It is important for those who are to take actions to own them. It is just as important as to have ownership of the hurt and the dream. A plan created during a team-building event will be a plan the participants own. An effective plan does not have to be elaborate, but it must contain actions that affect the aspects of the environment that are to be changed. Typical action statements for the dream of a better matching of people and work, stated earlier, might be:

- Train all professionals and managers in the concepts of person/job matching and career discussions.
- Establish a policy requiring person/job-matching interviews.
- Communicate the policy and establish target dates for the first discussions.
- Measure the results and make course corrections.

Each of these action items would be assigned to task groups or functional units of the organization in a good plan. Each of these action steps would have dates and schedules.

Measuring, Benchmarking, and Feedback as Factors

If the changes that have been decided upon are important, it is important to set up techniques for the measurement of change. Initial measurements can become benchmarks. A benchmark is simply a reference measurement; it is something to measure against, from which progress can be charted. Feedback is communicating the measurements. If the measurements are to be used to motivate further actions, they must be communicated and acknowledged.

The Recognition Factor in Managing Change

It is important for us, as individuals, to know that what we do is important to someone else. Recognition is demonstrating to someone that what he or she did was important to the organization. The recognition must be appropriate in the context in which it is used. This means that it must neither be too small or too large; it must fit the situation. If someone comes up with a new concept that makes a large difference in the implementation of the change, then some large recognition is appropriate. The most important part of this point is that there should be some form of recognition. Demonstrating caring, through recognition, is an important part of the managerial function.

As I write this, I am in the middle of an assignment to help a research group of professionals overcome poor morale, excessive discontent, rampant self-reinforcing negativism, and distrust of management. In searching for causes, one stands out as more important than any other. It is that this group feels that management does not care about them and their work. That this is a perception, and probably not the reality, makes little difference. The perception becomes the reality! One of my recommendations for improvement will be for management to establish many different action patterns that provide recognition and feedback, thus transmitting the feeling that what these individuals do is important to the organization. These actions will range from simply walking around the workplace and acknowledging the individuals to increasing their pay relative to that of others in the organization.

Course Correction for Enhancement of the Benefits

No plan can anticipate all the things that will happen. Managing change therefore requires that the measurements be used to establish the base for changes in direction, changes in tactics, and implementation of the new ideas that grow out of the change process. Deciding on these minor adjustments of direction (course corrections) is as important as is the initial process of determining the discomfort and what to change. If the course corrections are too great or seem to undermine the original intent, they may transmit the wrong message. For example, in a period of change, individuals are sensitive to cues, signals, which help them to establish comfort with what is happening. If a course correction can be interpreted as a change in the original goal, be sure that such an interpretation will be made.

Thus, each message, announcement, or communication should be examined not only for its content but also for the signal it may communicate. Each message has the chance to become an environmental statement, something where the action itself speaks louder than the words. Suppose, for example, that you have decided to implement the program that will increase the conversations about person/job fit. The training has been accomplished. You are at the stage where the first round of conversations between manager and individual is to take place and you discover that there is confusion about how this conversation relates to performance appraisal conversations. Sensing the danger that the implementation of the new program may negatively affect a functioning program of performance appraisal, you decide that some announcement should be made. If the announcement can be interpreted to mean that performance appraisal is more important, then you risk the possibility that people will interpret this to mean that the new program should take a back seat and is not really important. It is important to be sure that the message detracts from the importance of neither, but reinforces the need for them both to be integrated into a larger concept.

The Messages of This Book

In the Summary section at the end of each chapter, I have reinforced the points of the chapter. Thus, if you went through all the chapters and read the Summary sections, you would have a summary of the book. My feeling is that each reader needs different levels of summary; consequently I shall try to bring together in this one list what I consider to be the most important messages of the book:

1. Leading-managing in R & D is different from managing other functions. It is different because the organization is made up of professionals who come to work with unique values, unique personal characteristics, and unique expectations, which are, in part, the result of their extensive training. It is unique because of the goals, which combine the need for creativity (requiring an open or differentiated organization) with the need for results, which requires a controlled or integrated organization. It is unique because the leaders are drawn from the technical environment and most often emphasize technical aspects at the expense of the human aspects of managing.

2. The work environment, the characteristics of the work, and the needs of the professionals in R & D are changing. The changes require an increased emphasis on human resource management. Organizations that fail to improve the quality of the work environment (QPL) will soon find that they cannot attract, retain, and nurture the professionals they need to pursue the organization's goals. A central theme is understanding the importance of psychic income and how a culture, climate, and environment can be built that make its achievement more probable.

3. Because of the unique characteristics of the professional and the unique environment of R & D, there are difficulties in understanding and communicating between R & D and the organizations of which they are part. Improved effectiveness, productivity, and vitality depend on increasing the understanding across these organizational boundaries as well as improving the operations and environment in R & D.

4. In leading-managing R & D, it is important to understand the need for exciting missions and exciting goals. Professionals are achievement-oriented, probably as a result of both selection and training; thus, achievement in the

larger context of the organization and the profession is a strong motivating force. Managers need to work to gain goal congruence—compatibility of the goals of the organization and the individual.

5. Goals are important as a basis for providing direction and a reference base for decision making. There is a critical need for new goals, and vitality and effectiveness were proposed as coequals with results goals. This new mating of goals, with its heavy emphasis on improved human resource management, was proposed as a way to improve productivity.

6. Environmental design is a necessary managerial responsibility, and environmental design creates a climate that eventually results in a changed culture. Through environmental design, management can establish cues for behavior. Environment takes on a special importance in R & D because creative work is less directed than in other parts of the organization and the professionals are searching for cues as to what is needed and what is right. The properly designed environment can provide these cues.

7. It is important for leader-managers in R & D to develop styles that foster openness of communication and include nurturing, caring, attention, and recognition. In R & D, good management feels casual and nondirective. It is often composed of activities like just walking around.

8. Recruiting, selecting, training, and development are all important in building an effective research or development team. It is important that recruiting be honest and that new attention be paid to the development of the psychological work contract, the unwritten specification of what the individual expects to bring, find, and take away from work. Having world-class professionals and other collegial support in the organization is important in attracting and developing professionals. A screening and indoctrination process that includes the nonmanagement professionals is desirable.

9. Performance management, including joint setting of objectives, agreement on measures, feedback, appraisal, recogni-

tion, and reward, is a necessary process for the management of an organization's goal achievement as well as for the development of individuals. A viable performance management system must be built on an understood philosophical base, supporting performance management, which is part of the culture of the organization.

10. It is possible through creative, experimental design of organizations to improve the probability of achieving desired objectives. Organizational design is part of the managerial role.

11. The matching of people with work is a key responsibility of the manager, but it is shared with the professional. Improvement of the match is important in achieving effective goal achievement for the organization and psychic income for the individual. Both managers and professionals can and should be trained in the process of improving matching. In R & D, there are some special challenges in the matching process; they include the lack of a clear definition of what is to be done and the rapid change in technology, which changes what is to be done. The identification of job elements by using the conceptual approach that was presented can improve the negotiation between the manager and the individual over the job/person fit.

12. The implementation of change requires identification of the hurt factor, creation of a dream, buy-in on the part of the participants, planning the change, measuring, benchmarking, and feedback, with recognition of accomplishment and of contribution to the change. A major managerial role is change management.

Making This Book Work for You

My goal in writing this book was to present concepts, ideas, and suggestions that can help the leader-manager in managing R & D, as well as professionals, through their personal career/life management to create a more effective, productive, and vital organization. I have stressed the human resource side of managing as a way of partially offsetting the natural tendencies of the technically trained to emphasize the technical. I have stressed the human side because I believe that we are facing a crisis in which the human side is becoming increasingly important. I believe that more effective human resource management will make the difference between success and failure and is just as important as picking the right technology or making the creative breakthrough. In fact, I believe that the latter will follow if human resource management is done well. I have stressed the human side because in my consulting practice I see the problems caused by mismanaging people. I will achieve my goal if you take one or more ideas from this book and make them work for you. Throughout the book, I have provided scenarios that offer suggestions for using the ideas. In this last section, I intend to talk with you again about using the ideas.

Some of the ideas in the book can be used on a personal basis as an individual or as a manager. If, for example, you as a manager feel, as a result of your reading, that you should make your managerial style more caring and/or nurturing, you do not need a committee or a change of policy in the organization. You might start by listing the actions you can take that will have the effect of nurturing members of your organization. Then experiment with each of these ideas. Some will work for you because they fit your personality and the culture of the organization; others will not. Some will work for you because they fit your relationship with the other members of your team. Finding out whether or not they work depends on your experimenting, on your being sensitive to feedback, to responses from the individuals you relate to, and your observing the effects your actions have on others. If you observe that someone in your group rises to new heights of achievement after you have paid some additional attention to that person, then you may conclude that something worked. On a personal basis, you may keep the experiment under control, change at the rate you want to change, and make frequent course corrections. But experiment you must if an idea gathered from this book is to have any impact on the way in which you manage.

Transplanting an idea into a new culture on a broader scale, beyond the personal level, is not easy. The idea is fragile and needs care and nurturing. The idea needs to be adapted to the new culture, since what works in one organization will not automatically work in another. You and the members of your organization must take on the idea and make it your own. In consulting, I find that I drop ideas like seeds, but only some of them grow. I find that the ones that do grow are those which are owned by the members of the organization and which fit the need of the times. Thus, the ideas you take should not remain Miller's ideas, or "the ideas from that book." To be transplanted successfully, ideas must become culture-specific, and the timing of introduction must be chosen carefully to match the needs of the organization. Using one of the ideas in this book to solve a problem you do not have will not work. You and your organization must need the idea now. So, as in this chapter, you must start with an assessment; you must look for your organization's discomforts, hurts. Using a task force formed for the purpose of assessing and introducing needed changes is the mode that I suggest. You may or may not find that you need a consultant, an outsider, as a catalyst in the process. This book can become a source book for ideas for the task group. As on the personal level, you and your organization's members must experiment if the ideas of the book are to have any meaning or impact.

Summary

- Managing change is one of the key functions of the manager. Like other aspects of management, it should be fun for the leader. Change management starts with the identification of a hurt, a discomfort, which can provide the incentive and the motivation for the investment in change. The manager needs to carry on the identification process in a way that the hurt is shared and agreed upon by the members of the organization who will be affected by the change and who must implement the change.

- Once there is agreement on what is wrong, the leader must work with others to define the dream. The dream is a vision, a picture, which is communicable and which defines the improved state that will result from change. The dream needs to be translated into specific goals and an action plan.

• For people to invest in change, they must buy in, become the owners of the hurt, the dream, and the improvements that will result. Participation has been demonstrated to be the management approach that causes others to become owners of change and thus be motivated to change.

• In managing change, there is a necessity for measurement. Initial measurements become benchmarks against which progress can be assessed. Subsequently, measurements provide the necessary input for course correction, to ensure that the goals are met. Later measurements become the basis for reinforcing the change through feedback, recognition, and reward. Because change is uncomfortable, reinforcing it through recognition is very important in achieving success.

• Leading and managing in R & D is different from managing in other functions, and it requires a soft hand. Throughout this book we have emphasized the design of environments, as opposed to directing people, and participation as a management style, both because it is the right way and because the professional expects to be part of the management process. Self-management, having both strategic and operational autonomy, is part of the professional's definition of being a professional. Only a manager who understands this can improve the effectiveness of R & D by providing the opportunity for the professional to gain psychic income in the process of pursuing the goals of the organization.

▼▼▼▼▼▼▼▼▼▼▼▼

References

American Society for Engineering Education. "More Schools Found Limiting Enrollment." *Engineering Education News,* Nov. 1985, *12* (4), 1.

Arieti, S. *Creativity, The Magic Synthesis.* New York: Basic Books, 1976.

Badaway, M. K. *Developing Managerial Skills in Engineers and Scientists: Succeeding as a Technical Manager.* New York: Van Nostrand Reinhold, 1982.

Bailyn, L. "Autonomy in the Industrial R & D Laboratory." *Human Resource Management,* Summer 1985, *24* (2), 129–146.

Baird, L. S., Beatty, R. W., and Schneier, C. E. *The Performance Appraisal Sourcebook.* Amherst, Mass.: Human Resource Development Press, 1982.

Blake, R. R., and Mouton, J. S. *Building a Dynamic Corporation Through GRID Organization Development.* Reading, Mass.: Addison-Wesley, 1969.

Blake, R. R., and Mouton, J. S. "Don't Let Group Norms Stifle Creativity." *Personnel,* Aug. 1985, pp. 28–39.

Bolt, J. F. "Tailor Executive Development to Strategy." *Harvard Business Review,* Nov.–Dec. 1985, pp. 168–176.

Bonoma, T. V., and Slevin, D. P. *Executive Survival Manual: A Program for Managerial Effectiveness.* Boston: CBI, 1978.

Brooks, F. E. *The Mythical Man-Month.* Reading, Mass.: Addison-Wesley, 1975.

Carruthers, P. A., as quoted in W. J. Broad, "The Creative Mind: Tracing the Skeins of Matter." *New York Times Magazine,* May 6, 1984, pp. 54-62.

Cole, D. W. *Professional Suicide: A Survival Kit for You and Your Job.* New York: McGraw-Hill, 1980.

Culbert, S. A., and McDonough, J. J. *The Invisible War: Pursuing Self-Interests at Work.* New York: Wiley, 1980.

Cummings, P. W. *Open Management: Guides to Successful Practice.* New York: AMACOM, 1980.

Deal, T. E., and Kennedy, A. A. *Corporate Cultures: The Rites and Rituals of Corporate Life.* Reading, Mass.: Addison-Wesley, 1982.

Dowling, W. F., and Sayles, L. R. *How Managers Motivate: The Imperatives of Supervision.* New York: McGraw-Hill, 1978.

Drake, J. D. *Interviewing for Managers: Sizing Up People.* New York: AMACOM, 1972.

Drucker, P. F. *Management: Tasks, Responsibilities, Practices.* New York: Harper & Row, 1974.

Dyer, W. G. *Team Building: Issues and Alternatives.* Reading, Mass.: Addison-Wesley, 1977.

Fear, R. A. *The Evaluation Interview.* New York: McGraw-Hill, 1978.

Fournies, F. F. *Coaching for Improved Work Performance.* New York: Van Nostrand Reinhold, 1978.

Francis, P. H. *Principles of R & D Management.* New York: AMACOM, 1977.

Frank, F. D., Sefcik, J. T., and Jaffee, C. L. *The Assessment Center Process: A Participant's Workbook.* Orlando, Fla.: Human Resource Publishing, 1983.

Galbraith, J. R. "Designing the Innovative Organization." *Organizational Dynamics,* Winter 1982, pp. 5-25.

Gaum, C. G., Graves, H. F., and Hoffman, L. S. S. *Report Writing.* Englewood Cliffs, N.J.: Prentice-Hall, 1950.

Gellerman, S. W. *Motivation and Productivity.* New York: AMACOM, 1963.

Ginzberg, S., and Vojta, G. *Beyond Human Scale: The Large Corporation at Risk.* New York: Basic Books, 1985. Excerpted in *Hermes* (Graduate Business School Magazine, Columbia University), Summer 1985, *11* (2), 5-19.

Gomberg, W. "The Historical Roots of the Democratic Challenge to Authoritarian Management." *Human Resource Management,* Fall 1985, *24* (3), 253-269.

Gouldner, A. W. "Cosmopolitans and Locals: Toward an Analysis of Latent Social Roles." *Administrative Science Quarterly,* 1957, *2,* 281-306; 1958, *2,* 444-480.

Hackman, J. R., and Suttle, J. L. *Improving Life at Work: Behavioral Science Approaches to Organizational Change.* Santa Monica, Calif.: Goodyear, 1977.

Hall, D. T. "Project Work as an Antidote to Career Plateauing in a Declining Engineering Organization." *Human Resource Management,* Fall 1985, *24* (3), 271-292.

Harris, D. G. "How National Cultures Shape Management Styles." *Management Review,* July 1982, pp. 58-61.

Harris, P. R. *Management in Transition: Transforming Managerial Practices and Organizational Strategies for a New Work Culture.* San Francisco: Jossey-Bass, 1985.

Harvey, J. B. "The Abilene Paradox: The Management of Agreement." *Organizational Dynamics,* Summer 1974, pp. 29-46.

Herman, S. M., and Korenich, M. *Authentic Management: A Gestalt Orientation to Organizations and Their Development.* Reading, Mass.: Addison-Wesley, 1977.

Hersey, P., and Blanchard, K. H. "Leader Effectiveness and Adaptability Description." In J. W. Pfeiffer and J. E. Jones (eds.), *The 1976 Annual Handbook for Group Facilitators.* San Diego, Calif.: University Associates, 1976.

Hines, W. W., III. "Increasing Team Effectiveness." *Training and Development Journal,* Feb. 1980, pp. 76-82.

Hinrichs, J. R. *Practical Management for Productivity.* New York: Van Nostrand Reinhold, 1978.

Hofstede, G. "Motivation, Leadership and Organization: Do American Theories Apply Abroad?" *Organizational Dynamics,* Summer 1980, pp. 42-63.

Holland, J. L. *Making Vocational Choices: A Theory of Careers.* Englewood Cliffs, N.J.: Prentice-Hall, 1973.

Hower, R. M., and Orth, C. D., III. *Managers and Scientists: Some Human Problems in Industrial Research Organizations.* Cambridge, Mass.: Division of Industrial Research, Graduate School of Business Administration, Harvard University, 1963.

Hunt, J. W. "Applying American Behavioral Science: Some Cross-Cultural Problems." *Organizational Dynamics,* Summer 1981, pp. 55–62.

Institute of Electrical and Electronic Engineers. Career Maintenance and Development Committee. *Professional Practices for Engineers, Scientists and Their Employers.* Washington, D.C.: Institute of Electrical and Electronic Engineers, 1983.

Jansen, E., and Von Glinow, M. A. "Ethical Ambivalence and Organizational Reward Systems." *Academy of Management Review,* 1985, *10* (4), 814–822.

Johnson, R. G. *The Appraisal Interview Guide.* New York: AMACOM, 1979.

Jourard, S. M. *Healthy Personality: An Approach from the Viewpoint of Humanistic Psychology.* New York: Macmillan, 1974.

Kappel, F. R. *Vitality in a Business Enterprise.* New York: McGraw-Hill, 1960.

Katz, D., and Kahn, R. L. *The Social Psychology of Organizations.* New York: Wiley, 1978.

Kaufman, H. G. *Professionals in Search of Work: Coping With the Stress of Job Loss and Underemployment.* New York: Wiley, 1982.

Kerr, S., Von Glinow, M. A., and Schriesheim, J. "Issues in the Study of Professionals in Organizations: The Case of Scientists and Engineers." *Organizational Behavior and Human Performance,* 1977, *18,* 329–345.

Kidder, T. *The Soul of a New Machine.* Boston: Little, Brown, 1981.

Kilmann, R. H. *Beyond the Quick Fix: Managing Five Tracks to Organizational Success.* San Francisco: Jossey-Bass, 1984.

Kilmann, R. H., and Saxton, M. J. *The Kilmann-Saxton Culture-Gap Survey.* Pittsburgh, Pa.: Organizational Design Consultants, 1983.

Kilmann, R. H., Saxton, M. J., Serpa, R., and Associates. *Gaining Control of the Corporate Culture.* San Francisco: Jossey-Bass, 1985.

Kingdon, D. R. *Matrix Organizations.* London: Tavistock, 1973.

Kirkpatrick, D. L. *How to Manage Change Effectively: Ap-*

proaches, Methods, and Case Examples. San Francisco: Jossey-Bass, 1985.

Langbein, L. I. *1985 IEEE U.S. Member Opinion Survey.* Washington, D.C.: Institute of Electric and Electronic Engineers, 1985.

Lawrence, P. R., Kolodony, H. F., and Davis, S. M. "The Human Side of the Matrix." *Organizational Dynamics,* Summer 1977, pp. 43-61.

Leonard-Barton, D., and Kraus, W. A. "Implementing New Technology." *Harvard Business Review,* Nov.-Dec. 1985, pp. 102-110.

Likert, R. *New Patterns of Management.* New York: McGraw-Hill, 1961.

Lorsch, J. W. "Organization Design: A Situational Perspective." *Organizational Dynamics,* Autumn 1977, pp. 2-14.

McCulloch, K. J. *Selecting Employees Safely Under the Law.* Englewood Cliffs, N.J.: Prentice-Hall, 1981.

Marcus, A. A. "Professional Autonomy as a Basis for Conflict in an Organization." *Human Resource Management,* Fall 1985, *24* (3), 311-328.

Michael, S. R. "Organizational Change Techniques: Their Present, Their Future." *Organizational Dynamics,* Summer 1982, pp. 67-80.

Miller, D. B. *Changing Job Requirements: A Stimulant for Technical Vitality.* Continuing Engineering Studies Series, no. 7. Washington, D.C.: American Society for Engineering Education, Continuing Engineering Studies Division, 1972, pp. 133-146.

Miller, D. B. *Personal Vitality.* Reading, Mass.: Addison-Wesley, 1977a.

Miller, D. B. "How to Improve the Performance and Productivity of the Knowledge Worker." *Organizational Dynamics,* Winter 1977b, pp. 62-79.

Miller, D. B. *Personal Vitality Workbook.* Reading, Mass.: Addison-Wesley, 1977c.

Miller, D. B. *Working with People.* Boston: CBI, 1979.

Mills, J. *The Engineer in Society.* New York: D. Van Nostrand, 1946.

References

Mintzberg, H. *The Nature of Managerial Work.* New York: Harper & Row, 1973.

Morris, W. T. *Work and Your Future: Living Poorer, Working Harder.* Reston, Va.: Reston, 1975.

Naisbitt, J., and Aburdene, P. "Reinventing the Corporation." *Chief Executive,* Autumn 1985, *33,* 40–41.

Nash, M. *Managing Organizational Performance.* San Francisco: Jossey-Bass, 1983.

Nurick, A. "The Paradox of Participation: Lessons from the Tennessee Valley Authority." *Human Resource Management,* Fall 1985, *24* (3), 341–356.

Oliver, R. *Career Unrest: A Source of Creativity.* New York: Columbia University Center for Research in Career Development, 1981.

O'Toole, J. *Work, Learning, and the American Future.* San Francisco: Jossey-Bass, 1977.

Pelz, D. C., and Andrews, F. M. *Scientists in Organizations: A Productive Climate for Research and Development.* New York: Wiley, 1966.

Peters, T. J., and Waterman, R. H., Jr. *In Search of Excellence: Lessons from America's Best Run Companies.* New York: Harper & Row, 1982.

Pfeiffer, J. W., and Jones, J. E. (eds.). *A Handbook of Structured Experiences for Human Relations Training.* Vol. 1. San Diego, Calif.: University Associates, 1974.

Posner, B. Z., Kouzes, J. M., and Schmidt, W. H. "Shared Values Make a Difference: An Empirical Test of Corporate Culture." *Human Resource Management,* Fall 1985, *24* (3), 293–309.

Quick, T. L. *Understanding People at Work: A Manager's Guide to the Behavioral Sciences.* New York: Executive Enterprises, 1976.

Raelin, J. A. *The Salaried Professional: How to Make the Most of Your Career.* New York: Praeger, 1984.

Raelin, J. A. "The Dilemma of Autonomy Versus Control in the Management of Organizational Professionals." *Human Resource Management,* Summer 1985, *24* (2), 147–175.

Raelin, J. A., Sholl, C. K., and Leonard, D. "Why Professionals Turn Sour and What to Do." *Personnel,* Oct. 1985, *62* (10), 28–41.

Reed, P. R., and Kroll, M. J. "A Two-Perspective Approach to Performance Appraisal." *Personnel,* 1985, *62* (10), 51–57.

Riggs, H. E. *Managing High-Technology Companies.* Belmont, Calif.: Lifetime Learning, 1983.

Ritti, R. R., and Funkhouser, G. R. *The Ropes to Skip and the Ropes to Know: Studies in Organizational Behavior.* Columbus, Ohio: Grid, 1977.

Roberts, E. B., and Fusfeld, A. R. "Staffing the Innovative Technology-Based Organization." *Sloan Management Review,* Spring 1981, pp. 19–34.

Rosow, J. M. *The Worker and the Job: Coping With Change.* Englewood Cliffs, N.J.: Prentice-Hall, 1974.

Sarason, S. B. *Work Aging and Social Change: Professionals and the One-Life Career Imperative.* New York: Free Press, 1977.

Sayles, L. R. *Managerial Behavior: Administration in Complex Organizations.* New York: McGraw-Hill, 1964.

Sayles, L. R. *Leadership: What Effective Managers Really Do, and How They Do It.* New York: McGraw-Hill, 1979.

Schein, E. H. *Organizational Psychology.* Englewood Cliffs, N.J.: Prentice-Hall, 1970.

Schein, E. H. *Career Dynamics: Matching Individual and Organizational Needs.* Reading, Mass.: Addison-Wesley, 1978.

Schein, E. H. *Organizational Culture and Leadership: A Dynamic View.* San Francisco: Jossey-Bass, 1985.

Schmidt, T. D. *Managing Your Career Success: Practical Strategies for Engineers, Scientists and Technical Managers.* Belmont, Calif.: Lifetime Learning, 1982.

Schmitt, R. W. "Engineering Research and International Competitiveness." *High Technology,* Nov. 1985, *5* (11), 13–14.

Selye, H. *The Stress of Life.* New York: McGraw-Hill, 1978.

Snow, C. P. *The Two Cultures and the Scientific Revolution.* New York: Cambridge University Press, 1959.

Steele, F., and Jenks, S. *The Feel of the Workplace: Understanding and Improving Organizational Climate.* Reading, Mass.: Addison-Wesley, 1977.

Strauss, G. "Managerial Practices." In J. R. Hackman and J. L. Suttle, *Improving Life at Work: Behavioral Science Approaches to Organizational Change.* Santa Monica, Calif.: Goodyear, 1977.

Sudhalter, D. L. *The Management Option: Nine Strategies for Leadership.* Boston: Human Sciences Press, 1980.

Tichy, N. M. "Managing Change Strategically: The Technical, Political and Cultural Keys." *Organizational Dynamics,* Autumn 1982, pp. 59-80.

Tichy, N. M. "Foreword." *Human Resource Management,* 1986, *25* (1), 1-7.

Toffler, A. *Future Shock.* New York: Random House, 1970.

Von Glinow, M. A. "Reward Strategies for Attracting, Evaluating and Retaining Professionals." *Human Resource Management,* Summer 1985, *24* (2), 191-206.

Watson, T. J., Jr. *Business and Its Beliefs: The Ideas That Helped Build IBM.* New York: McGraw-Hill, 1963.

Weick, K. E. "Organization Design: Organizations as Self-Designing Systems." *Organizational Dynamics,* Autumn 1977, pp. 31-46.

Weinberg, G. M. *The Psychology of Computer Programming.* New York: Van Nostrand Reinhold, 1971.

Wiggins, L. A., and Johnson, V. R. "The Demand for Engineers: A Predictive Model." *IEEE 1975 Manpower Report: The E/E at Mid-Career, Prospects and Problems.* New York: Institute of Electrical and Electronic Engineers, 1975, pp. 2-2 to 2-34.

Wolff, M. F. "Managers at Work: The Joy (and Love) of Matrix." *Research Management,* March 1980, pp. 10-12.

Zukowski, R. W. "Managing Technological Career Transitions." *Enhancing Engineering Careers by Fulfilling Individual and Organizational Goals.* New York: Institute of Electrical and Electronic Engineers, Conference Record, Palo Alto, Calif., Oct. 27-28, 1983.

Index